Marco Bonafini

Stoned Angels

Club memoirs of our legendary nights.

An Angel on the roof of the Baia degli Angeli club.

For the Angels of Baia degli Angeli club.

When friendship and solidarity still had value. Music played and danced from the first to the last record. Time stood still and the magic and carefreeness of those years will remain forever in our hearts.

A true story.

Stoned Angels.

Fee fie fo fum. We're looking down the barrel of the devil's gun. Nowhere to run...   (C.j & Co. - Devil's Gun)

A Vespa[1], shrouded in fog, trumpets toward a friend's house. The motorbike doesn't have a souped-up exhaust yet, the one that makes you feel cool when you drive along the main street of the village, but in the dark winter, with no living soul in sight, it hardly matters. His balls are freezing and to fight the bitter cold, he sits on the edge of the seat and risks his arse slipping off. The inner parts of his kneecaps brush against the scooter's central axle. He shelters behind the fenders. The way he is sitting causes the rest of his legs to diverge towards the footboard, in a "∧" shape. His nose knocks against the windscreen but, between the mist of his own breath on one side and specks of dust on the other, he can't see shit. He tries spitting on it, as you do on a diving mask, but spreading slithered saliva with phlegm has no effect. "Fuck off the tips of some folk", he seems to say, as he struggles to dry the slime with his forearm. He has to lean half his head out sideways and look at the roadside. Sinusitis is looming. At last, he arrives at his destination. The road from London to Verona is particularly long in these conditions.

'Hi Freddy, you okay? Any news?'

Freddy usually answers with a French "r":

'Crap, crrrrraaaap, I'm full of crrraaaap!'

It's a typical expression to show that he hasn't found a girl yet. If he is above the shit level, that means everything is fine, but if he is below, as we imagine, when Angie asks:

'Hiiii, Frrrreddyyyy how'rrrre you? Rrrrr you full of

---

[1] *The Vespa motorbike is a world-famous icon of Italian design and life. It was patented by the Piaggio Company on a project by aeronautical engineer Corradino D'Ascanio, who is also the inventor of the modern helicopter.*

crrrraaaap? Frrrreddyyyy?'

The house is quite unique. Surrounded by three four-storey buildings, it's low, simple. It's immersed in a clearing and kissed by a channel where water flows in the summer to irrigate far off fields. Nothing strange so far, except the fact that, once you go in the living room, you are shrouded in a white blanket. No, it isn't the fog again, it's the linen sheets that his friend's mum places on every piece of furniture to protect them from wear and tear and keep the dust off. They stand in this room a while, just long enough for some bullshit, a sip of Martini taken from his dad's alcohol cabinet and then, as usual, away they go on the motorbikes. Except this time, Freddy introduces something new:

'Do you know who's coming?'

'No, I don't, who?'

'Mark, yeah, Drill!'

'Wow! I can't wait to hear which story he's got for us this time.'

Mark. He's a classmate and a friend from adolescence. He knows how to change society and he does. He lives with a semi-invalid fascist uncle. To be honest, no-one knows where he learned his antagonistic lifestyle and behaviour that would go on to influence many young kids belonging to the "Bay Of Angels" generation. Ever since he got his Ciao[2], he goes around in a white T-shirt and bleached, wrinkled and patched dungarees, his haircut down to his eyebrows like Dee Dee, Ramone, yellow lensed glasses and white clogs. All the girls turn their heads. All of them.

That's where the trend for white clogs that rages among the young in every corner of the city, particularly in local clubs, like Piqu, Vrrrr2000, and Papillon, comes from. They often hang around with torn, skinny-leg, tube-like jeans with the frequent addition of black and white cloth patches sewn on the rear pockets, apparently depicting some transgressive myth of the past, such as Marilyn Monroe and others.

'Here you are, hiiii Maaaark!

'Hi guys, look what I've bought!'

'What? A mega stereo?'

'Yeah, yeah, besides the stereo, it's the tape inside that's awesome!'

---

2 The Piaggio Ciao was one of the most popular mopeds in Italy and Germany.

You look so self-possessed. I won't disturb your rest. It's lovely when you're sleeping. (Ian Dury - Wake up and make love with me)

Each generation grows at its own pace. Music goes hand in hand with life but the music of your youth vibrates more than any other that accompanies you in everyday life as you get older.

'This is some serious Baia degli Angeli [3]shit! This'll freak you out, guys!'

'Okay, I got it from the club in Gabicce[4].'

Freddy looks at Angie. They sense that something new is about to happen. That angel with a halo and wings, the Baia symbol, would make them dance differently than at home, alone, watching Piccolo Slam[5] or Discoring.

Chains, your chains of love. When something is busting loose, and your heart needs a boost.(Gregg Diamond&Bionic Boogie - Chains)

Now they understand the reason for those patches sewn on the jeans. The most successful of Baia nights was the Marilyn Party. Giant Marilyn posters covered every corner of the club. And yet, it was Mozart and Baldelli's[6] wild splashes of disco-funk that echoed in the room where Freddy, Angie and Drill danced, trying not to spill their Martini.

'Listen to thiiiis!' shouts Drill.

*Listen to the beat! Listen to the beat! The beat! The beat!
(Hamilton Bohannon - Bohannon's Beat)*

'Come on guys! Pancho tonight okay? Smoke red, smoke sound, smoke black Pakistan! And then to the discooo!' Cheers Drill.

What this meant, they found out soon enough (they were types of hash). London was mentioned but it's only the nickname for Raldon, a village where, in 1969, a pizzeria was founded, perhaps

---

[3] Baia degli Angeli or Bay of Angels. A famous Italian club where the story began.
[4] Gabicce Mare, a resort where Baia degli Angeli is situated.
[5] An Italian music chart TV programme similar to Top of the Pops in the UK.
[6] Bay of Angels' DJs.

the first pizzeria in Italy. This hamlet near Verona is where Pancho can be found and is therefore a hangout for specific occasions. Among other things, it preserves old friendships, like Poplar. He was the one who introduced Angie to a discotheque in the city, a real dive called the Papion disco, which was totally forgotten the moment that the Vrrr2000 disco's coaches started to leave from the city centre headed towards the Verona suburb where the club is located. It would be well to point out here that friends are often not called by their real name but rather by a nickname that recalls or evokes something personal or perhaps historical. Poplar, for example, stems from the fact that he is very tall and Angie is named as such because he used to hum that old Rolling Stones' song at school. Similarly, Freddy named Mark Drill due to the vicious drug circle that led him to shoot up.

'Hey! Old guys! Don't you know?' continued Drill.

'Spill the beans!'

'A new disco is opening at the lake and it seems that the DJ is from the Bay of Angels.'

'Noooooo! Awesome!'

Freddy and Angie are genuinely surprised. Since the Vrrr2000 is an indispensable meeting place for thousands of Angels[7] from and outside the province, a new disco, with a DJ from Baia degli Angeli, was bound to be of considerable interest.

'Are you sure? Aaaand, when will it open?'

They ask Drill, greedy for news and the chance to exploit it by airing their knowledge to their friends.

'I heard it should be this spring, May or June; I'll let you know, okay? Come on, let's enjoy this evening.'

You can get to the Vrrr2000 disco, commonly called "2", any way you want. The most pleasant means though, is on a souped-up moped. It is not easy to ride with a passenger, but a friend or girlfriend can sit uncomfortably on the luggage rack or the seat. However, if you install a double seat or footrests on the rear wheels, everything becomes much more accessible. A motorbike is just the sexiest thing. If you have a Ciao or any other two-wheeler, you try to accelerate so that the girl behind sticks to your hips and then, when you brake, you feel her tits pressing into your back.

---

7 People that belong to the generation of Bay of Angels.

STONED ANGELS

I believe in miracles. Where you from, you sexy thing, sexy thing you.
(Hot Chocolate - You sexy thing)

Funds are meagre, just like the vast majority of young people, except for those who started working at fourteen and have some extra money. It's therefore decided to go to the disco on Sunday afternoon at three o'clock. Saturday night is a little trickier, even if, most of the time, you always manage to find a way to breach the rules.

The ticket office and wardrobe are on the right just inside the entrance and, immediately after the ticket inspector, the bathrooms are on the left. What is the first thing you do when you go in? You go to the bathroom because they are lined with mirrors. Even though you have smeared your face with Topexan[8] at home, a pitstop by the mirror before the disorienting array of Angels by the dancefloor is still essential.

Disco bathrooms are a must for many. Side bangs are carefully cultivated, while others comb their hair with precision, curving it forward to cling to the forehead. Some even change here, their disco outfits in danger of freaking out parents. In the end, someone weird inevitably pops up, like Drill. Friends often see him in a red satin suit, Amii Stewart style. The music begins softly, like the soundtrack to a porn movie. The Angels turn anticlockwise and clockwise to make eye contact, copy a style, find a soul mate and leave uniformity behind. Sofas, arranged on various levels, surround the dancefloor. You pass through the middle now and then to look for a free seat, perhaps near a couple of girls, in an attempt to start an approach, a conversation. There is a bar, or preferably two. The one you see on the other side of the entrance is larger and is where hardened clubbers consume the tough stuff, standing apart from the neophytes. There is also an upper floor. It's the "skulk zone", dotted with sapphire-blue sofas obscured by a faint light that allows you to put your hands down your partner's trousers without attracting attention. To be honest, once there, nobody cares what anyone else is doing even if you are nearby or sitting on the same sofa. The only thought is tongue contact and finding pubic hair.

---

8 *A product for pimple problems.*

I'd give you everything and more, and that's for sure. I'd bring you diamond rings and things right to your door. (Chilly-For Your Love)

Meanwhile, those who remain downstairs continue circling, sometimes reversing their direction, like a roaming herd of cattle. There is a bottleneck right under Rudy Corradi, the DJ, and that bottleneck is in conjunction with a secret entrance, a sort of tunnel where you go to fuck. Suddenly the theme song starts. An echoing "VRRRRRR" interrupts the vintage restaurant music and the explosive opening of 'Espanolada' by The New Trolls begins. As if the song were a catalyst, the aimless mass flips over to the dancefloor and, in order to exchange audible bullshit, you have to wait for the slow dance. Yes, the slow dance, a nightclub that leaves a small space for lovers. The quality of the track determines the flow on the dancefloor, any slip and it's back to the sidelines for a smoke. There's always a chance for one of the fly-guys to get on the floor and bust his moves, but it's the girls who invariably win the spotlight, arranged in circles with their hippie bags in the centre.

Every morning they gather in the city centre, the point of arrival for buses and gaggles of students from all over the province. Among all the stupid things that involve this generation, some passionate news transpires. Spring has arrived with the promise of balmy days to come and the time of year that makes any boy's mouth water. The heat leads to the unveiling of personal tastes and graces and T-shirts and bodies are the perfect combination for comments to go from an endless exchange of bullshit to appreciation. However, Drill arrives and delivers some important news. He alights from the bus sporting a yellow satin jacket and a fringe covering one eye. His fringe requires constant attention since his ear fails to provide the required support. The nervous tic is distracting. The news is that the much-anticipated Cosmic has finally opened in Lazise. The initial four nights in April were insufficient to cope with the unprecedented demand from the Angels.

☺

It all started in the late '70s and early '80s. In 1975, the Baia degli Angeli nightclub in Gabicce Mare marked the birth of the Angels, a new generation of clubbers was born in one of Europe's most trendsetting clubs. This generation was hugely influenced by the styles and sounds emanating from the US and UK with bands such as the Rolling Stones, Janis Joplin, The Doors and The Who.

Taking these trends as their cue, the Angels dressed in wildly divergent styles that included stonewashed jeans, Indian sandals, oversized jumpers, Clarks shoes, denim jackets festooned with patches, Indian scarves, Marilyn and Vagabond ("the man with the guitar") logos and especially the mythical "Woman with pot" poster design. Much of these fashions and love for disco music were fuelled by a reaction to the dominance of rock music.

The trend fanned out from the Baia degli Angeli into other regions and clubs, such as Cosmic, Typhoon, Melodj Mecca, New York, Les Cigales, Chicago and hundreds of others, where the music was a bewildering range covering funk, disco, Afrobeat and offbeat electronic sounds. Their icons were bongos, the djembe drum, a guitar on the shoulder, mixtapes with the original disco nights, the chillum[9] and big nightclub stickers. Even their means of transport became iconic. Angels hitchhiked to the Saturday night disco, Vespas were adorned with stickers, such as the stylised angel with the word 'cocaine', the glovebox was transformed into a stereo system with two woofers and luggage racks, front and back. Then there was the Ciao and the Cagiva[10] with alloy wheels. But it was the Citroens that were the most popular. The 2CV, the Dyane, the legendary DS Pallas (known colloquially as 'Shark'), with home stereo, woofers and interior red lights. Lastly, the Renault 4 with the man with the guitar sticker on the hatchback. They slept anywhere and everywhere outside in tents with the radio on. Perhaps in the company of a joint. Perhaps on a trip or an alcohol spree, or even with love which could, as far as was possible, even have been free.

---

9 A chillum, or chilam, is a straight conical, tube-like pipe traditionally made of clay and used in India since the eighteenth century.
10 The Cagiva Motor is an Italian motorcycle manufacturer. It entered the motorcycle market in 1978 after having taken over a factory which produced Harley Davidsons.

The woman with pot.

STONED ANGELS

The Shark. *The Vagabond.*

Gabicce Mare, near Rimini, a club called Baia Imperiale, a tacky structure overrun with porticoes and plaster centurions; it looks like a garden centre run by hairdressers. Legend has it this was the site of Baia degli Angeli – the Bay of Angels – a breathtaking nightclub overlooking the sea, designed to hold 3,000 of Italy's wealthiest, most beautiful people. As the cocktail hour descended, actresses, artists, playboys, designers and heiresses would gather, framed by the startling scenery around them, either indoors or under the darkening sky. The DJ booth was built in a glass lift so the 'discaires' could play for four different dance floors at once, gliding from one to another as they selected their tunes. Everywhere was a snowy white, including the dust that made the night sparkle.

(Bill Brewster, Frank Broughton – Italian afro-cosmic)

The Bay of Angels today. Baia Imperiale.

Angie is still with Freddy. Their sole interests revolve around two things: girls, where to find them and having fun. Added together, they lead to the same result: a nightclub.

'Well, did you hear about Cosmic? Apparently, it opened and all hell broke loose!'

'Wow! How did that get to be nationwide news?'

'I don't know, maybe something amazing happened?'

'Sure, Drill told me that people came from all over, by car, by Vespa, on foot. It might have something to do with the music.'

'We just have to go! But we've got to go in Bay of Angels' style, what do you think?'

'Shit, that's right! God knows what I'm gonna wear but I can ask Drill if he can lend us something second hand.'

'Great idea! But, how do we sneak out with that kind of gear on?'

'Don't worry, I'll bring a bag. We can put everything in there and then change on the way to the Cosmic.'

'Good thinking!'

There was a time when the mania for second-hand clobber reached fever pitch, especially among the Angels. There was actually a second-hand shop called America in Via Roma. It was totally unique. When you went in, it looked like one giant closet with everything hanging, layers of sweaters, shirts and jackets, while on the floor, like a superannuated jumble sale, there were rows and rows of trousers and garments of all stripes and sizes. Rather than aim at a particular target – hippies, punks, bikers etc. – it was a vast melting pot of the entire world's clothing options. You could find a denim jacket with the American eagle sewn on the back next to an Indian sari. You had to rummage and dig to find things because even the shop assistant had no idea where anything was. As soon as order was restored another group would arrive and chaos resumed. Prices appeared to be made-up on the spot, often with no discernible logic, but were undoubtedly advantageous, thanks to a few little tips from clued-up parents.

A moped approaches. It enters the courtyard. It stops. The engine dies. A strange guy gets off. It's Hugo. Why strange? Because, apart from the red trousers and curly hair shaped like a bush, it's perhaps more interesting to know how he acquired those ring-like abrasions on his chin and cheeks. Hugo has a beard and to shave it completely, he presses the heads of the electric razor on his skin. Result? One strange guy.

'Hi, Hugo! There you are! How's it goin'?' Asks Freddy.

'Yeah, good! I feel good!'

'Perfect! Let me introduce you to Angie, a pal we used to go to motocross competitions with.'

'Hey! How's it goin'?'

'Great! I'm here at Freddy's because we're thinking about goin' to Lazise by moped, you know, to the Cosmic. D'ya wanna come?'

'Why not? What's the plan?'

'Well! The main problem is finding the right clothes but it seems Drill can lend them to us.'

'Oh, yeah? What kind of clothing?' Hugo asks inquisitively.

'Well, first we need to go into town and buy Indian sandals at America. White clogs are so last year and we'll need to ponce some stonewashed jeans and stuff like that from Drill,' Angie suggests.

'Perfect! I'll see what I can find at home, maybe something weird in my dad's drawers, you know, hippie shirts or, I don't know, let's see.'

June 1979. Early afternoon. Freddy, Angie and Hugo set off in three on two motorbikes. Destination Lazise. There is only one road. They head towards Lake Garda. Bums are fraying as they travel the 30 km that separate the city from Lazise sitting on the rack or on a Ciao bicycle saddle. Never mind, this time they have a comfortable Vespa 50cc seat.

Along the way we see boys and girls, two by two on motorbikes, all heading in the same direction. Some of them are practically perched on the rear wheel as they cling to the rider's abdomen. Legs and feet hang loose so as not to touch the asphalt. The most technological of them have foot pegs installed on the wheel's axle to provide some comfort on the journey. The other option is for both passengers to sit on the seat but in that case, the driver is a bit uncomfortable due to the tip of the seat separating his buttocks and slipping into the arse. Setting off is really affected by the extra weight and requires Flintstones-like running to pick up speed. Travel is alternately in a line or in pairs. The journey is also slowed down by intermittent conversations that break out between the various riders and pillion passengers, to-ing and fro-ing as riders slow down, like an elaborate motorised dance. So much to talk about, so long to get there. The biggest danger is the police. Getting a fine, no matter how small, is a catastrophe for teenagers on virtually zero pocket money. There is one simple tactic. When a patrol is spotted, the passenger swiftly jumps off the back while the driver continues and picks his friend up again once past the traffic cops. The only other alternative is to find a different route.

The primary concern is not getting a fly in your eye but how to fix your fringe after the hot air has ruffled and messed it up. Never mind, the notorious disco bathrooms will be ready and waiting.

'Do you know what time it opens?'

'It opens at three.'

'Can we make it in a couple of hours?'

'We have to, at all costs! Don't forget we also have to change so we need to find a place.'

'Yeah! Where are we goin' to change?'

'Look, to get the Cosmic, instead of taking the lake road we can take a country road and get there from behind.'

'That's right! Once we take the country road, it'll be easy to find a place to change!'

'Of course, the two cool Angels know alternative roads!'

Remarks Angie.

'Great! Jamboooo[11]!'

Shortly before Lazise, they turn left onto a narrow road that runs parallel to the lake. They slow down to search for a suitable place in which to change their clothes. They find one. A corn field very close to the disco. They stop, leave the motorbikes down the road and, taking the bag, make their way into the field. They go deep enough so as not to be seen.

'What you got for me?' Hugo asks inquisitively.

'Drill's jeans, the old, faded and tattered ones,' Freddy assures him.

'Great! They're a bit greasy but I can still wear them.'

'No wonder. Half the city has worn them!' Quips Angie.

'Okay guys, come on! Here we are! I can feel the Cosmic getting closer!'

They return to their motorbikes, which either with a pedal or kick-start, cough into action. They ride around the bend. An extremely high hedge along the road seems to hide goodness knows what secret. They see nothing except several cars parked on the side of the way that, as they advance, multiply as if leaving a coded message with their number plates from Milan, Verona, Turin, Reggio Emilia, Florence and even Austria and the Netherlands. Nerves give way to a sense of keen anticipation. They glimpse the end of the hedge and, travelling at walking pace, head towards what appears to be an opening to the car park. They move gingerly forward along a road teeming with Angels, their left feet trailing on the asphalt to make sure they don't get knocked off. There have been many cases of two guys on a motorbike who, either at a traffic light or a give-way sign, were both convinced of the same thing. The driver thinks "the one behind has put his foot down", while the passenger thinks "the driver has put his foot down" with the inevitable result of a dramatic tumble.

They finally enter the square, and there, right in front of them, a unique sight opens up. Even if they don't have such a great knowledge of the world of discos, at a glance, this place seems highly unlikely. Hugo immediately gets off from behind and says something that none of the others understands. It looks like a square

---

11 Jambo in Swahili, one of the most widespread languages in Africa, means "hello"

that doubles as a Sunday market, yet it is a kind of "anarchic" and lawless territory. The Angels mingle with incoming and outgoing cars, groups of guys and girls gather while others wander alone, bouncing from here to there like a pinball. Cars from far and wide - Ferrara, Mantua, Brescia, Piacenza and Pisa – are parked everywhere.

'Hold on, how did they know about this place?'

The answer was soon to become evident. They were witnessing the start of a new culture and musical movement that sprung from clubs like Cosmic.

The "Afro"[12].

> Africano: When it comes to this Deep Disco cut, Africano is one of those tracks that probably never got much shine in America, but has since become a dancefloor favorite of underground disco DJs worldwide. Curiously, years after its release, its biggest supporters were Italian DJs like Danielle Baldelli, Mozart and Gianni Maselli who during the 80s played Disco, African records, American R&B, and reggae to create what has become since known as the Afro-Cosmic scene at the height of Club culture in the discothèques of Northern Italy.

---

12 Afro means: coming from Africa. For example, there are types of hairstyles in "afro" style, "Afro" food, clothes and all manner of things, including music. The Afro Italian music trend should not be considered a genre of its own, which it is not, but rather a container of various musical experiences and indicates any kind of music strongly influenced, whether directly or indirectly, by tribal rhythms and African culture. Afro-jazz, afro percussion, afro Brazil, afro funky, afro Cuban or just African music, such as afrobeat, juju music, high life, reggae, blues.

They try to park their motorbikes somewhere among the Vespa ET3s, Citroen 2 CVs, Renault 4s and DS Sharks, whose owners, on seeing them arrive, greet them in the mutual understanding that: "they belong to our tribe". They finally find parking space and there, right next to them, is the Cosmic. Their eyes settle on the façade for what feels like an eternity. It's just a building with a spaceship painted on it but, nonetheless, time seems weightless as the entranced onlooker registers every last delicious detail.

Entrance with the spaceship.

Someone is lying on the ground, sleeping bag cast aside from the previous night's long wait. Others are leaning against cars smoking spliffs, cigarettes or sipping beer. You can tell from their clothes that this wonderful gathering of youth are all Angels. Dialects intermingle, all gender, class and age barriers melt away. You can speak to a stranger as if he were an old buddy and no-one blinks an eye. It's as if everyone has known each other forever. They are a tribe. Our tribe. We notice the luggage racks on some Vespas.

'Look, have you seen what those guys have on their Vespas?'
'Oh yeah! They must have come a long way and slept over...'
'Yeah, of course. You do see, though, that it's a new life, don't you? It isn't about goin' to the club, having sex with some bird or dancing, always in the same place...'
'Shit, that's right! For them, it's travel, freedom, adventure...'
'Riiiiiight! We should organise something bigger too, I don't know, a disco faraway, always new people, what do you think?'
'Sure thing. We'll meet up at my house one night and work something out, okay?'

They walk towards the door that looks like a large pipeline coming out of the wall. The entrance ritual has yet to come and their eager anticipation is fed further as they approach amid the full volume stereo systems installed in the boots of cars, whose blast ingeniously shuts off when the hatchback is closed, leaving the woofers fixed on the decklid in plain sight. They cross the threshold. The tunnel is slightly cold. You cannot see the end because it has a curve highlighted by two, bright, parallel stripes running underfoot and veering left. The passage is studded with silver stars. They sense they are about to break into something "cosmic". You don't hear the music, just something soft, indicating that the show hasn't started yet. An opening smothered in stickers serves as a ticket office on the left. Two beautiful girls, framed by this little window, welcome everyone with a smile. One in particular fondles the coloured Cosmic stickers so bewitchingly that she almost charms everyone into buying one.

At last, they are in. The refreshing breeze on their faces is replaced by a heat that grabs them by the neck. The dance hall is already crowded with Angels. They slowly make their way in and their eyes are immediately struck by two contrasting colours. The first is a dark band that reaches the average height from the ground of the people it consists of and is surmounted by the second, which is a blaze of brushstrokes of lights all over the ceiling seemingly joined to the silhouette of the crowd by columns of light. The music is still playing in the background so the usual perusal seems the next logical action. DJ Daniele Baldelli's console, set up inside an emerald green astronaut helmet, is also immediately striking. You can barely see the lighting guy, who is called 'Lucifer'. There doesn't seem to be much going on there, so the three decide to walk around the perimeter before taking a much closer look at the helmet. They notice that a few steps covered in a sapphire-coloured velvet separate the dance floor from the disco wall. The room seems to go on forever and the intermittent spot lights converge endlessly like straight parallel lines. They realise that the effect is due to a large mirror covering the entire wall at the end of the dance hall. A small bar serves drinks in paper cups with "Cosmic" printed on them. Coming out of the Angels' ranks, they enter a cube of light: the dancefloor. Curiously, it is still empty. True enough, the space is small in comparison to the "2" disco but, if you add the world that is inside to what is outside, it's an immense universe. At around three o'clock, the intro theme starts. Electronic notes bounce into the dry ice emanating from the enormous helmet and the DJs are no longer visible. The Angels group on the dancefloor and the Cosmic comes alive with all its luminous power and, in the loudness of this brand-new genre, they start to dance.

Livin', livin' in the jungle. Lovin', lovin' in the jungle.
(John Tropea - Livin' in the jungle)

You don't talk at the Cosmic, you dance and you get high. There is no interval at the Cosmic. Slow dances don't exist. You don't think about anything at the Cosmic. You close your eyes and watch the flashes of light penetrating your eyelids. There is no time at the Cosmic. You stay alive right through to closing time.

On the other hand, you can say that time doesn't exist at all...
(Richard Wahnfried - Time Actor)

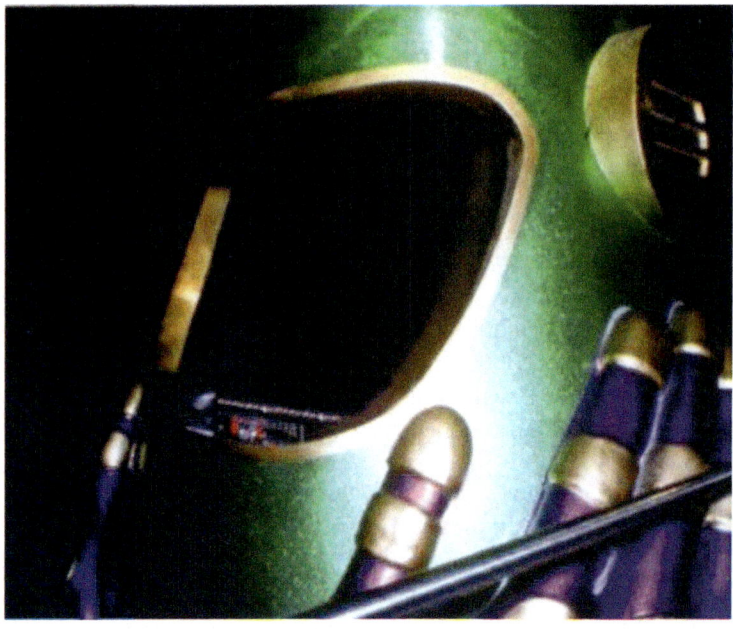

Cosmic Booth – Console.

Freddy says he wants to smoke, needs a break. He asks Angie and Hugo if they want to go out as well to see if he can scrounge a cigarette. They nod and, making their way to the entrance, ask if they can go out. The girls on either side of the tunnel nod, but first, they have to show their wrists and then, one at a time, they each receive an ink stamp[13] on their skin by way of a re-entry pass. They walk out into the large square and even though two hours have passed since their arrival, chaos still reigns.

While smoking a fag, they can't take their eyes off a beautiful girl with long, blond hair, dressed in a full-length, close-fitting white dress with a wide, shiny white belt falling onto her hips. She is hugging a guy. She puts her arms around his neck and glues herself to him. The moment she kisses him, she begins to slide down with her head. She loosens her arms, leaving them stretched as her face

---

13 *An ink stamp on the wrist so that those who go out of the disco can come back inside later.*

slides down his chest and her knees bend. Her arms, still completely stretched, are no longer on his neck, only her hands are still on his chest. Her knees touch the ground. The girl's position, rather than looking like someone doing penitence, takes on the aspect of a blowjob. She is stoned. This is the Cosmic. You go in and out all the time, you see all kinds of weird stuff both inside and out. The first signs of demobilisation can be seen after four hours of cosmic vibrations. For some, tomorrow is Monday, perhaps.

'Guys, have you seen all those slackers over there with sleeping bags and tents?'

'Yeaaaah! I'd like a wandering adventure too...'

'Riiiiight! That's what I'm talking about! We have to do some trips, further away from the lake. We have to do the same as them, maybe to some other disco...'

'That's right! That's the only way we'll ever be truly cool. We'll have to get together and decide where to go next time. Maybe in Emilia-Romagna! They say the clubs there are full of the most beautiful chicks in summer. Full of pussy!'

'Great idea! We have to get a radio though so that we can fool around along the way.'

'Shall we go back in and buy their latest tape? I see they're selling them in the DJ's helmet and they're numbered with the letter C, C1, C2, C3?'

Cosmic mixtapes, C numbered.
☺

    Poplar's house is huge. Nestled in the countryside, it dominates the neighbouring houses because it's higher up. An embankment gently descends towards the fence along the road, forming a beautiful garden. You go in through a large sliding gate and park your motorbike near a wide descent. That descent will make history. It leads to a basement den, an excellent hangout for friends, especially during the winter.
    'Hi, Poplar! Everything ok?'
    Whenever Poplar meets his friends, he always greets them with one arm held high, hand open and a fag perched sideways between

his lips.

'Heyyy! Great!'

Lamp, whose name derives from his ability to change light bulbs, is with him. Yet another weirdo, when his parents bought him a Vespa, he spent the whole night in the garage pretending to ride it.

'Guys, I just wanted to get to know it, bond with it.'

His bike flaunted a sticker on the headlight: "Your summer is called Lamp".

'Hey! I have something to tell you. I went to the Cosmic with two pals from Verona, I want you to meet them!'

'Coolio! Next Sunday, okay?'

'Perfect!'

Sunday arrives at last. Introductions over, this time there are five of them going to the Cosmic and, to top that, they have also managed to scrounge a lift from Savage and Bulldozer, two guys who are heading to the lake by car.

'What's so special about this Cosmic club?' the car guy, who usually goes to "2" or Thucana, asks.

'It's the DJ, he's different from the rest. The music he plays, the way he mixes, the people, everything!'

Daniel Baldelli stood out from his peers, most of whom played more commercial sounds, because he had a particular take on the music he played, which eventually became known as the 'Cosmic sound' or, as some dancers called it, 'Afro'. Baldelli bought and listened to a lot of vinyl, especially anything off-the-wall, unusual or plain odd, something that fitted into the menu he held in his mind, combing them into a strange and unique fantasy. He was also notable for his experiments with speed, often playing 45s at 33rpm and vice versa.

While my mind struggles to remember things from last week, I will never forget the time when I was first exposed to a mix from Daniele Baldelli, cruising around the bends on the Great Ocean Road. This audio paradise completely transcended my deep escapism. Synth pop 12"s played at half speed and morphed into this slowmo evil? Reggae LPs at 45? Somehow all magically blended into a sonic excursion of electronic kraut, afro boogie, jazz rock and disco staples. With three turntables (pre-pitch control), a reel to reel and home engineered filters, this legendary Italian would make Phil Collins sound like the most epic shit ever recorded. DJing at Baia degli Angeli between 1977-1978 and then at Cosmic Club 1979-1984, he had an output of over 100 mixtapes, many of which were created with his likeminded cronies Marco Maldi and TBC. They still sound as visionary to this day and Baldelli continues to spread his original style across Europe, simulating the Cosmic experience for new comers.
(Noise In My Head)

His tapes, which became legendary, were released onto the market to hungry clubbers as well as other DJs. Freddy, Angie, Hugo and many others were besotted with this style.

'So? What should we do? Should we check out some other places?'

'Yep! Did you see how hot those Emilia girls were at Cosmic?'

'I've no idea where they came from, but yeah, they're hot.'

'Fair enough, but what I like is that they're friendlier, not as snooty as others.'

'Well, if you say so. Why don't we check out some other Emilia clubs?'

'Hummmm, which ones?'

'Well, someone, told me that the Picchio Rosso is a cool spot.'

'Where is it?'

'Close to Modena, in Formigine.'

'OK, but how would we get there?'

'If we left in the morning, we could take the train and come back late.'

'And what do we tell our folks?'

'That we're going to the lake for the day. Simple.'

'All right, I'll bring a radio for company if you check out the timetables.'

'Let's all meet at mine later.'
At Angie's house, it is already midnight.
'Let's meet back here tomorrow morning.'

☺

That night Angie paces around the house until 3:30, anxious about the plans for the following day. He eventually falls asleep only to wake again at 7. Hugo arrives at about 8.

'Alright geezer, everything okay?'
'Cool man, think we're gonna have a great time today.'
'Yeah, we'll be fine, buuuut, where's Freddy?'
'I haven't seen him yet. Has something happened?'
'I don't know but it's already 8:30. We absolutely must leave now!'
'Let's try and catch up with him. Maybe he got stuck on the way.'
'Come on! Let's get goin'!'
They bump into him along the way.
'Holy shit! We've gotta take the bus to the city!'
They reach the village and park the motorbikes in a private garage without a proper door. They don't even know who the owner is – but at this stage, who cares? – and run to the bus stop. It's already gone nine o'clock. The bus has just left.

'Shit. Now what? The train to Modena leaves at 9:30. How the fuck can we get to the station? I definitely don't think it's safe to leave the motorbikes at the station.'
'Come on! Come on! We'll hitch a ride! Jamboooo!'
All four - the three boys and the radio - hit the road. Two walk forwards and the other, being out of his mind, walks backwards like a shrimp.
'No-one's gonna give a shit about us on a Sunday morning!'
'Chill out, mate.'
They're in luck. An Austrian guy stops and picks them up. What an Austrian is doing on the road is not clear and they don't bother to ask. They are too focused on the time. Twenty minutes later he drops them at the station. There's not even time for a thank you.
'Auf Wiedersehen! Danke schön!'
Those are the only German words they know.
They rush into the station and hit the ticket office. Return to Modena. They check the platform number and make a dash for it.

The train is about to leave and they make it by the skin of their teeth. They dive into the first empty compartment. The sweat from their frantic scramble glues them to their seats. They look at each other, smile and burst out laughing. They get the fags out and turn on the radio to improvise dances. It takes about two hours to reach Modena station and, once off the train, they ask a railway worker for directions to Formigine.

'Christ, Formigine is twenty kilometres away, you'll need to take a taxi!'

'But if we're on foot, which way is it?'

'Fair enough. As you get out of the station car park, take Via Giardini and keep going.'

'Thank you, Jamboooo!'

'I have to call my girlfriend, just give me a minute!'

'Come on, it's almost noon! The club opens at three!'

Maybe she's in need for a kiss. I said hey, what's your name, maybe we can see things the same.   (Witch Queen - All Right Now)

'Really? I'm starving. Can we stop for something to eat at a pizzeria? Just a quick bite?'

'OK, but it'll have to be somewhere cheap, I don't have much money with me.'

'Don't worry; we're all in the same boat.'

They leave the station and start walking.

'Look, this place fits the bill. Cool with you lot?'

'Let's do it.'

They have a plate of spaghetti with tomato sauce and a glass of water, after which they set off again towards Formigine but not before Angie makes another call to his new girlfriend. His old one dumped him and he doesn't even know why.

'Jesus, stop making bloody phone calls, we really don't have time for that shit.'

They resume their earlier formation: two walking in front, the third, with thumb out, moving like a shrimp.

They get lucky. An Angel in a Dyane 6 stops and sees that they are from the same tribe. Solidarity among brethren.

'Hi guys, where'ya heading?'

'We're going to Formigine, to the Picchio Rosso.'

'Get in! You're in luck, that's where I'm heading too.'

Fifteen minutes later they are standing in front of the club. 'Amazing, we made it!'

There is still half an hour to go before it opens so they have plenty of time to look around. There are already scores of people gathered in the large square waiting for the club to open. A bit of chat and they soon find out that the place hosts anywhere between three and four thousand clubbers on Sundays. As opening time approaches, the Angels form an exhausting crush around the entrance. Here and there, they hear snippets of information about its history. Artists like Donna Summer, Ray Charles and John Miles have all played here in the past.

The building itself is impressive with its accurately-designed, rounded and oblique turrets. They wonder what the inside will look like since each club always has its own unique style. The clock strikes three at last.

Picchio Rosso Club (Red Woodpecker).

Slowly, step by step, the Angels squeeze through until it's their turn. They're out of their comfort zone here. Who knows whether it will have the same impact as the Cosmic club.

'Excuse me, where do you think you're goin'?'
'Me?'
'Yep, you!'
'What do you mean, where am I going? I'm here to dance. What're you on about?'
'You can't come in.'
'Eh?' They chorus.

They've already handed in the radio at the cloakroom. 'You can't come in with those! What are they supposed to be anyway? Trousers?'

Hugo is sporting a pair of pants, somewhere between over-plumped cushions and a Persian carpet.

'What, why? What about the others?'
'There's a dress code.'
'Hold on, mate. I came from Verona practically on foot. It's summer, it's fucking hot and I'm here with my pals. Come on, give us a break.'

The bouncer ignores the pleas.

'Listen, just this once, okay? It won't happen again.'
'This is the first time we've ever been here, don't spoil it!'
Disgruntled Angels begin to moan...
'You're blocking, everybooooodyyy.'
... and persuade the bouncer.
'Just this one time. Get out of my sight.'

You're damn right. Who is the man that would risk his neck for his brother man?   (Issac Hayes - Shaft)

They get through. After missing the bus and then almost the train, they risked a club-based disaster. But the stress swiftly evaporates when they start to dance.

Do it any way you wanna do it. Do it any way you wanna do it! Do it! (Peoples Choice - Do it any way you wanna)

There are three levels inside and a myriad of still and flashing lights. Laser traces illuminate the Plexiglas handrail while brightly lit steps and gangways with rotating colours suggest the designers had definitely been to Las Vegas. The tacky decor, gaudiness and tasteless fun are all part of the club owner's armoury. But at the end of the day, it's still all about business.

Two hours fly by and it's time to leave. They are exhausted. They never stopped dancing and because one track merges into the next, there was no break, just one continuous groove. The signal that the party is about to shudder to a halt comes from playing a downtempo track. It's about half five. They leave, somewhat sweaty, and hit the road to Modena train station. Thumbs out, of course.

'What time is the train?'

'Half six.'

'If we get a lift in the next 20 minutes, we'll just about make it.'

Once again, they set off. Cars drive by but nobody stops. An hour ticks by and still no-one has stopped.

'Guys, shall we see if there are any buses?'

'On a Sunday?'

They keep on walking. Thumbs out, still hopeful, when a black BMW pulls over. They run towards the car.

'Hi, cowboys!'

It's an American with another guy. Quite what a yank is doing on this road, God only knows.

'Where're you heading?'

'Modena station.'

'Come on, get in... where're you from?'

'Verona, you?'

'San Francisco.'

'Nice, what about you?'

'I'm from Belgium.'

They never did find out what an American and a Belgian were doing on the road to Modena. Twenty minutes later, they are dropped off in front of the station. There's no time for pleasantries but they thank the driver for everything and rush into the station. They've missed the train.

'Shit! What now?'

'Let's see when the next one is.'

9.15 pm.

'We've got a 90-minute wait!'

They call home to let their parents know that they will be late and Angie calls his girlfriend. Again. Rather than hanging out near the ticket office, they head out and start wandering aimlessly around.

After countless laps around the station without finding anything interesting, they sit down in the square and listen to the radio until it's almost time to catch the train.

What an awful day. What a terrible day. All day. All day.
(Throbbing Gristle - What a Day)

'It's time to go home. Thank fuck for that.'
It's a local train and stops at every tinpot town and village along the route. The journey home is painfully slow.
This time there's no private party in the compartment, just shooting the shit, smoking fags and telling stories.
'What do you call a woman with no legs? .... A snail.'
At the umpteenth stop, which happens to be Mantua, a voice rings out:
'Allll change please!"
'Shit! What the fuck are we gonna do?'
They get off the train to ask for information. There's a bus that leaves outside the station. Unfortunately, it makes the train journey feel like a Japanese bullet train in comparison. The radio is the journey's lifesaver.

My happy radio is never too far. I just reach out my hand, turn the dial and I know it will make me smile (Edwin Star-H.A.P.P.Y. radio)

They get back at 11.30 and rush to the bus station.
'Fuck, are there no buses back home?'
'Please don't say we have to walk home!'
'How much money have we got?'
'Come on, we can afford a cab.'
The taxi stops in front of the place where they left the motorbikes. It's midnight. The motorbikes are still there.

And when the sun goes down, my fantasies gone wild when midnight comes around...   (T Connection - At Midnight)
☺
The summer is about to enter peak season. Freddy's birthday comes round and it's another excuse to socialise.
'Easy mate, how's everything?'
'Wicked. Fancy a tipple?'

'A Vov[14].'
'Come and meet Jake and Claudio.'
'Not seen you guys around here much before.'
'Well, we live on the same street.'
'Thing is we work, so we're out during the day. We usually hang out at night.'
'Man, I need some cash too! I've heard there's work on a farm somewhere.'
'Yeah, we've heard about your club adventures!'
'Innit! Freddy, did you tell him about our little jaunt to Picchio Rosso?'
'Well yeah, we're planning another sortie out there too, aren't we, Angie?'
'Could be a pretty cool little expedition, for sure.'

On summer evenings, it's customary to take a little ride around the local villages, get in a few beers, some wine and maybe even a joint. The perfect setting, in fact, to make new friends. These trips into unknown territories swiftly bolster up the gang, so Claudio and Jake soon become tight friends with Poplar, Lamp and Volt, who manages a little video store. As the crew expands, it becomes increasingly difficult to find a house to hang out in, so the village square becomes the meeting place par excellence.

'Easy, chaps!'

These loose configurations of youths, whose connections are based on friendships, school or location, gather wherever there are free steps, walls or benches to sit on. These are the tribes of various genre that populate the streets of Verona: Paninaros, rockers, punks and heavy metal freaks. The latter category, a rarer form of species festooned in studs and shrouded in grubby leather, frequently shares the same space as punks.

Ring! Ring! It's 7:00 A.M.! Move y'self to go again. Cold water in the face. (The Clash - The magnificent seven)

Even during the peak years of disco, it's worth noting that punk rock was the most pervasive of all the youth cults in Italy. But

---

14 Vov is a famous Italian liqueur made with Pellegrino Marsala, free-range egg yolks, Madagascan vanilla, milk and sugar. This versatile drink can be enjoyed on its own, either chilled or warm, or even as a topping for ice cream.

perhaps the most notable gang of them all was the Paninaros. This subculture, which originated in Milan in the 1980s, was the most stylish and, it has to be said, also the most fun. Each city had its own brand of Paninaro, who were so committed that they would happily skip a meal if it meant being able to afford a Lacoste polo shirt. Battles raged between these two divergent youth cults, the press comparing them to the iconic New York gang movie, The Warriors, while the police kept a tight lid on anything getting too out of hand. This fertile scenario of youth included the Angels.

We are assassins. We are not evil. We act with reason and heart. Your heart. (Gary Numan - I assassin)

'Right guys, I'm off on holiday for a while, if you see my gal, say hello from me,' Freddy pleads.

'Don't worry; we'll take care of her.'

'I'm splitting too, I met a couple of birds called Stump and Frog, give them a nod if you see them,' adds Poplar.

'No worries, squire.'

These exchanges of favours and especially where to find the place to go, lead to a decision to divide the city into sectors: A, B, C, D, E, F, G.

'Anyway, which club is next on the list?'

'What about Les Cigales in Brescia? It only just opened.'

'After the last train, plane and car caper, how about we just try going on our bikes?'

'Cool, it's a plan.'

Those left behind decide to put their new money-making scheme into action. Facing the simple equation, no money = no club, they head into the city centre every Saturday around 2 pm. At that time, it's teeming with people and motorbikes. Vespas and mopeds snake round the flower beds that dot the entrance to the old town. They also park there and, once the bikes are secure, set off for a stroll. Dressed in full Bay Angel regalia, and therefore a little tatty around the edges, they hit the high street and start asking:

'Can you spare a bit of change, please?'

'Excuse me, any small change going spare?'

But they're not only on the scrounge, they also want to make new friends and take note of any new trends. For example, Indian sandals are losing ground to espadrilles. Indeed, the shop that sells the Indian kicks are also selling espadrilles in a bewildering variety of colours.

'What do you think about white, guys? Do you think it suits me?'

'Easy Jake, did you make any dough?'

'A bit, yeah.'

'Shall we scoot?'

'Let's wait for Freddy and then go. What's the score for tomorrow?'

The plan is to meet up with mates camping by the lake.

One is particularly highly rated. Mauro, nicknamed Camel, due to his addiction to the singular American cigarette brand. He even has a poem dedicated to him.

THE CAMEL.

IN THE ARID DESERTS THE CARAVAN PASSES,
WHERE THE BLAZING SANDS DREAM OF A FOUNTAIN...
THE CAMEL DOESN'T DREAM. CALM, TRUSTING HE GOES,
THE WATER FOR HIS THIRST
WILL NEVER BE LACKING.
IN HIS NATURAL "PIGGY BANK"
HE STOCKED UP AT THE START:
HE WILL HAVE SOME FOR A GOOD STRETCH YET.
A PRECIOUS INSTINCT SO COMMANDED HIM.
SAVE IT, AND YOU'LL HAVE WHAT YOU SAVED.

'Can you see the pissing man?'

To save money, the same pals spend Sunday hitchhiking with a pitstop at the Cosmic in the afternoon. Sometimes they buy a mixtape at the DJ booth and then zip round to Volt's to make bootleg copies. Sometimes, they don't even bother going in, partying by the boot of the DS. But this Sunday is different. It's Les Cigales in Brescia.

'Look, I haven't got my Vespa so I need a lift.'

'I don't have my moped either. It's my brother's and he needs it.'

'OK, so I'll take Claudio and you can take Hugo.'

'Hugo's gonna have a square arse travelling on the Ciao.'

'Tell you what, drop me off at the station and I'll take the train to Peschiera and you can pick me up there. I think the club is outside Brescia.'

'Sounds like a plan, there and back.'

When you ride a motorcycle, you usually go at full throttle. When the petrol tank is getting low, you can sense it by the dull noise of the engine and the drop in speed. One little trick is to swing, sway, hop and pull it up hard with the handlebars just to coax that extra mile to the nearest petrol station.

After collecting Hugo in good time, they start to ask around.

'Excuse me, do you know the way to Les Cigales?'

'The what?'

'It's a club near Brescia.'

'Don't know, try asking once you get to Lonato.'

Several similar answers swiftly follow until, further on, they finally hear the answer they are looking for:

'Bedizzole! Follow your nose and you'll be there!'

They make frequent stops and that's when the chatter kicks off.

'That guy's got such a huge overbite, when it rains, his mouth turns into a reservoir.'

'What the fuck are you on about?'

They reach Bedizzole at last. Finding the club is a cinch. They are soon standing in front of the entrance:

"Club closed this Sunday. Sorry for the inconvenience".

They go back with their tails between their legs. They mirror the outward journey and pick Hugo up at Verona station.

☺

The summer days are long, languid and carefree. Casual meetings are a daily occurrence and sometimes they even get to take some girls home, packing three on the motorbike. Any chance is right to get talking to the opposite sex.

Poplar always says:

'Even the ugly ones are good; they always have a pretty girlfriend.'

Afternoons are spent hanging out with various members of the crew. The old Saturday and Sunday routines fade away since Drill is rarely around these days.

'We went to Les Cigales but it was closed.'

'That sounds like a waste of time.'

The old Drill seems to have been replaced by a new, quieter version. He rarely talks and when he does, his teeth look bad. They are turning black, rotting. When he laughs, he puts his hand in front of his mouth or clamps his lips tight shut. Thankfully there was no Pancho today with his spliff and marijuana oil. Freddy pipes up:

'Right, I've got a suggestion. There's a new place called Caravel in Mantua. It's definitely open.'

'What about transport?'

'We could use the Picchio Rosso method but it'd be a trek.'

'What does everyone else think?'

'Claudio's up for it, Hugo's a don't know.'

'Jake?'

'Not this time.'

It's a tried and tested method. Bus to the station. Train to Mantua. Then thumbs out. It's only five kilometres to the club and Angie, Freddy and Claudio start walking down the main street. This time they are lucky. An R4 with three Angels on board stops almost immediately. We're quids in here, they think.

'You guys goin' to the Caravel, by any chance?'

'Yep!'

'You're in luck, get in.'

'Six?! Tight squeeze...'

'No problem, jump in!'

Unfortunately, the Carabinieri are on patrol in their Gazelle[15]. As soon as they spot the traffic cop, the driver slams on the brakes and drops them off. The trio walk on as though nothing has happened. They amble past the Alfa without the officers even noticing them. They never see the occupants of the car again.

---

15 *Alfa Romeo car for the force.*

They dance barefoot. Unfortunately, someone nicks their Indian sandals. They feel a keen sense of betrayal that someone might do this. They leave, shouting:
'This club sucks!'
'Even the music is shit!'
'And the people!'
At this point, someone asks where they are from.
'Turin!' they reply.
They trudge down the road, thumbs out, barefoot. Luckily, a black Shark driven by two Angels pulls over.
"This looks exactly like the kind of car that would get pulled over," they think.
'You heading anywhere near the station?'
'Smoke? Trip? Joint? Hash? Pot?'
'No mate, just the station, ta.'
On the way, they bump into the Carabinieri again although this time they are in the service station on the opposite side of the road. The officers look at the black car without doing anything other than tap the signalling disc repeatedly on the bottom of their boots. Amazingly, given their previous bad luck, they make the train and arrive back in Verona. They do, however, end up walking barefoot back to the village after the bus breaks down. Can't win 'em all, eh?

☺

    The gang also hits the city on some summer evenings, especially in Sector C, where they meet up with two blondes known as the Gypsies.

    'Hi Luke, how're ya doing?'
    'Good mate, listen, I need to talk to you about something.'
    'I'm all ears, bro!'
    'There are these hotties in Vicenza I'd like to meet up with. There's one in particular, see.'
    'And?'
    'Fancy coming with me?'
    'You need a wingman, do you?!'
    'For fuck's sake, it's not like that. She's got mates and I was thinking we could meet them in a club there.'
    'What, there are clubs in Vicenza?'
    'There's the Pub Club. It'll be fun.'
    'Train? Hitching?'

'They'll meet us off the train.'
'Oh, aye, how's that then?'
'They've got wheels.'
'Ooh, proper grown-ups!'

Angie and Jake head off towards the station in the early afternoon where Freddy and Luke, who's walking as if he's got a melon up his arse, are waiting for them. As with all club adventures, the trusty radio accompanies them in the carriage for an impromptu train disco. The girls are waiting for them when they arrive. One, the brunette, is called Emmanuelle, the other has red hair and goes by the name of Roxanne. She drives a red R4 and is Luke's love interest, the primary reason, in fact, why they are here.

'She's a redhead?'
'Yeah, do you know that Police song - Roxanne, you don't have to put on the red light?'

The club is full of Angels and the brunette doesn't waste any time in introducing them to as many friends as possible. The other is engrossed in Luke. Sometimes they hit the dancefloor. The DJ plays pure disco here.

Don't you wanna dance? Everybody, get on up and dance. Get on up, yeah!   (Hamilton Bohannon - Let's start the dance)

They dance.

Dance, dance, dance dancing to the tip. Take me all night. Dance, dance, dance dancing to the tip. (Free Life - Dance Fantasy)

They keep dancing.

Movin' it together. Bursting lights all around me. Now were here forever. (Peter Jacques Band - Fire Night Dance)

These afternoon club sessions last two and a half hours, so the time to head home comes round all too quickly. Luke and Roxanne remind them it's time to go. Shame, they were really feeling the music. In a generous gesture, Angie gives the brunette his much-coveted Kappa polo shirt.

'Kappa?'
'Yeah, it's the one with the index finger though.'
They never see the girls again.
☺

The assaults on the cities, the club jaunts and new friends all seem to become a weekly occurrence as their friendship circle widens and diversifies. Going to a club while Genny plays a faggot is a brave act. His crazy dancing, frequently off the actual dancefloor, gets him into constant trouble. Once he ended up in a fistfight with a barman. A regular stoner, he'd carry a stash the size of a shopping bag around. Girlfriends, fleeting and temporary, come and go: Lucy, Susy, Ornella, Juliet, Roberta, Lilly, Niki, Rita. The only thing that lasts are their hickeys.

'Hi gorgeous, what's your name?'
'Hugo.'

That's not how it's done in an Italian club. Everyone has their own personal technique for pulling. Take Volt. Now, he will perch on a sofa, squeezed in among two or three girls, and start talking. Endlessly. Nobody really knows what he's saying but one by one, the girls leave. However, if one of them manages to go the duration, he's closed the deal. Poplar, however, hits on everyone. It's almost systematic.

'The law of large numbers,' he says.

Having said that, he's happy just to make friends too. He'll get invitations to private parties through his recent encounters. He's like that. Now Jake tends to attract stoners, possibly because he's always got a ready stash in his pocket.

'Hi, what you doin' here?'
'Hmmmm, have we met before?'
'Not really, are you from GolosAngeles[16]?'
'Santa Lucia.'
'Ah! We knock around there occasionally. Nice place. What's your name?'
'Rita.'
'Fancy meeting some of my mates? Maybe we've got some mutual buddies.'
'Okay, where are they?'

---

16 *Veronese neighbourhoods.*

'Over there.'
Angie, Claudio, Freddy and Jake converge.
'Guys, this is Rita. Oh, and how did it go?'
'Me, nothing.'
'Me neither.'
'Neither did I.'
Nobody gives a shit about hapless Rita. The four guys look at each other.
'We've won the beeeet!'
Earlier in the evening the two duos – Claudio and Angie v. Freddy and Jake – bet on the first to pull.
Rita, who is waiting to be introduced, asks what the fuck is going on:
'A bet? Who wins and what do they win?'
'A vodka!'
'Fuck the lot of you!'

☺

The gang creates chaos even in private. Take Jake, for instance. He decides to have a party at his house but predictably it gets trashed. His father is less than happy, especially since he is in the middle of renovations. The immaculate whitewashed walls are splattered with graffiti lampooning Jake's parents (and Jake himself); Jake blissfully unaware. In between chucking cream cakes, they get out the last album Jake bought: Dynasty, by American cock-rockers, Kiss. They play mean tricks on each other. Lucy fools Angie into thinking she's pregnant with his baby. But the crowning moment is Jake's impersonation of Kiss star, Gene Simmons.

Well, my name it's a number. It's on a piece of plastic film, and I've been growin' funny flowers... (Kiss - 2,000 Man)

'Hold your horses! Stooooop everybody!'
Jake writhes on the floor, air guitar in place, with his tongue wildly lolling about. Gene Simmons would've been proud.

Is it my fortune or my fame? Is it my money or my name?
(Kiss - Charisma).

'Here it is! Here it iiiis! Bleahhhhhhaa!'
It's the climax to every Kiss tune. A minute before, Jake closes

his mouth and with some serious dumbfuckery, manages to perfectly time opening his mouth and sticking his tongue out to coincide with the last note, producing blood from God knows where, that dribbles down his chin. Ladies and gentlemen, he is Gene Simmons personified.

'Happy birthdayyyy! Jaaaake!'

(*Kiss - I was made for lovin' you. Top disco-song in the UK and the Netherlands.*)

☺

The end of the summer is nigh and they already know that there will not be another like it. They have already noticed, as they cruise through the city, that there are scores of bigger and better wheels than theirs, particularly the Vespa PX, a marked step-up in quality. If they can't take their driving test yet, they can at least take the A licence for a 125cc motorbike. Almost all of them enrol at driving schools in the autumn and while some have ordered the new Vespa, a major expense for any family, several are all on the desperate hunt for a decent second-hand one. It's occupying all their minds, an obsession, an object of exquisite desirability.

Angie is intent on finding adverts for Vespas for sale in the local papers. Autumn is fast approaching and they now have to rethink how to occupy their time. There is not an endless number of options: birds, music, parties. Some are still on the scrounge for cash to buy tapes so Volt can bootleg them for various members of the crew.

There's an ever-dizzy roundabout of girls and boys dating and falling out. Jake is with Rita, although a few weeks later he's seeing Susy. But then Susy is seen with another member of the gang. Freddy, surpassing them all, is seen with both Roberta and Lilly on the same day. Meanwhile, Lilly is dating a neighbourhood mate.

Hugo's been spotted with yet another girl.

'How's your new girlfriend?'
'Dunno, mate.'
'What do you mean? What's her name?'
'No idea!'
'How come?!'
'Didn't even have time!'
'What do you mean?'

'She's already dumped me.'

Two birthdays are coming up, Poplar's and Stefan's. Throwing a party is simple. Make an invitation, do photocopies, give them to any likely candidates in the clubs and then see who turns up. No door policy, doesn't matter how old or beautiful, everyone gets in. Poplar's always popular.

'So, what's the plan?'

'We need a sound system.'

'No problem, Volt can sort that out.'

'What about lights?'

'He's got three different colours but we need to see if he can get a strobe.'

'What about food?'

'Crisps and popcorn and we're sorted.'

'Drinks.'

'Oh yeah, we need something that's, like, burnin' with desire, benzene for the party.'

'Ha! Ha! Ha! Good one! Benzene ha! Ha! The benzeneeee.'

'Let's get some bottles of Martini, Vov, Cointreau, beer and maybe Prosecco. Poplar will sort.'

'Perfect! Benz is perfect.'

This just goes to show how easy it is to coin new words, new urban slang. The term "benz" is one of these.

People in the bottle. There's people livin' in the bottle.
(Gil Scott - The bottle)

Each crew has its own slang and, like a disease, it spreads easily and quickly between different groups, disseminating, travelling, mutating, until completely new words emerge. For example, "fixa". Fixa is an obsession. When something enters your head and refuses to leave. It could be an object or a person. Angie's latest fixa is for a girl named Spice - until he got dumped. Stefan, one of the crew's latest recruits, goes for the obvious. Like his bloody scooter.

'Did you know my Vespa does 20 km to the litre?'

'Er, tell us something new. All Vespas do that.'

'A litre, though!'

'I'm sure Jake will be keen to hear your revelation.'

Poplar's party is going well.

'The beeeeenz! The beeenz!'

Someone drunkenly shouts.
'Where's the loo?'
'Outside.'
'Outside, where?'
'Round the back. Lift the seat up on Jake's Vespa, open the petrol cap and bingo.'
'Ha ha ha!'
Jake is industriously nipping back and forth into town on his Vespa, despite it being used as a urinal, to bring yet more people to the party, though nobody has quite figured out how.
'Shit! But, how come it's still working?'
'I'll put a stop to it!'
Freddy, who is the company's bomber, shoves one or two cakes into the tank but even so, for the next two days, Jake still goes around on the Vespa at breakneck speed.

☺

As the autumn evenings draw in, almost everyone is busy with driving lessons although meetings still take place around the phonebooth near Jake's place.
'Jesus, it's bloody freezing.'
'What really? You noticed?'
'Dunno what you mean, mate.'
'When are we off into town again?'
'Downtown?'
'Well, unlike here, there's always something happening. Sector C maybe? It's closer, if nothing else.'
'We've had more luck with birds there, so seems like a plan.'
'There are loads of cool meeting spots there, too.'
'We also need to start thinking about New Year's Eve. It might be a little way off yet but we need to make up our minds about who to invite. The more the merrier, eh?'
As the days get shorter, opportunities to socialise are fewer and farther between so using clubs as a means of handing out flyers to likely candidates is a must. There are a few local clubs worth trying, among them are Lem and the Cupole. Nothing ventured nothing gained.
'Fancy coming to our party?'
'You wanna bring your other half? Sure, no probs.'
'How many do you reckon you'll bring along?'
'We've got plenty of space, booze, nibbles and full throttle

disco.'

Nonetheless, there's still a ton of work to be done.

The three key ingredients: sound, booze, grub. Thankfully, Volt comes to the rescue. One of his jobs is installing TV aerials and car stereos, so his store is well stocked with amps, equalisers, lights and so on.

'I've got the sound sorted. Lamp's bringing his decks and I've got some tapes in case we need to use them.'

'Perfect! Tonight's gonna be rad! Tons of Angels, food and benz.'

'Eight sharp, right?'

'Eight!'

The afternoon goes by without incident other than Freddy and Angie being stopped in the city centre by a pair of Angels from Lecco looking for a local club called Torricelle.

'It's that way.'

'It's a dump,' he adds in a whisper.

Lamp's bar is under the family laundry and you have to go down a narrow and quite steep staircase to get to it. Before you get to the room, though, a half-open door offers a glimpse of mountains of pillows waiting to be washed and thoughts wander to a secret hideaway for shagging. The room itself has tables set out with Martini, Cointreau, Vov and bowls of crisps and popcorn.

'Come on! Put the C8 on.'

I have been on outside looking in for too long, too long...
(Carlis Munro - Outside Looking In)

Hugo gets pissed at double-speed, dutifully followed by Freddy.

'Need condoms?' says a wandering Matthew, not that any are needed at this stage of proceedings.

You are dancing on such way show. How can i keep in touch with you.
(The Hamilton Affair - How Can I Keep In Touch With You)

Partway through the evening there's a blackout.

'I'll sort it,' says Lamp.

The party somehow continues, crisps are eaten. A couple huddle together, steadying each other, the effects of Martini having already hit them hard.

The party continues. Crisps start to fly and there's some mouth-to-mouth breathing. Liquids are exchanged."

'Anyone need a rubber?'

There are no takers.

'Put the C17 on or do you have something else?'

The room is spartan and without chairs. Some are already sitting on the floor with their backs against the wall.

'Hit the strobe!'

The blackout is followed by another power failure, then another.

I wake up every day to the boogie, to that boogie, that boogie woogie. (Controllers - I Can't Turn the Boogie Loose)

'What the fuck is going on with this party? It's like a circus.'
'Yeah man, it's just like a Disco Circus by Martin Circussss!'
'Anybody need a rubber?'
'For fuck's sake, piss off.'

There are grumbles of discontent, firstly from the girls, then someone else not connected to the party organisers suggests an alternative strategy.

'Oh, don't leave. Come here and gimme a hickey.'

Blackout.

'Listen, let's get the hell out of here and go to Prince's party.'
'What? You suggesting we leave our own party?!'
'Fuck it, let's do one.'

Wanna be a great dark man. Nothing but a lesbian. You are perfect, you are sheer, if you are a red-haired queer. (Gina X- No GDM)

The gang sneak out into the street and, swaying ever so slightly, mount their Vespas. Singing, they head off to Prince's house, leaving their guests behind at Lamp's.

Papa said "You will ruin my house. You and that hand jive have got to go". (Rinder & Lewi - Willie and the hand jive)

'Hi, Prince'
'What the fuck are you lot doing here?'

'Cheers!'
'Hold on, have you bombed out your own party?'
'Ours was a technical washout, so here we are!'
'Whatevs. Come in.'

Baby give it up or turn it a loose like sex machine. Huh, ha Baby give it up or turn it a loose. (James Brown-Give it up or turn it a loose)

Lamp is not sure and asks Volt.
'Hey, what the fuck do you think was wrong with the electrics?'
'Christ knows. I've done a thousand installations. I've checked and double-checked. Still no idea what the fuck was going wrong.'
'What a pain in the arse.'
'Fuck all of that. Happy new year!'

Five, four, three, two, one! Lift up!   *(Rakotto - Boogie on up)*

The hangover passes fairly swiftly and for those more sensitive souls, disco sofas are always an aid to recovery. And if they can't remember who was at the party the previous day, the girls certainly can.
'Hi there, how're you?'
'Eh?'
'It's me?'
'Have we met before?'
'Er, yeah we copped off.'
'Do we have mutual friends?'
'At the party yesterday? We were kissing. Remember?'
'Really?'
Well, that one didn't work out, although not unsurprising in the circumstances. Angie's girlfriend is nowhere to be seen. And when Angie was engaged to the infamous Spice, she told him he made too many idiotic speeches. Who remembers Stump and Frog, so called due to one having small hands and the other a wide mouth? Perhaps not the most heartening of nicknames, but it was the girls themselves who used them to take the piss out of each other. Jake says:
'Shall we go to sector G again tonight?'
'Why not?'
Every night, they meet for a walk in the same spot in

GolosAngeles while pausing to exchange love bites. One night, one of the girls says:
'We need to split. See you soon.'
'Coooool.'
They walk back to the Vespa with the intention of heading home when one of them suggests:
'It's a bit early to be going home. Shall we go and check out what's what in Santa Lucia?'
'Sounds like a plan.'
They bump into the girls, who were only pretending to go home, a devious ruse to get rid of the guys. Another one bites the dust.

☺

More importantly, however, the first motorcycle licences are arriving for Licence A. Angie finally gets his. He has been on the lookout for a second-hand Vespa PX for a long time and now, much to his good fortune, he has a bit more time because the kids are on strike from school due to there being too little cream in the doughnuts.
'Hi Claudio, what're you up to?'
'Not much. A tree died in my garden so I'm pulling it up. Shouldn't you be at school today?'
'Strike, mate. Shame, I like chemistry and don't mind an experiment or two....'
'Like calculating and tying helium-filled balloons to fly a Vespa?'
'Exactly. That looks like a big job.'
'Well, it's dead and I've got to dig up the roots and all this black shit.'
'What black shit is that? Charcoal? Maybe you could turn it into a bomb.'
'Do you take drugs, by any chance?'
'Er, might do. Just throw in a bit of saltpetre and sulphur.'
'Where might you get the saltpetre?'
'Is it not that white stuff you get on bricks? Just scratch it off.'
'Give it a rest, mate, you've completely lost it.'
Angie digs up all the black stuff under Claudio's watchful eye, elbow resting on the shovel handle, legs crossed. He shakes his head in a disbelieving fashion.
'Relax buddy. Did we have a razzle at that New Eve Year's party

or what?'
'No-one has any idea it was us that kept switching the leccy off!'
'Is anyone still pissed off?'
'No idea. What're we up to on Sunday?'
'Well, there's a new club just opened?'
'Which one? It feels like there's a new one every week at the minute.'
'Le Pwwwah!'
'Le what?'

Everyone remembers the amazing nights with DJs Rubens, Spranga, Ebreo and Mozart at Les Pois. You could see the place miles away, like an Arabian palace jutting up into the sky. Some notable Spanish architect designed it. Its overwhelming white aspect dominated the valley's verdant green. It was known for its particular light installations which were spectacular and avant-garde with ceiling and floor-led strobes. People said it was similar to New York's Miramare.

'Look, everything is fucked up, we can't even move!'
'The traffic isn't moving. Good job we're on our Vespas!'
'Okay guys, let's dump them in the car park and go in.'

The music is completely commercial, nothing like the electronic experimentalism of the Cosmic. Not even as good as the "2" or Thucana, in fact.

☺

Thanks to a flooded basement, school is out again, so Angie is waiting outside the local college for Hugo to try and convince him to go into town for a mooch and a slice of pizza. The best and most popular is the one on the corner of Piazza Erbe, although there's another behind the council offices that gives student discount. The coolest place in the city centre, however, is the kiosk by the station which does mega panini. There are a thousand types of sausage and umpteen trays of fillings for every option imaginable. The first thing Angie notices on arriving at the college is an ad: "PX for sale."

"Booom!" he says.

He pulls the ad off the board and pockets it before anyone else sees it. All thoughts of his plans with Hugo evaporate as he heads back home to call the advertiser. In any case, the basement wasn't flooded. The school doesn't even have one.

☺

It's a cold evening. Angie is wearing a beautiful showy

sheepskin coat with buttons. The freezing air slips between the buttons onto his chest. A headwind dramatically increases on a bigger and faster motorbike, creating a centre parting and leaving the face and forehead unprotected. Even in motion, everyone still wants to be noticed as an Angel par excellence so, as you enter the square, you turn your head slightly so that the wind blows your hair sideways, giving you a fringe that settles nicely to one side. It's snowing. Angie is not slow in showing off his white **PX** to any or all of his friends. The first in the crew to have a **PX125**.

PX. (This pic is not from the British drama film Quadrophenia ☺)

The others are still waiting for theirs to be delivered. Sometimes it can take several months. In the meantime, trips are planned by divvying up the seats for those who have Vespa ET3s, so evening raids on Sectors C and G continue at warp speed. Besides, there's a new buddy in their crew now: Pepper. He can often be seen prowling at night on his dark Ciao on the hunt for either Pakistan hash or pussy. He has curly locks and when he stops, he slips his five fingers in the middle of his hair like a comb and ruffles it further. While Poplar applies the law of big numbers when on the pull, Pepper instead uses dialectics or maybe, is just relentless. He doesn't take no for an answer.

'You know you have a great smile?'

He delivers it with a theatrical flourish. She turns around.

'What? Excuse me, how can you see it from behind? How do you know?'

Like a musketeer, he doffs a make-believe hat and bows, extending his arm forth:

'Apologies, I meant perfume.'

He wants to know her name, where she lives and if he can come and hang out.

But friendships run much deeper than boys on the pull. 'Hi Stefan, listen... I know, it's freezing and the others wanna go to "2", but do you fancy coming with me to the Cosmic? We can go on my PX.'

'Mine's on order but is nowhere near being delivered so why the hell not?'

'Great. I'll pick you up tonight at 1 o'clock.'

'Fab.'

Whatever mealtime it is, everyone always wolfs their food down in five minutes flat. While they are permanently famished, the thought of missing out on the action far outweighs the feeling of hunger. Parents scarcely have time to form a sentence before they are out of the door and back into the fray. And while they might wish they had lingered a little longer over the food, the fact is that it tastes so good that one forkful rapidly follows another and there is rarely ever a scrap left on the plate. While the mouth is doing the eating, the head is processing plans, ideas, theories and gossip and the call of the local square is far more insistent than spending time in the company of parents.

'You good to go?'

'Sure, what's everyone else doing?'

'They're off to "2".'

'Cool! We can catch up with them later.'

'Come on, let's smash the PX!'

It is early February and the boys only have padded jackets for protection against the bitter cold. No-one with any self-respect would fit a windshield on their motorbike. It would totally spoil the look. What's a little cold compared to having the right look? No self-respecting Bay Angel would even consider wearing a hat or gloves.

It doesn't take long for the hands to go numb with cold, even though they are needed for gear change and the front brake. The solution, albeit temporary, is to alternately warm each hand between bollocks and seat. If it's the throttle hand, then the pillion takes over speed-administration duties. Somehow it works.

'Stefan, you can feel the difference, right?'
'You're not kidding!'
'Listen to this, it sounds amazing.'
'What?'
'Can you hear it?'
'What?'
'The clack!'
'The what?'
'The clack. When I change gear, listen to the clack!'

It's a whole different journey, even if they run the risk of accumulating fines for being two on a one-seater. They travel along the lake and spot the sign for an alternative route to the Cosmic. As they leave the main road and head into a side street, it feels as though they are leaving civilisation and heading towards a cosmic void.

Cosmic sign.

They drive into the car park and notice the Cosmic has changed. It now sports a dark façade embedded with neon stars and signage in the style of the Commodores. Cosmic. Changes have been made inside as well.
'What's going on?'
'Dunno, the helmet's gone, they've installed a spaceship.'
'Look at the bar.'
'Who's that with Baldelli?'
It's TBC.

STONED ANGELS

The new star-studded Cosmic façade.

Claudio Tosi Brandi, aka TBC, is now side by side with Daniele in the spaceship. History states that he prefers the leftfield sounds of Cosmic to straight-up disco and that he comes from the Papillon in Rimini. It is immediately evident that they are not here to work but to have fun. Claudio has brought all his ideas into the Cosmic DJ booth and, together with Daniele, is busy on the crossover, which is used as a musical instrument and, by manipulating the buttons and sliders, either kills or enhances different parts of a song, voices, bass, hi-hats, as if remixing live. The Angels frequently crowd round the DJ booth to find out exactly what is happening and how it's done.

The Cosmic entrance.

In command of the crossover, Baldelli plays the role of de facto torturer, rhythmically directing the current to cables attached to the balls of a prisoner or rather, to Sheev Palpatine who, with his hands, blasts Luke Skywalker with electric shocks. During their performance, they also use percussion and scratching, a cornucopia of new techniques to delight the audience. The duo also has a keyboard and, perhaps most innovatively, flick between 33rpm and 45rpm playing music at the 'wrong' speed, as with 'Frequency 7' by Visage, which totally pisses foreign holidaymakers off.

The new booth at Cosmic.

'Sie ruinieren die Musik!'
'Was zum Teufel tun sie!'

Don't say I know what you're thinking. It's plain to see...
(Classix Nouveaux- Guilty - 33 rpm)

Although Baldelli claims that it was all a happy accident, there are two reasons why it worked so well for them. Firstly, Italians don't speak English and therefore the lyrics just became sounds that merged into the music, as though playing an instrumental. Secondly, there were so many drugs being consumed in this Italian Bangkok that the dancers preferred a slow groove, with small swinging steps, arms aloft as though controlled by some unseen puppeteer and head dipped towards this slow psychedelic sound.

In this real spaceship of "Afro cosmic sound" Baldelli no longer gets angry since it is now impossible to ruin the records, which is what happened in the past when the Angels surrounded and constantly banged on the "helmet" booth.

This visit inspires Stefan to throw another party.

'You ready to sling a hook?'
'Cool. Let's go to "2".'
'Think I'm gonna throw another party?'
'What ya' got in mind?'
'A carnival party.'
'Wow, not a bad idea, where?'
'At my house. And I already have the theme song in mind. We'll start with Jazz Carnival by Azymuth...'
'Where did that idea come from?'
'The Cosmic's spaceship.'

Do you wanna go party, well get funky there, party. Drink a little wine, party. (Kc & Sunshine Band - Do you wanna go party)

The party begins. Angels turn up in numbers this time and the organisers are well-prepared, much more so than for the New Year's Eve do (they could hardly be less, to be honest). Bottles of the hard stuff on the tables with "*Latte di suocera*[17]", a powerful benz, first and foremost.

Na, vermisst du mich, wenn die Nächte lang und kalt sind?
(Nina Hagen band - Alptraum)

Even the food – and taste – is better this time and, instead of the usual snacks, there are also some tasty cakes and pastries. The organisers have obviously got their shit together for this one.

'The state of Jake!'

Jake is in a Kiss outfit. They keep him away from the tables so he doesn't spit blood on the snacks.

'Cooool!'

---

17 *Mother-in-law's milk (7.5% vol.) Label with white skull on black background. The bizarre name refers to the sense of burning that is felt in the throat following the intake of the liqueur, which, by analogy, recalls the stereotypical figure of an acidic and poorly tolerated mother-in-law.*

Freddy has come as a cowboy, Claudio, in Bermuda shorts, is sporting an African look, while Hugo is a whore.
'You look a bit cold, mate.'
Stefan has a beautiful big house, the perfect business card for all those participating at a party thrown by this gang. They come from all parts of the city and province. There's a certain amount of pride involved in throwing a party as good as this.

There's always something left inside here. I've really nothing much to lose. It seems so sentimental. (Japan - Life in Tokio)

'How about changing the style of music for a bit? How about a bit of rap...?'

Now what you hear is not a test I'm rappin to the beat and me, the groove, and my friends are gonna try to move your feet.

....hip hop, or whatever the fuck it's called.'

I said a hip hop the hippie the hippie o the hip hip hop, a you don't stop. (Sugarhill Gang - Rapper's Delight)

A little later there's a visible sign of movement. Jake, under close observation because of his considerable alcohol intake, is staggering around in a blizzard of objects being thrown across the room.

We got a new thing out, gonna make you shout. Got rhythm, got heat, gonna move your feet. (Joe Bataan - Rap o clap o)

The objects in question are the pastries thrown directly up and sticking to the ceiling. The forlorn-looking cakes look down on the party from their privileged vantage point. The end of the night is decreed by Jake's predictable collapse as, using a wall for support and comfort, cheek, chest and knees all caressing it, he leaves drool marks trickling down the painted wall. Stefan steps in.
'OK that's enough.'
'Ah for fuck's sake...'
'How we gonna get this lump home now?'
'You take his Vespa and we'll take him.'

'Hugoooo, you coming?'
An otherworldly gargling noise emanating from Hugo suggests a big fat no.
'Which idiot chucked pastries on the ceiling?'
'Ask the terrorist.'
'Let's go.'
Jake lives on the first floor and, after dragging him upstairs and standing him in front of his door, they look for his house keys.
'Shit! He doesn't have the keys on him.'
'Nor in the Vespa.'
'Are you sure you've looked properly?'
'How can I look properly, if I don't know where the fuck they are?'
Jake's mother is a gentle, kind, welcoming woman, a family person and a particularly devout Catholic, who, together with her husband, has raised her kids to appreciate Christian values.
'What we gonna do?'
'Dunno, can we leave him here?'
They lean him against the front door, feet well-planted, propping up his body. They ring the bell and run down the stairs. Suddenly there are three noises. The first, the door opening. The second, a loud thud on the floor and the third, the mother's voice.
'Ja..., Jaaaake!'

☺

Sector C is a densely populated residential neighbourhood. Upon arriving in the local square, teenagers gather in groups by the flowerbeds, benches or in front of the bar, chatting amiably and aimlessly. It is also why Freddy, Jake, Angie, Claudio, Stefan, Poplar, Lamp, Pepper, Hugo and Genny have claimed this district as their own. Besides the presence of Angels, they are also on friendly terms with the neighbourhood girls. Moreover, now that the crew had grown to accommodate youngsters from all over the city, it is a good geographical compromise. They claim a spot beside the steps of the shop, in front of the church bar, the crew's effective office. It has a good and strategically important vantage point over the square, so anyone else entering the bar has to walk past, acknowledge and smile at these friendly citizens and, if someone is walking directly by to meet his pals, he can stop and ask:
'Easy guys, What's happenin'? Where're you from?'
Or, if you're particularly daring, you can slip off and join the

company of another group of kids. This was how the company of the steps gets to meet with Vange, Grape, Pylon, Icy, Theo, Rhino, Crime and many others. These guys, especially the first two, have ET3s with mangled rear number plates, the result of excessive wheelies. They're wheelie freaks. They're always pulling damn wheelies. They are the master jugglers of the clutch, brake and throttle. They ride side by side, front wheels up, so that all their passengers can see is the sky. Everyone has heard about it, no-one actually saw him do it, but legend has it that Vange, with the throttle wire broken and pulled out of its sheath, travelled 20 kilometres from the city towards Lake Garda with the front wheel of the Vespa never touching the asphalt. A wheelie all the way!

'With a broken throttle cable?!'

'Right on! Thing is, he held and handled it with his hand. Christ knows how he did it.'

Here's a guide to the perfect wheelie. As you set off, you must simultaneously press the brake pedal, hit the gas and pull and release the clutch. If you go up too high, you have to press the brake pedal; if you are dropping too much, you have to hit the gas. It's a game of balance. Balance is everything because, if you don't, you'll find yourself with more dents than a stock-car.

Danger, be careful, be cautious. I'll catch you unaware. Look out. I'll get you. Look out son. I'll get you.   (Pylon - Danger)

'What the fuck did you do, Angiee?'

'For fucks sake, I crashed, what do you think happened? Can we change the subject?'

'Listen, I've got an idea.'

'And...?'

'We can fit this stereo in the glovebox aaaand, as it has two outputs, we can ride with headphones on. What do you reckon?'

'Shit Gennyyyy! Good thinking, a PX disco.'

No sooner said than done. Now Genny has some cool reggae sounds in his ears instead of constantly thinking about smoking pot.

Wheelies.

This ya music, reggae music, as far as I can see. This ya music, reggae music, it's got a spell on me. (Peter Tosh - Buk in-hamm palace)

The combination of PX and headphones is pretty unmatchable. It no longer matters where you go or why you're going, you just go. You can ride round in circles, passing the same starting point a million times, as though stoned, happily ignorant of the fact.

The road of life is rocky and you may stumble too.
(Bob Marley - Could you be loved?)

In only a short amount of time it seems as though everyone in the neighbourhood has a 125cc and a new obsession is born.
'What did you do to your side panels?'
'Well, I took another tumble before I scratched this panel so now it's on this side.'
'Listen, everyone nicks those panels. Maybe we could organise

a night raid and look for a new white one?'

The PX has side panels to cover the engine that can be lifted with the simple turn of a lever. If a scooter rides without them it means they have either been nicked or they are at the body-shop being re-sprayed.

It's evening. The steps gang, Pylon, Icy and others set off in search of panels to nick. They travel the city all night, long and wide, but without any luck and return empty-handed. Angie's panel will have to wait for another day.'

'Guys, don't worry about it, I'll just plaster it with stickers.'

Stickers! Of course. As well as club stickers, there are also those from boutiques. For example, the owners of Cosmic, two entrepreneurs from Verona, run a chain of boutiques specialising in designer-wear and The Chiocciola is one of these famous stickers. Although the Angels look slightly 'weird' in their second-hand gear, you can still find the same brands as in the boutiques. The guys who have a bit more cash to spare might buy a pair of Levi 505's or a Martin Guy shirt and plaster their Vespas with stickers of aspirational brands and boutiques.

The most coveted shops are Grand Prix, Lion Road and Coin. As wages increase or a little more disposable income comes in, a few affordable pieces might be bought at Fiorucci, Wrangler or Americanino, but the Moncler and Timberland brands would always be avoided since they stock the uniform for the Milanese Paninaros.

'Have you heard about the fashion show event at "2"?'
'A fashion show in a club?'
'Yes! Why not?'
'When?'
'Saturday night, at 9.'
'We mustn't miss that!'

Admission is free and the world and his wife has turned up. Despite this, you now recognise many more faces than you did before. While you could once walk through a club without bumping into too many acquaintances, now it can take half an hour to get from one side to the other. It's hard to go ten metres without meeting someone you already know.

The steps gang sits on the dancefloor. All the gang in one place, together, excited. The music is chilled and instrumental and the lights, all muted colours, have not yet sprung into action. After the inevitable delay, the show begins.

Take from the constellation of Capricorn, I've been seen all the mission so special. (Simonetti-G. Meo - Capricorn)

A presenter emerges from behind a big blue curtain on the catwalk and, despite being dead centre, it isn't clear what she is saying. Her voice can barely be heard above the hubbub of the slowly settling crowd as people carefully weave among the limbs of others or clamber over arches to find a free spot. One guy struggles to stay upright as he steadies himself on someone's shoulders before regaining his balance. Someone else fares even worse.
'Mate, what're you two doin'? Get up.'
'Fucks sake, they're already pissed.'
'They came in stoned.'
'Chuck them out, I wanna see this show.'
The first hotties come out modelling Fruit of the Loom clothes and the music that accompanies them raises the enthusiasm of the crowd.

The wheel was spinning away my earnings and the bets had stopped across the table...   (Sniff 'n' The Tears - 5 & Zero)

Next up are top models sporting the Stefanel brand and soon the crowd is on its feet. Within a short space of time, the whole dancefloor is standing and straining to catch a glimpse. The Angels start to move until the dancefloor finally reaches lift off.
Spitfire, Rifle, Wrangler, Americanino, Benetton.
'Angie!'
'Spiiiice, you're here too?'
'Yeaaaah, I heard about the show, so I've come with my girl friends.'
'How're things?'
'Cool, you?'
'Well, I'm alive.'
'Yeah whatevs, mate.'
'Did you hear that I bought a PX?'
'In that case, maybe you can give me a lift home later. Someone else can ride mine home.'
Spice and Angie had had a fall out but this chance meeting is

an opportunity to forgive and forget and renew the friendship. Angie dives into the contingent of Angels to look for the rest of his crew before heading off with Spice's mates. They rendezvous outside "2" but it has turned a little cold. They wrap themselves up to their eyeballs and shoot the breeze with some girls before the square empties out. A strange game of coupling ensues. Who will go with whom? Looks dart from one eye to another as an evident awkwardness sets in. There's no exact science to these things and who knows who will end up with whom. The worst thing is when the girls intervene and start making their own suggestions (the very cheek of it).

'So, I'll go with him and you go with that other guy, okay?'

A counter suggestion.

'She can come with me, but that means you'll have to take her friend.'

There are also those situations where someone is left playing gooseberry but still tags along in the vague off-chance of pulling.

When they finally leave it's at breakneck speed. The fuel burns so caustically that plumes of smoke dull the effect of their disco lights. They brake to get onto the main road - the side effect of braking helps push the girls into the small of their backs. They accelerate into wheelies and power on along the back roads as if their lives depend on it, snaking through the narrow alleys as if their sole purpose was to scare the girls to death. Now it's so narrow they can only follow in single file. A long terrace of houses runs down the left while wisps of fog rise from the fields on the right.

At that speed and in those conditions, you can only mimic what the scooter ahead is doing. After some slaloming, Angie notices that a part of either Lamp or Poplar's ET3 has come off and, as he corners, he realises something is wrong. The girl's hand, which was clinging to the rear rack, suddenly somersaults. He hits the fence that separates the road from the field and then all he can see is a concrete pole and blackness. Angie is catapulted into the middle of the field. The girl has also fallen nearby, her face going from confused to frightened and finally to furious.

'Come on, it's just a scratch!'

They never see the girl again.

The two-month-old PX is completely destroyed.

☺

The others are finally taking delivery of their own PXs while

Angie is already without wheels. Somehow, he always manages to scrounge a lift to Sector C and, between his buddies in Borgo Roma and the steps crew, he always gets a lift home. These cashless transactions only increase the intensity of the friendships established on the steps. One night, for example, Water gives him a lift, a guy who's second job is painting Vespas. Another evening, along with Claudio, they are invited to Jeep's home. Jeep is a strange guy. The cut of his long, smooth, light blond hair looks like it underwent some catastrophic razor-based experiment. He is always mimicking and exaggerating the others' gestures and his speech is littered with twisted sentences and absurd exclamations. For example, if you greet him by raising your arm, he reciprocates by raising his arm and then bending backwards.

'Look at him! Beep at him!'

They meet his cousin Giby. His girl-crushes are notoriously intense. He develops lightning-quick crushes and completely loses his head (and shit) in a completely illogical infatuation. But his ardour decelerates and disappears just as quickly. He can fall in love and break up in a matter of hours.

'As soon as they fix up your PX, let's go on a nice little lake tour.'

'The whole crew?'

'Why not? Almost everyone's got a 125 at this point, it would be a fun little outing.'

☺

This Sunday is a bright, blue day. The crew pack into the square. Angie has almost finished resuscitating his PX having had to readjust almost everything from changing the front fork onwards. He now has a free back seat. He's introduced to a girl who is willing to be his pillion passenger for the trip.

'Hi Angie, this is Carla.'

Carla is beautiful. Blue eyes, long, straight dark hair, slender, with the body and face of a goddess.

'Hi there, where're you from?'

'I live in Argentina but I come here to visit relatives occasionally.'

'Fancy a lift?'

'Sure. But I've heard about your riding exploits, so drive carefully or I'll get off and walk.'

'Don't worry, it's gonna be a beautiful day on the lake.'

'Well, it better had. I've gotta make it back to my grandparents in one piece.'

'No problem. Look at my pristine white PX, you don't think I wanna smash this beauty up, do you?!'

There are several places on the lake where you can plot up but San Vigilio Bay is lovely and the Bay of Sirens is particularly unique. There's also another lovely spot just past Cisano which is super social with a pebble beach and a very deep shoreline. Besides smoking spliffs and drinking beers, the main pastime is making man pyramids. Clambering one on top of the other, grappling arms and necks as you go, the trick is to belly flop like a deadweight into the water. Although the water is a little chilly for the season, they hardly notice while playing a lengthy game of 'it' finishing off with a mega water balloon fight. In between spliffs and beers, spliffs and music and radio and spliffs, it was a pretty good day.

'Hey, San Vigilio Bay, Bay of Sirens, Bay of Angels, we're bay Angels!'

They collect their things and pack the scooter racks, the bulk seemingly doubled since setting off. They go down to the lakeshore and, on reaching Lazise, turn left and head out. Just as they leave the town, there's something odd in the road. At that speed, you're only watching what the rider in front of you is doing. If he leans to the left, so do you and vice versa. As Angie enters the curve, he instantly realises something is wrong. Carla grips harder as he hits a black spot that suddenly appears behind Rhino's PX and loses balance as the Vespa slides away, the crunch of steel panels bouncing on asphalt. Luckily, as she lands kerbside, the girl's fall is softened by the grass verge. Angie slides through the oil patch. Everyone stops and rushes over.

'Fucking hell! Angie, you ok?'

'Fucks' sake, my Fiorucci cyclamen trousers are ripped! Only bought them two days ago!'

He never sees the girl again.

☺

The Sector C gang is intrinsically linked to the steps crew and any and all ideas that constitute fun or mischief are activated immediately and passed from peer to peer, which further builds the square's population. One day, an intruder, a punk, comes out of nowhere (well, not exactly nowhere, since punk was the height of fashion).

'Hi I'm Paul.'

Paul is not the typical punk of Mohican cliché but is dressed simply in white tennis shoes like Steve Jones of the Pistols (or the Ramones): frayed jeans, a faded denim jacket and, despite being blond, a rather fine yellow mop on top.

'Fancy going for a ride into the city? I've got to do some shopping.'

'What do you need?'

'I want some pins to hang on my jacket.'

'Pins?'

'Yeah. Let's go, I'll show you when we get there.'

They leave for the city and park in the central square by the traffic lights as usual. By this time on a Saturday, Piazza Bra is already filling up with motorcycles. It's first come, first serve for the parking places near via Mazzini. The others park along the road around the square forming a perfect arc of Vespas and Cagivas.

'Where are we actually going?'

'London Shop.'

'Where?'

'The London Shop, of course.'

London is now the epicentre of the punk movement. Two friends went for a brief trip to the British capital and returned to open this store, filling it with all sorts of imported gadgets and nicknacks.

Man watching city fall. The clock keeps on ticking. He doesn't know why. He's just cattle for slaughter. (Killing Joke - Requiem)

For example, when in London, if you want to buy a Hearts football strip, you head to Soccerscene and knock yourself out with the myriad of items to choose from. There you can buy the shirt of any British football team or any scarf, in wool or satin. You can buy badges or flags or any other paraphernalia of pretty much any team you can conceivably name. Whereas here it is pot luck. It is either available or your mum has to knit it for you. London Shop marked the birth of merchandising. Here you can buy anything from a badge of the band of the moment, to posters, Union Jacks of all sizes, belts and even records. Wearing something bought in the London Shop to a match, immediately made you cool.

'Have you got any punk badges with the Union Jack in the

background?'

'Have a look in that container.'

'See this? Punk's Not Dead.'

'What about this one with the skull?'

'I'll take the Destroy And Punk, please'

Angie watches him proudly march out of this eccentric store with badges pinned to his denim jacket.

'Happy?'

'Yeah, and since you gave me a lift, I'd like you all to come to my birthday party.'

'Hold on, bru', it's not gonna be a load of punks, is it?'

'Nope, people from various areas and you'll know a lot of them already.'

On the way back, they stop by a couple of Paul's non-punk friends: Moreno, the owner of a white PX, and Adon with a similarly delightful red Vespa TS.

'Hi Paul, this is a happy coincidence. We've been looking for your friend here, mate.'

'Cool ok,' answers Angie.

'This girl we know wants to meet you. Chiara, she's called.'

'Intriguing.'

'We're coming to the party so we'll bring her with us.'

'Cool bananas.'

I see your picture, what do I see, the face of an angel staring at me. (Shock - Angel face)

Only a small representative faction of the steps crew turns up at Paul's party, namely Angie and Genny "The Bitch", who acquired his new nickname after a series of slutty acts. Everyone else had other interests with hotties from Santa Lucia. He's here because he's going out with Marcy, a friend of Paul's. The significant activity around the house makes it relatively easy to spot. Once inside, they mingle with various pals including Jeep, Giby, Grape, Vange, Tits, Sheep, Water, Pope and Pink Panther, so named for her love of pink dresses.

The security is lax tonight. The front door is completely open and anyone can come and go as they please. Icy, for instance, keeps popping into a bar down the road for a beer as if the party were a dry-zone.

Everybody up, it's time to party now. Turn up the music and let's get on down. (Ray Parker jr. & Raydio - It's time to party now)

It's a large place with two floors and numerous rooms running off a substantial central corridor. A room on the ground floor is packed full of people aimlessly wandering about with glass and fag in hand, casually bumping into all and sundry. The guests are roughly divided into three groups. The Smashed, The Amoebas, The Lurkers. The Smashed speak for themselves though they're divided into two categories, the Intentionals and Accidentals, The Amoebas don't give a shit about anything and the Lurkers are permanently on the pull. Directionally speaking, the Smashed tend to be in and around the bathroom vomiting. The Amoebas wander about mindlessly while the lovebird Lurkers are upstairs.

Loud music and fashioned column lights. Pretty girls wearin' that jeans too tight. (Ray Parker jr. & Raydio - It's time to party now)

'Fancy going upstairs so we can be on our own?'
'Okay, let's go.'
'Through this door.'
'Shit, is that Pylon!?'
'Takennnnn! Bugger off!'

Most of the girls seem to have a secret plan. They didn't come to dance. (Ray Parker jr. & Raydio - It's time to party now)

'Let's try this one. Oops, sorry, Arse!'
'Piss ooffff.'
'This one?'
'This's mine!'
'This one, then. I'm running out of options here.'
'Hi guys.'
'Sorry, Moreno, I didn't realise.'
'No, come in! It's in a bit of a state, but we don't mind if you hang with us.'
'Thanks, that's cool of you.'
  The other two groups contribute to the mayhem, the Smashed barge in without a thought, the Amoebas gingerly intrude, both of

them major pains in the arse.

The boys sleep with girl. The boys sleep with boy. Never find that high. Never acting coy. (Fad gadget - Coitus interruptus)

It's chaos. But on the command "the cake has arrived!" the rooms empty and everyone converges into the one big room on the ground floor. The cake is placed on a long table, surrounded by party debris and weed smoke. It looks more like the Mad Hatter's Tea Party than an 18th birthday.
'Where's the guest of honour?'
'Yeah, where's Paul the Punk?'
Angie goes looking for him. Nobody in the kitchen or the study, someone pissing in the sink in the toilet, though Angie's not sure if he saw what he saw. A couple fucking in the corridor.
'Stop knobbing, the cake's downstairs.'
No answer. Angie continues his odyssey until he opens the bathroom door.
'What the fuck are you doing in here?!'
Paul is lying is in the bath immersed in water, completely naked.
'I'm freshening up!'
'Come on, mate, the cake's here.'
'Give me a sec, I'm comin'.'
Angie goes downstairs to warn the others that he has found the birthday boy.
'Found him!'
After a while, he shows up but only those with sufficient brain power are fully able to comprehend the sight before their eyes:
'Paul, mate, you appear to have forgotten your clothes!'
'Look at his dick hangin' out!'

Look up I hear the scream of sirens on the wall. I see a policeman crying in the backseat of a dying Ford. (Gary Numan - Bombers)

Time's up. Paul's parents and his brother Bert are due back any moment. They all parade out like a line of zombies. In the commotion inside, they missed the thunder of an impending storm and within minutes everyone is soaked. They look at each other, barely comprehending. Rivulets of black mascara run down the cheeks of the girls, while hairstyles turn into floor mops. Without looking up or around, the crowd disperses and dissolves into the night. Angie has one last chinwag with Jeep.

'Don't know if anyone's going to Chicago tomorrow, do you?'
'Don't know, but we could still get together?'
'My dad's staying in a caravan in Valverde near Brescia, if you fancy that?'
'Cool. Should I bring a sleeping bag?'
But the conversation comes to an immediate halt with the arrival of Bert, Paul's brother.
'What the fuck is going on here?!'

Punks. An underground movement at the top during Afro Cosmic age.

☺

The trip brings to mind that fateful expedition to Les Cigales but all negative thoughts evaporate as the morning sun burns through the little cloud that still persists in the sky. Green hills, a gentle breeze and lake views are the setting for the first stop on the schedule. A quarry.

'Jeep! But this is a gravel pit. What the fuck are we gonna do here?'

'Motocross!'

The beaten tracks on the dunes are perfect for launching their PXs as if they were motocross veterans, no match for KTM, TGM or SWM maybe[18] but enough to let fly and dream for a moment. The fun ends quite suddenly as they break just in time at the edge of an abyss. It's near impossible to separate pleasure from catastrophe when the ground is an even white.

The village is beautiful, inspiring thoughts of freedom and renewal, especially as they get closer to Les Cigales club. The summer season is now in full flow. Armed with 125cc of scooter power, the gang can now go anywhere they like and not feel obliged to return the same evening. Freddy's black PX recently arrived, a blue one has just been delivered to Claudio and, unlike Angie's, their indicators work. And, after seeing one in the square outside Cosmic, a tightly-rolled sleeping bag is set to be this season's quintessential luggage rack accessory.

'Sleeping bag? I love sleeping with a 'bag'.'

'Dirty bastard! Everyone's up for going to Chicago next Sunday. It's a new club near Bologna, one of the big DJs is the new resident there, Ebreooo!'

Chicago's original resident DJ and its owners decided to transform the club into something new and entirely innovative and he was now joined by both DJ Ebreo and Spranga. But to understand how and why Chicago played such an important role we need to step back in time a little and consider the influence of Italy's original innovators, American DJs Bob and Tom, the rulers of the Bay.

This duo stopped the talking and kept the music flowing, changing the country's whole disco culture with their 'mixing'. They were the base from which sprang important first- generation Italian DJs like Daniele Baldelli and Mozart, who took over from them at Baia degli Angeli, and Rubens, Spranga, Ebreo and Meo, who all carried on the traditions set by the New Yorkers.

An old club called Pap used to be on Chicago's original site but

---

18 Austrian and Italian motocross bikes.

Meo's stay there was short because he left to work on rotation with Rubens at Les Cigales. Meo's return to the newly opened Chicago received countrywide acclaim. Ebreo, taking his cue from Daniele Baldelli, who was considered one of the major architects of this new movement, delved deep into ethnic cultures of music from Brazil, Jamaica, Africa and worldwide funky sounds.

Sunday morning comes and Angie and Jeep leave on the latter's PX. The others have already left but the meeting point is under the Bologna sign at the entrance to the city. The PX mileometer reads precisely 3655. Even clocked-up mileage has cult status among scooterists. Not only do they compare where they went and with whom, but also how many kilometres they travelled, the greater the mileage, the bigger the badge of honour. Consequently, a broken front cable that measures the mileage is considered a disaster, a prestige-killer, so much so that, when it is eventually repaired, the mileometer is adjusted accordingly (any suggestions that this might occasionally have been doctored are, of course, mere lies and smears).

☺

The adventure begins. This expedition is very different from the previous ones and the enthusiasm doubles in proportion to the distance. Mantua - a first quick stop to check the route. River Po - another stop to check on the facial redistribution of gnats. Modena – a further stop, this time forced due to getting a fine for having two people on the same scooter. Bologna - finally meet the others under the city's first sign.

'Here they are.'
'All cool?'
'Apart from the square arse after three and a half hours' riding, we're fine.'
'Does anyone actually know where Chicago is?'
'We know it's in Baricella but we need to go via Ferrara.'
'Jesus, what a trip'
'Okay, so let's follow directions to Ferrara.'
'Don't s'pose anyone's got a map?'
'A what...?'

Together now with Icy, Sardine, Cypress and Homo, they all head north. It's half one in the afternoon and, since the club opens at 3, they know they're in good time. At last, after a few wrong turns, they arrive in front of the Chicago gate. It's exactly 3 pm.

"Chicago is closed today."
The red sign of the club seems to look at them with a sarcastic air as they become increasingly deflated. There's not a single person in sight.

'There ain't no DS Sharks swimming here today, that's for sure.'

'What the fuck are we gonna do now?'

'Let's go to Ciak!'

'What?'

'Let's go back to Bologna and go to Ciak.'

'Never heard of it, any cop?'

'The DJ and club are supposed to have won awards. Let's give it a go.'

Bologna natives know the Ciak as the "nice Castle". It's a medieval castle capable of holding 1,500 people indoors and up to 4,000 if you include the outdoor summer space. The main hall features a seven-metre cinema screen projecting films and cartoons, etc., while people are dancing. The DJ booth is four metres above ground level and is the size of two rooms. The DJ's name is Miki and, with relatives from New York and having been a reporter for singers and bands in the States, his sound arrived somewhat later in other Italian clubs.

The gang feels at home as soon as they arrive. They are met outside with the classic Angels' world mix of Vespas, Sharks, VW Beetles, 2CVs and, of course, sleeping bags. They're late for a Sunday but the first impressions are good. It doesn't last long, however. There's something very wrong and it's the music.

'What's he playing?'

'Sounds like rock music.'

'I think he even plays punk now and again.'

'Let's do one.'

Despite their late arrival, they're among the first to leave. The ride home feels longer and more arduous than their more optimistic outward journey. Morale is low after the failure of this doomed expedition. They try to strike a positive note when they stop to eat in a bar and refuel with plenty of beers. It's already night. They manage to get back home in one piece. They never go back to that club. It burned down after a short-circuit started a fire and all its contents were destroyed, including 7,000 records.

☺

But they're not ones to give in. Rather than let the bad vibes of their misadventure taint the optimism of youth, they decide to recruit yet more into the crew and press on with the exploits. Nothing ventured, nothing gained.

'So, where is it this week, then?'
'Let's spread our wings: Brescia.'
'Where exactly?'
'The Cupole, Brescia province.'

As with the previous week, Angie is late but this time the arrangement is to rendezvous in front of the Cupole with Rhino. They already know the route, the memory of their ill-fated jaunt to Les Cigales still vivid in their minds. Angie arrives to find the others waiting outside.

'Man, this club is a shit-hole!'
'Er, have you actually been in it yet, hmm?'
'Never mind that, look at the state of it!'
'Yeah, but the music?'
'Dunno, mate.'

They buttonhole someone outside.
'Hey, who's the DJ in here?'

'It's Beppe Loda aaaand....'
'He plays afro music?'
'Yeah, think so.'
''K. Let's do it.'

While the music meets their exacting standard, the club sucks. It is more of an open-air dancehall than a modern club. Although they were late going in, they leave early. The disappointments of their fun-seeking were almost solidifying into habit. And to make matters worse, Angie discovers he's been dumped by Chiara.

The reasons for the dumping are many and various. In this instance, it was because Angie was never around to take her out. But it could have been one of several: "I'm fed-up with it all", "It's impossible to be together", "You always act weird", "You've changed", "You're not you anymore", "Just today, eh? Then get lost".

Oh, don't look back. Don't look behind you. Reckless drivin' on. (Dirty back Road -The B-52s)

While ill luck is following them around like a bad smell, things look up during the week spent hanging out on the steps in Sector C. Laughing, smoking, pissing about and trying to work out who sent the letter to Angie, allegedly from his ex, Stump. Hugo spilled the beans. Some even suggested this fuckery was done to cause friction among the crew.

It doesn't particularly matter who is in the square or who isn't. The only important thing is that there is enough of a quorum to hang out, talk bullshit and always be available for new recruits. The latest candidate is a guy called Finger, whose every other word is a profanity and he has an unmistakable laugh that echoes around the square every time he guffaws. He is a bullshitter par excellence, telling tales that are long and tall, but always as though he is merely passing on information from someone else, rather than his own concocted nonsense. His hair is long and wavy, covering half his face and hanging down over his shoulders. He is so thin that, if you look at him sideways, it seems as though he is entirely made of hair and little else. He always wears a non-descript jumper and his jeans are so tight that he's forever rearranging his balls. Finger introduces himself to girls in a singular manner.

'What do your mates call you?'

'I... finger... you?' Classy.
Perched on the steps of the shop, his usual spot, he says.
'Fancy coming over to mine for a bevvy?'
'Cool, what drink should we bring?'
'Don't worry about that. I'll make one of my specialities.'
'Sounds like a plan.'
'Good for me, too.'

Finger's mum is a kind-hearted lady. She opens the door smiling and watches them march through the house in single file, as though watching a rally at Wimbledon or a F1 race. Finger is a model of politeness.

'Hi guys, what would you like to drink?' asks mum.
'Shut up!'
'Crisps?'
'Shut the fuck up!'
'Snacks?'
'Piss ooooff!'
Despite his rudeness, she lets out a squeaky laugh.
'Wow, your mum's got an interesting laugh.'
'Yeah, she sounds like a strangled chicken.'
'Right, everyone, try and imitate her laugh.'
Now, each time she laughs, they mimic her, and she says:
'You do realise you sound like a chicken?'

Finger pulls out oranges, lemons, wine, rum and various ingredients. He turns on the stove and begins to boil some sugar, adds the other concoctions and an intoxicating smell begins to emerge from the kitchen.

'What the hell is that?'
'What, the smell?'
'Gimme a beer, I'm not taking chances.'
'I'm making rum punch,' reveals Finger.
'Fuck's sake, it's summer aaand you're makin' punch?'

The punch is served in any container going: jug, bowl, pan, whatever. The boys get howling drunk, slumping on the couch or lying on the ground, in the loo, laughing like strangled chickens. Now they know that Finger is one of the lost souls, one of them.

The following evening, they run through the previous evening's agenda - or at least they try to piece it together as best they can.

'That was a proper burpathon, Finger.'
Which brings us to another of Finger's previously undisclosed

qualities. He can gulp in air and regurgitate it in burp form. During the holidays, this talent is particularly exploited to its fullest extent. Whether they meet in the square or the local pizzeria, burps pepper the conversation.

'Christ knows how many burps I've done but they said they could hear it in the street.'

'Well, since we're talking bollocks, I have something I wanted to say.'

'You mean everyone's lost it?'

'Well, there is that. I was thinking more that we should give our crew a name.'

'Like the ones in The Warriors?'

'Well, we are the lost souls so...'

'Soooo, the Lost Gang!'

'There are already Two Bells, the Wall Gang...'

'And we're the Lost Gang!'

Weekday evenings are always spent in a similar fashion. Another evening, Angie is hanging out with Freddy in front of one of the skyscrapers.

'Hi Freddy, how's the PX?'

'Awesome thanks and now that it's summer, I'm planning a little jaunt.'

'Where?'

'To Baia degli Angeli.'

'Have you got a sleeping bag?'

'No probs, I have everything I need, old chap.'

Drill shows up mid-conversation.

'Well, I'm a scout so...'

'Drill! What the fuck are you doin' here? Did they let you out?'

Drill was busted for drugs and was last heard of in the clink. He might not be looking 100% but he looks cool in a jumpsuit.

You've got the stuff to pick me up. You've got the stuff to pick me up. (Bill Withers - You've got the stuff)

'You ok, Mark? Where're you hangin' out these days?'

'Out and about, mate. You?'

'We were just making plans for this summer...'

'OK. Who're you guys seeing at the moment?'

'I'm going out with a girl from GolosAngeles and...'

'I've just dodged a bullet, mate, someone tried to pull a fast one on me.'
'What's that?'
'I was told that this girl called Sony was interested in me, but then found out these fuckers were all shittin' me.'
'Ha ha! Seen what I just bought?'
Drill's sporting a pair of light leather boots with a square toe.
'They're Fryes. I got them at Madras in via Mazzini.'
'Coolio.'
There's a little pizzeria on the ground floor of the skyscraper. Periodically, someone comes out to smoke a cigarette before throwing the butt on the floor and getting back to work. Freddy pounces on any butt left on the ground, examines its veracity, calculates whether there's sufficient tobacco left and then takes the last few sneaky puffs. Drill is suitably impressed:
'You animal! How the fuck could you smoke that stuff?'
'You do what you have to, brother. I don't always have the cash to buy fags.'
'Mate, it's just a stub.'
'And it's just a puff! Shit, I'm smoking the filter...'
'In any case, I remember when you used to piss on people from buildings!'
That was the last they saw of Drill. They never see him about, in the clubs, or anywhere else.

☺

It is scorching outside and, even though the prospect of tramping about in a pair of pristine Vaqueros boots is not the worst thing imaginable, attention is focused on meeting spots. The Lost Gang now almost always meets in Sector C with no stops anywhere else on the way before arriving at the steps in front of the church. Those who stay on the steps are the ones that, after hearing numerous tales about Drill and hard-drug use among others, have found their comfort zone. Most evenings revolve around the steps and this square. Each night they arrive in dribs and drabs before a quorum is reached. Other crews know exactly where to find them and often pass by to talk shit.
'We could do with a local bar, really.'
'That one sucks. Nobody should have to live in a world without Martini.'
'What about Tacky's bar.'

'Where's that?'
'The barman's called Tacky and the bar is down there.'
Tacky's bar is the perfect place for them. Located just across the square and down an imposing staircase, there's no sign outside and if you don't know exactly where it is, you might even miss it. It's a miracle anyone knows it's there at all.
'Angie, let's go get a bevvy.'
'Shall we give Tacky's a go?'
'Yeaaaah, let's do it.'
'Cool. Listen don't sit on the PX, the stand's fucked.'
Once the rubber pads have worn on the two-legged stand, the Vespa will typically only stand if the asphalt is hard. In the summer, when the road surface is malleable, the scooter sinks into the charcoal mire.

The grey staircase that leads down to Tacky's bar is illuminated by a rectangle of light coming out of the bar's door. The door opens and a curtain of cigarette smoke billows out forming a cloud that spirals up as if the air pressure were higher inside the room. They go inside. A long counter fills the width of the room to the left while there are a few tables, a pool table and a lot of empty space on the right.

It's a nice crowd with several familiar faces from the neighbourhood. There are a few quizzical glances thrown their way as they head for the bar where the ever-smiling Tacky, always in on every joke, is at his station behind it. It is as though everyone has known each other all their lives. Angie instantly feels at ease. Now he understands the popularity of the bar. Tacky is one of them. An Angel.

'The best on the Earth!'
He repeats it.
'There's a gang out there gagging for a Martini!'
Angie goes outside, drink in hand and runs into a girl:
'Hi, will you take me home, please?'

Oh, this time, baby. We won't be in and out of love. In and out, baby. (Jackie Moore - This time baby).

It's Sony, the butt of the joke. Once in front of Sony's house, Angie says:
'Listen, since you've now met my gang, you should know that

these arseholes' matchmaking skills are based on mischief rather than love.'

'Maybe, but, in this instance, it's true.'

She and Lipgloss are among the first girls who join the Lost Gang. The mating begins.

The arrival of women into the picture brings fluidity of movement and plans. Those with girlfriends might wait on the steps or swing by hers on the way, for instance. One night, Angie gives Jake a lift to Erika's place in GolosAngeles because he's on foot.

She sits alone waiting for suggestions. He's so nervous avoiding all the questions. (Rod Stewart - Da Ya Think I'm Sexy?)

With them are Claudio and Freddy, who Drill nicknamed Stub.

'Easy, boys!'

Claudio, Angie and Stub are keen to find out who Jake's new buddies are but Jake offers them some cocky advice:

'Well, you lot can fuck off!'

'This is what we get for taking you back and forth every night, you twat?'

'Piss off. But don't forget to come and get me later.'

To kill time, they head out of the city up to the Torricelle hills, which overlook Verona. Emerald green, lush and full of little gullies perfect for fucking. Parks, mini-golf, castles and pitches where you can stop to admire the city from above or the Milky Way from below.

Take me to your place in space. I'm simply tired of mad rage. On rocket ship no time to wait. I just want to gravitate. (Galaxy - War)

In short, a place for star-crossed lovers but not for the trio on this particular night. The most fun thing you can do, armed with scooters and a significant amount of testosterone, is take the 'lasagna'. This is the name given to the medieval roads that snake off the main carriageway and descend steeply down the hills into a thousand narrow curves and bends, bordered by high drystone walls and creepers. The roads are cobblestone with a polished marble raised strip down the middle. Angie and Claudio take one and bomb down, swiftly followed by Stub. The challenge is to ride the central

strip right to the end of the lasagna. Doing it at night is even more perilous and adrenaline-fuelled because of the light. To the ears of those below, the cavernous PX 125 rumble is amplified as the three descend the slope, clearly visible from the juddering headlights powering down towards the abyss. The exit is wide enough to make but tight enough to cause panic. But this time the screams come from somewhere else.
 'Whhhhaat the fuuuuck...'
 The screams mingle with the clatter of Vespa metal.
 'What the fuck are you doin'! Look the fuck out!'
They collide into two girls on a Ciao right at the lasagna exit. Who could have imagined such perfectly disastrous timing!

To my surprise, one hundred stories high. People getting loose y'all, getting down on the roof. *(Disco Inferno - The Trammps)*

The Lasagna. (no Bolognese ☺)

'Look at this! You've twisted the front wheel...'
Fortunately, the bend leaving the lasagna is not sharp so the two scooters mainly emerged with scraped side panels and hurt pride.
'Look at what? Have you seen the state of my mudguards?'
'You dickheads!'
'Tell you what, give me your phone number and, to make it up to you, we'll invite you to one of our parties.'

Thankfully, Stub's got a bottle of Martini stashed away at home and a few sips on that soon settled any aftershocks the boys might have had. While sorting the glasses:
'Hang on, we forgot Jake!'
'Jake?'
'Weren't we supposed to pick him up? You know he's on foot, right?'
That night Jake walked several kilometres home.
No-one has seen Claudio for a few days. There's a reason for everything and this is no exception. He has a new girlfriend. Someone reckons they know where he's gone too. So, instead of winding up Jake, this time they turn their attention to Claudio.
'Where is he then?'
'Up in the mountains.'
'He's got a new girlfriend called Lily and they're planning to go up to the mountains this weekend. I have a good idea where as well.'
'Don't say anything. Let's go fuck him up.'

High on mad mountain. You and me fall the ground.
(The Mike Theodore Orchestra - High on mad mountain)

'Why the fuck would he go up to the mountains. Doesn't make sense to me. If he wants peace and quiet, he could go to the local nunnery or cemetery.'
'For all you know he might have a house in the mountains, in which case, it's a free weekend away, innit?'
The mountains would not be their first port of call. It's a beautiful day and their plan is met with enthusiasm. A couple of the girls they know from the steps decided to join them, so the scooters are soon laden with two per vehicle.
'Poplar, why you ducking out?'
'I'm still a bit spaced-out from last night.'
'What happened last night?'
'Er, me, Hugo and Stub went on the piss. I'll be at mine later if you wanna come by.'
They finally leave for the mountain village where Claudio is allegedly holed up. They take their time almost to the point where the mission appears to have been forgotten amid wheelies, joking, overtaking and general high spirits, but they reach the village with renewed purpose.

'Let's ride round and see if we can see Claudio's scooter.'
It's not long before they spot it parked on one side of the road along a row of houses. Everyone is keen to get in on the high jinks. The Vespa is equipped with a screwdriver and spark-plug spanner under the seat. Since it's not secured properly to the body, they unscrew his seat and take it with them.

The day flies by and they ride over to "2" since entry is free 90 minutes before closing. It's a chance to save money since there are Frye boots to be bought in the not-too-distant future.

Poplar's fabulous dinner is awaiting them. They head for his basement after waiting for Claudio to get back from the mountains.

'Well, Claudio? Everything okay?'

'Fuck you all!'

On finding his scooter sabotaged, he had also seen their instructions on where they would be later on, smeared on the shop window right where he had parked. Despite the mean tricks they play on each other, nobody ever gets angry. On the contrary, taking the piss out on each other is infuriating but usually ends up in a party.

Poplar's parents are splendidly hospitable people and have practically prepared a banquet. Once served, they gracefully withdraw from what will soon become a battlefield. Poplar's parents are farmers and know how to make good wine. Smashed, the boys try to make sensible conversation despite slurring.

'So, Jake? Did you like the cat?'

'The cat?'

'Yeah, yeah! The cat you ate.'

'Shit! Wasn't it rabbit?'

'Come oooon, noooo! Rabbit tastes just like cat, and we ate a cat.'

'Oooh yeah! Poplar's dad hit it with his car and he thought he'd cook it.'

It's automatic. As soon as someone comes up with a load of bullshit and makes someone else believe it, everybody plays along and, in this case, it's Jake's turn to be the victim.

After the first alcohol binge, someone is already suggesting something different, as if the evening should not end this way.

'Shall we go downtown and see how much the Frye cost?'

'You're crazy! There are still some half-empty bottles!'

'We'll take them with us and go to the downtown gardens.'

The Frye boots cost a bunch of money. They realise that they will have to scrounge money much more regularly and jump harder on the petrol pipes at the service stations to get the last drop into the tanks of their scooters.

Eyelids are drooping but, despite the fun-filled day, they still have one grain of common sense left.

'The bottles are all empty, shall we leave them here?'

'Are you mad? Do you want to trash this beautiful lawn?'

'We'll take them to the Sector C steps.'

They leave them there on the steps of the shop where they usually group. They realise that, amid all the boozing and eating, they haven't yet decided what to do over the next weekend. So, the next night sees them at Jake's house and, between one Martini and another:

'So? Any ideas?'

'Shall we go to the Bay of Angels?'

'Wow! You're so cool! You're as smart as a hare.'

'Uh? I'll slap you on the dick!'

'Come on! Don't be such a dick!'

'Hmmm, a new disco would be nice.'

'Mountains? Lake? Sea?'

'Well! Let's do this, let's do all of them! Who can, comes and who can't, doesn't...'

'Where do we start?'

'Seaside! Come on!'

With unprecedented organization, they type every detail of what to take with them on Hugo's typewriter. Cigarettes, radio with tapes, bottles of Martini....

☺

The early morning air stings their nostrils, goes up their noses, continuing on down their larynxes, outlining the entire anatomy of the respiratory system. Even their cheeks notice, but not them. They open their mouths like a hippo emitting its first verse of the day, composed of one or two letters at the most vomited into a loudspeaker. The air is cool. It's cool because, as Poplar says, it has been out all night. Wearing white trousers, the current trend, they push their Vespas out of the garage. The meeting point awaits them. They can be sure that, by this time of the morning, someone is already swearing about the ignition pedal because, if your foot accidentally slips as you give it a kick to start the motorbike, you can

bump your right ankle bone. And it hurts! One by one, they converge on the starting point. Those wearing a jacket only have the sensation of damp hair while those without also have damp arms.
'What a fuckin' freeze!'
'A little bit.'
'We forgot something at Jake's that night.'
'What?'
'Well, since Frye cost a bunch of money, we could go to some other city to see if they cost a little less.'
'Ah! Right! We'll talk to the others on the way.'
They are all there. Everyone has a slightly red nose and tears in their eyes from the cold. In the ever-present silence of the early morning, they can just begin to make out the trappings around the door of the newsstand, bar and shop, while the sun gains space between the houses, lighting up the windows in silver. The morning air gives them all a gift. A sense of wonder because the world before them is about to open up. It always takes some time between the first and last to arrive but finally, they leave. It's six o'clock. Villages flip by one after another.
It's 7.25.
'By the way! If anyone gets lost, we'll meet at the Chichito nightclub.'
Needless to say, once they get to remote villages, they find themselves on a country road bordered by stretches of dried corn. If it was hard to keep an eye on the motorbike queue before, just imagine it now! They stop for a moment to take stock of the situation although someone already has other intentions.
'Stub! Have you lost your mind?'
'What's up? Can't I have a fag while I wait?'
'Wanna set a fire?'
'That's why, within a radius of 10 - 20 metres, all the corn plants have been dug up.'
'Aaaaall right! So, we can smoke in peace.'
'No one's coming, we've lost Claudio.'
'Come on! Come on! Let's get goin'. We'll meet them in front of the club.'
Continuing along the country road, they finally reach a village and, although the scooters are camouflaged by the corn stuck in the luggage racks, with some suspicious looks from passers-by, they manage to get directions to the seaside. They get to the disco at last

and take a head-count. It is actually only a little way from the village but Claudio is still missing. Before long he saunters up to join the rest of the gang and, upon his arrival, they dedicate a song to him, putting the tape in the radio on the right track.

Everybody move. Feel the groove. Feel the groove. Boogie down get funky now. (The Real Thing - Boogie Down - Get Funky Now)

'Where shall we put the Vespas? I don't want to leave them on the road. There are fuckers goin' round these days nicking spare wheels.'
'Right! In that case, you could go and nick one yourself.'
'Yeah! You talk like that because you've got an ET3, which has no spare wheel.'
'I have an idea! Let's put them in a garage.'
'Garage?'
'Yeah! We'll just wander around the village and see if there's an open garage and stick them in there.'
The idea is not new. The technique had already been tried and tested when they went to the Picchio Rosso. And that's exactly how it goes. After a few comings and goings along the waterfront, they see an open door which leads into a sort of boathouse. They angle-park the motorbikes there and, after a few steps, already have their feet in the sand at Hardy Bagni, a nearby beach establishment. It's a beautiful day, sunny and still. One of those days when you only hear the flapping of the umbrella canvas when a light breeze comes up from the sea. The silence is only interrupted by the odd shout as a mother calls her children back or by someone playing some bullshit on the beach. The quietness, however, doesn't last long. Half an hour after their arrival, they bury Stub in the sand up to his waist, digging a hole of a metre and more and leave him there to ask for help. After filling their swimming trunks with cotton to make their genitals look bigger, Pepper starts hassling all the chicks with his classical approaches, such as:

'Hi! Listen, a pal of mine is fucking in love with you. Do you wanna meet him?'
The answers are all negative:
'Not today, thanks!'

You got to get an' wail an' shake your big tail. Get up an' go when you got it to show. (Frantique - Strut your funky stuff)

At noon only Claudio and Angie decide to get a pizza for lunch, the others are scattered on the beach.
'A pint of beer!'
'Pint of beeeer!'
'Can I have another one?'
'Me too, thank you!'
'Claudio! Fancy a pint of beer?'
'Pint of beer!'
'Two pints of beer please!'
After pizza, they decide to have something else to drink and between one laugh and the next, looking through the stained-glass window, they notice a guy making strange movements in front of the pizzeria customers. A waiter goes up to him gesturing animatedly. Then, the same waiter comes towards them because they had given him a sign to ask for the bill.
'Look at these people! Why in the world do they come here to do this shit!'
They teeter over to see what is going on and see Genny, the Bitch, washing his hair with coke from the diner's freezer.
'Shit, Genny! The showers are there!'
'Yeah, but this keeps my hair curly.'
The day goes by and the last hours of the afternoon are spent improvising some ballet on the beach and watching Pepper pretending to swim on the strand.

Down by the docks, yeah, down by the docks. It's a place where you don't go down. If you want to go fancy. (Sailor - Down by the docks)

It's time to go home. They all stand up, flapping their towels, blinding the other bathers' eyes with grains of sand. Then, with the towels wrapped around their waists, they all busy themselves in the act of taking off their swimming trunks and wringing them out in front of the other people.
'Look at those rude boys! Do they have to come here and do this shit?' The other bathers are disgusted.
The last performance sees everyone making superhuman efforts to get their clothes back on to their damp bodies.

'Everybody here?'
'Holy shit! We have to pull Stub out of the sand!'
Back home, they're trying to take the piss out of Pepper.
'So, Pepper? How many hotties did you meet in that faggot thong?'
Pepper, much to their astonishment, takes out a piece of paper with the addresses of all the ones he met.

☺

Since the first scheduled outing went so well, in the wake of this enthusiasm, they decide to meet, as usual, on the shop steps in Sector C with the promise of bringing further good suggestions for subsequent outings.
'Who's missing?'
'Pepper and Stub.'
The words were hardly spoken when they see a black PX whizzing through the quarter with a DANGER road sign on the rear rack. Pepper is driving. His body is bent forward, chin touching the odometer, shoulders tight around his neck, mouth wide open and elbows spread outwards. He seems to be on the verge of taking a triple leap forward. Stub is sitting behind, his arse hovering on the seat. His legs and arms outstretched and a bottle of Martini dangling from one hand.
'The beeenz, the beeenz,' they repeat at every fly-by.
'Listen to me, folks! Okay! We'll reschedule for the next expedition, given the situation.'
A whole series of evenings follow without the gang meeting up in full. One night Genny, Jake and Stud leave to smoke a joint, another night Poplar and Pepper show up drunk but with excellent news.
'We made pals with the Wall gang!'
'Yeeeah! And we paid for drinks all round! Martiniiii for all the chiiiicks.'
'But, were they able to wet their whistle?'
It's useless. It is still impossible to gather the whole Lost gang because some of them are going on holiday. It is also quite absurd to wait for everyone to be there, so decisions have to be made.
'Well! Let's do this! Let's go swimming at Lake Garda and then go to the disco.'
'Yeah! Thucana?'
There's little going on at the Thucana disco so they choose not

to go in.

'What shall we do then, go in or not?'

'No! No! Come on! What do you think we bought all those bottles of Prosecco for?'

'Come on! Pull up a chair!'

And so, Stub, Pepper, Jake, Angie and Genny pop the first bottle.

'When we're all here, can we go to the mountains?'

'Ooookay, sure, mountains disco?'

Meanwhile, the first bottle is over and done with. They put it on the ground, easy prey for a road sweeper, who appears from one side of the club and picks it up.

'Well, since some have decided to go to the sea on holiday, what's our next expedition?'

'I'm sorry, we're going to the sea too, this time with Luke and his gang.'

'Yeeeah, the one who walks like he's got a melon up his arse.'

Meanwhile, the second bottle is over and done with. They put it on the ground, easy prey for the road sweeper, who, lurking at the side of the club, comes out and picks it up.

'Shit! That means there are only a few of us left! Well, where can we go?'

'In a club, somewhere!'

'For example?'

'Have you ever heard of the Picchio Verde?'

'Ha! Ha! There's also the Verde one, and where is it?'

'In Carpi!'

Meanwhile, the third bottle pops the cork.

'I know the way! I went there with Jeep not long ago!'

'But, why right there?'

'Why? Surely you know that the chicks from Modena are beautiful? They're hot!'

'Yeaaaaah! Hot stuff!'

On the point of leaving for home, just as they were about to put the bottle on the ground, the sweeper comes out and, with an acid look, follows their every movement, even pretending to sweep the square. The bottle, among other things, is still half-full, so, they put it under the seat of Angie's PX.

'Hey! Sweeper! We haven't finished it yet!'

'Oh, yeaaaah! You thought we were gonna leave it for you,

huh?'

And off they go.

☺

The appointment is for the early afternoon. They are a small group, only Genny, Claudio, Angie and Stub. The others are still at the seaside.

Hot day, nebulous start, reduced speed due to Genny, sitting on the Vespa seat with his shoulders turned towards the driver, holding onto the rear rack with his hands. The journey continues calmly and quietly. It's almost boring until Stub reveals that he has become an adult.

'What? Adult?'

'Oh, yeeeeah! It's my birthday today; I'm 18 years old, crrrrraaaap!'

'Stop! Stoooopp! We should make a toast!'

There's plenty of "benz". Angie pulls the half bottle of Prosecco left over from the last trip to the Thucana from under his seat and they drain it, performing dances around the Vespas.

Jingo Jingo ba Jingo ba lo ba, ba lo ba, ba lo ba. (Candido - Jingo)

'Okay! We've got nothing to drink now. Will there be a bar?'

'Imagine there not being a bar in Mantua!'

Stocked up on beers, they continue their journey to Modena. On reaching Carpi, they start asking for directions to the disco.

'Beeeer, beeeeer for freeeee!'

'Free beer for anyone who can tell us where the Picchio Verde is!'

'Beeeer! Beeeerrrrr!'

'No! You no! We only give it to chicks!'

And so, after several rejections, they meet two beautiful girls who explain to them that the Picchio Verde is just around the corner. They were lurking right there for the mere purpose of making these kinds of approaches.

'Wow! Right around the corner?'

It has to be said that the girls of Emilia-Romagna are super-friendly and chatty up to the point that you lose the conception of time.

'What brings you here? It's usually only boys from Mantua who come here.'

'Well, we met a lot of easy-going people from Modena at the Cosmic aaaand, we wanted to come to a different disco.'
'And you came here? It's a little bigger than the Cosmic but nothing more.'
'Have you tried any of the thousands of clubs we've been to? For example, the Picchio Rosso.' Say the girls.
'Sure! We know that one! Awesome! But, did you say thousands?'
'Yeaaah, you know that you're in the disco triangle here, don't you?'
'Really? For example?'
'For example, the Kiwi, the Snoopy, the Piccadilly, the Marabou, the Mac, there's also one in Nonantola, if you want, or the Charlie, oooor the New World.'
'Mmmmm! We tried a couple in Bologna but it didn't go so well.'
'In Bologna? The Chicago, by chance?'
'Yeah, that's right!'
'Good! But, if you want, you can go one better. Do you know the Arlecchino?'
'Hmmm! It's not new to me, I've heard of it.'
'Anyway, if you just go further to Reggio, there's plenty.'
'Fuck! It's 4!'
'Look! You're missing Equinoxe, the theme song.'
They go in but they only have about an hour.

People say you're tough, I can't figure it out. It's so good so good so good so good. (Pamplemousse - Wanna make music with you)

The disco is not very big, the usual dance floor surrounded by sofas and a DJ who, quite frankly, they don't think much to. Like all discos of this type, the busiest evenings are Friday and Saturday nights when there are loads of young people. Sunday afternoons are also busy but that's when 14 and 15-year-olds go too. Sunday evening is the least exciting when mutton dresses as lamb, hoping to meet a soul mate.
'Should we stay, or should we go?'
They prefer to stay outside next to a chip truck and watch the gangs go by. On the return trip, they decide to stop at Poggio Rusco because the fries had given them a thirst which they promptly

quench with a bottle of Prosecco.

Picchio Verde club. (Green Woodpecker)

☺

And here they are again, gathered in the square near the steps. It's time to seriously lay the foundations for the next expedition. The schedule foresees a trip into the mountains. The decision is made within a few seconds.

'Trentino!'
'You plan the route.'
'Aaaaall right! I'll think about it! And now let's go and pay the Wall gang a visit.'
The biggest probability of making a fool of oneself, in other words, smashing up a motorbike, happens on the journey between Sector C to the place they are heading for. The problem stems from the fact that, when you do a wheelie with a Vespa, you need to find the balance by speeding up, braking, as well as steering the handlebars slightly to the right or left while you are at the top. But, if the motorbike comes back down and the front wheel touches the road before you get it back into line with the rear one, you lose control and you end up scrambling on the side. Poplar is the one who disgraces himself tonight by tipping over right around the wall where the Wall gang gather.
'Did you hear that bang?'
'That's Poplar, he touched down.'
Those who rush to the street behind the wall see Poplar, already on his feet, contemplating the Vespa which is still lying on the asphalt.
'I can't have sex with her tonight,' Poplar blurts out.
'Poplar! Are you OK? The Vespa?'
'Holy shit! I wanted to look cool for her and I fucked myself up.'
'Who?'
'That chick who just got dumped.'
'Can't be helped. Buuut, do you really think someone who has just been dumped by her ex-boyfriend already wants to go out with someone else? The first guy to come along?'
'Sure! It's a chance. I hunt out those who have just been dumped because they're looking for consolation, right?'
'But, didn't you say that the best technique is to go out with the girl's best friend? Because surely, she won't say anything?'
'Yeah! Yeah! Come on, let's back to the wall.'

☺

Hair is worn long, touching the shoulders. Some have a centre parting, letting it fall naturally with no help from the barber. Some have a slight all-round trim to avoid split ends. Others have a fringe cut just above the eyes like the Ramones. Wearing white trousers, they introduce themselves to the Wall gang and to all those gathered in other squares where everyone recognises them immediately. This recognition label is also applied to their motorbikes since they are scratched by numerous accidents similar to Poplar's. Angie's PX has suffered the same fate more than all the others and, since he can't always take it to the body-shop, he has to find a gimmick. Like all self-respecting Angels, stickers come in handy. This time, however, the scratches on the side panels are very long and need a big patch to cover them completely. A particular Cosmic sticker might be the optimal solution but it costs too much. He has to find something else.

'Did you ever notice that giant sticker at the Lion's Road boutique?'
'No! Where?'
'In one of the dressing rooms.'
'What kind of sticker is it?'
'By Martin Guy. I saw it when I went to try on a shirt.'
'Buuuut, would it be big enough?'
'Trust me! Go and buy something and see if you can get it for free.'

Most of the time when you go shopping in a boutique, the salesgirl puts a sticker in your bag, either one of the boutique's or of the brand of the product purchased.

'That's a great idea. In any case, we know the salesgirl.'
'That pretty blonde chick with the bob haircut?'
'That's right! We'll make sure she serves us.'

Once they enter the shop, feigning indifference, they begin to scan the merchandise on display, pretending to be interested in everything. They casually look through the shirts and T-shirts, trying not to attract too much attention and avoiding serving themselves by picking up an item because the first sales assistant in the vicinity would have stuck to them like a gnat on a bottle of new wine. They greet the blond, trying to invite her to serve them, even if she has already labelled them as "prospective" customers.

'Can I help you?'
'Sure! I'm looking for a shirt.'
'Plain, patterned colours?'
'Aloha shirt, Jamaican.'
'We have Jamaican T-shirts but these are the only shirts.'
'Mmmmm, I'll try these four then.'

Fortunately, the dressing rooms are free and the curtains are half-open. Angie immediately locates the dressing room with the sticker. It's just what he needs, almost as big as the side panel of his Vespa. He goes in, pulls the curtain, tries on the first shirt and starts to peel off the cyclamen-coloured, Martin Guy sticker with the nail of his index finger. He takes off the shirt as well as his own T-shirt and tries on another one as proof that he has had them on and then, using all his fingers, he pulls the sticker as hard as he can. A loud ripping noise comes out of the dressing room and Angie stops immediately. He isn't even halfway through yet! He listens carefully to catch any comments that might compromise the success of the operation and then starts again with short tugs. The sound is tolerable and so he carries on with more confidence. The big sticker comes off at last and is entirely in his hands but how can he get it out? Angie turns his T-shirt inside-out and presses the sticker onto his chest and then turns the T-shirt he was trying on inside out as well. Next, he takes off the shirt and puts his own T-shirt and shirt back on. Now the sticker is underneath. No one can see it.

'I'm sorry; I don't like any of them.'
'Would you like to try something else?'
'Nnnooo, thank you but, I'll be back sooner or later, byeeee!'

They leave the boutique and dissolve into the crowds of the old town.

'You could hear everything from outside the dressing room.'
'What! Shit! And her?'
'She played it cool.'

Now he can show off the patched-up side of his PX and what better opportunity than to be part of the planned mountain expedition.

☺

Expeditions.

Everyone gathers in the morning, all strictly wearing white trousers, ready to leave for Trento. To share the fuel expenses, a petrol-oil mixture, they are once again riding in pairs on the Vespas, especially those with luggage racks since today they are also taking a windcheater, radio/stereo and some beer. Finger is riding with Angie.

'Remember! Drive properly, no accidents today.'

'Easy! We're all coming back today in white trousers.'

They set off. The weather is good. Eating up 200 kilometres for them is an awesome experience. The rider behind follows in the wake of the one in front as if to overtake. The rider in front continues to zigzag so as not to let the one behind overtake. If the motorbikes do pair up, the two sitting behind the driver will join the battle. They spread their legs to give those overtaking less space. They try to kick each other but after a while, probably halfway, they decide to stop to have a break. What better way to lighten the Vespas' loads than drinking all the beers. They set off again. The weather is still good. Maximum speed is 50 km/h.

There is a substantial difference in travelling northwards into the mountains than going south into the country and this considerable difference can be measured by a sandwich. You divide it into halves and continue driving with the sandwich open against the wind. When travelling north, you don't have any filling but if you go south the sandwich is full of flies. They get to Trento at last, starving hungry because no flies are filling their sandwiches. They look for a pizzeria and, as punctual as a Swiss clock, at half-past noon, they are sitting at a table.

'Margherita!'
'A poison mushroom pizza for me, I'll die for it!'
'Ham and mushrooms!'
'Margherita for me, too!'

It's an easy order since the menu only offers 7-8 types of pizza at most. Those who order a Margherita are saving up to buy Frye boots.

'A pint of beer!'
'Me! A pint of lager!'

And the Frye's savings go into beer, even though it's normal for them to take coke from the supermarket into a pizzeria.

They're off again. The weather is really splendid. Finger salutes the pizzeria with a noteworthy burp. In a short time, they arrive at Lake Caldonazzo. They have reached an altitude of 1,400 metres and it's freezing.

'It's bloody cold!'
'Yeeeeah! What's more, there's a storm brewing. Look at those dark clouds.'

Jake has a solution.

'Hey! Lost folk! Look what I've brought with me.'
'Shit! Our jackets? Weren't you supposed to take the jackets?'
'Calm down! Look, I brought a little blanket. You know, in case we lay on some grass,' Jake says.
'You moron! You're nothing but useless! You left our jackets at home for a fucking blanket!'
'Eaaaasyy! I brought something else too that wouldn't have fitted with the jackets.'

Jake has brought bottles of wine which blow away all fear of the storm. They set off again. The weather is terrible. Claudio is drunk as a skunk and is singing at the top of his voice. The sound of engines covers his toneless racket but, when they go into the many tunnels that follow on one after the other towards the Vicenza plateau, the echo restores his blissful happiness. Pepper is also showing signs of instability. Whether it's the trip, the air or the environment, he starts to see Shark DS everywhere. It's the famous "fixa". Every now and then, he urges the cavalcade to stop and, dismounting, gesticulates in the middle of the road trying to stop the cars.

'The fixa! The fixa! The Shark! The Shaaark!'

He does the same at a level crossing. He stops cars in the middle of the road invoking the Shark. The drivers are not too taken aback because they think the crossing bar is broken but this is not the case. As soon as the "fixa" drives off into the distance, Pepper gets back on the Vespa and, just on the point of leaving again, the crossing bar comes down. That's when it starts to rain and there they are, staring at the unknown, with only a small blanket for cover. They set off again. The weather is prohibitive. Vicenza suburb. Vicenza. The long march continues without further hindrance since Pepper's fixations no longer cause them to stop. But, on entering the city in the rain at a sharp bend, Angie begins to lose control of his PX. The bend, together with the wet asphalt, is a perfect recipe for making the small wheels of the Vespa slide. Finger's hands, which were hooked to the rear rack, suddenly grip Angie's arms. He is losing his balance. The Vespa leans and runs away. You can hear the screech of the sheet metal on the asphalt. In an instant, Angie and Finger hit the ground with the sides of their bodies. They start to glide on the asphalt, coupled to the motorbike until they see the PX crawling fast ahead of them, indicating that they have stopped first. Sitting on the roadway, they look at each other. Finger thunders:

'Fuckin' hell! I knew we were going to have a fuckin' accident! What did you say?'

'The sticker! The Martin Guy sticker is ruined!'

The Lost gang soon starts jeering, especially Jake, who mocks Angie with roaring laughter as he rolls on the ground.

Filthy, stained and cold, they head back home in the rain that shows no signs of stopping. Coming up to a junction, where the lane is wider, Jake is the one to show indecision. After revving up the Vespa to overtake everyone, he realises that he can't stop at the give-way sign. In order to brake in as little space as possible, he also pulls the front brake lever, which, combined with the wet road, is just perfect for taking flight. No sooner said than done, Jake and Volt,

who, at that moment, is wearing Jake's blanket, start to glide on the asphalt coupled to the motorbike until they see the ET3 crawling fast ahead, indicating that they have stopped first. Sitting on the roadway, they look at each other. Jake cries:
'The blanket! Shit, Volt! The blanket is ruined!'
Twelve hours since their departure, they finally return to base camp, stunned and filthy, their clothes fit only for the dump.

☺

Because of the latest accidents, Jake decides to switch from small to wider wheels. Tonight, he joins the gang on the seat of a new entry: a Cagiva. This model is becoming more and more popular among Angels. They are beginning to appear increasingly more frequently and are said to rival, in terms of sales quantity, the many and highly popular Vespas. A motorbike with harmonious lines, simple to drive since the gears are lengthy so you don't have to change continuously. Fuel consumption is reduced and maintenance is almost non-existent. Moreover, the front brake is not drum but disc, thus, increasing the motorbike's safety. Even if they take the piss out of him every night because he is the only one without a Vespa and ruins the photos when they line up the PXs or ET3s to immortalise the gang, he has more news to impart.
'I'm goin' to Bay!'
'You what?'
'To the Bay! To the Bay of Angels, to Gabicce. Me, Stub and Claudio. Who wants to come with us?'
It's the consecration of an Angel. Although in the end only the three of them are able to go, it's as if the whole gang has been baptised.
Originally a members-only sporting club, an entrepreneur later transformed the venue into a disco. The club was set up in a theatre that had previously been a television studio and was given the name Baia (Bay) due to the shape of the theatre. This entrepreneur often went to the United States for business where he took to going to famous nightclubs in the evening and was so dazzled by the style of the environment, the people and the music, that he decided to import it into Italy. The building overlooked the sea and the walls and furnishings in the large and elegant rooms were white. Marilyn Monroe was everywhere on the walls to show the owner's connection to the United States. A laser beam traced the way from the roof to the people of the night that, at the theme song, "Ju Ju

Man" by Passport, poured onto the dance floors, immersed in a sound that filled the dream-like atmosphere. The sounds sneakered among the flow of the fountains and dove into the colours of illuminated pools. The Angels could either dance on the central dance floor in the middle of two swimming pools or on a crystal walkway overlooking another pool, all inebriated by the scents emanating from the sea. The whole interior was illuminated by a battery of headlights placed on a mechanical arm that could move from one dance floor to another. The DJ console was in a glass lift with which the DJ could, at his own discretion, go up to the first floor, where he had a full view of the outdoor dance floor, adjacent to the pool. There was a problem, though. When the lift came down from the upper floor and touched the lower floor, a tiny landing bump made the vinyl pin jump. Such an important audio system should never have featured this anomaly. Bob Day and his life partner Tom Sison, the two American DJs in white salopettes at the time, solved this problem by using a tape recorder. The moment the lift approached the end of its run, they mixed the record with the recorder to avoid distorting the sound with the final jerk. When Daniele Baldelli arrived, however, the turntables were replaced with new tonearms with anti-skate control able to withstand the bumps. Baldelli and Mozart had so much fun going up and down because they could easily mix the songs, having learnt from Bob and Tom's experience. Another new idea that originated at the Bay of Angels was the way to mix. To overlap two records tracks for a few moments, American DJs had to hold the one about to start on a turntable with a finger and drag it. So, they came up with the idea of putting a 45-rpm cover between the turntable and the vinyl to use as friction. They could then hold and release the record at will even though the underlying turntable kept spinning. Baldelli and Mozart, however, improved things by placing a simple cloth in-between.

With its breath-taking sea view, accompanied in the night by the lights of fishing boats, the rocks and palm trees, the Bay of Angels boasted a desirable location and, with closing hours at six in the morning and business cards from famous artists like Grace Jones, attracted thousands of people.

And if I wander down the wrong road, it's alright baby, just let me go. (Grace Jones - Bullshit)

STONED ANGELS

On the notes of "Bolero Ravel" by Kubra Electric, which decreed the end of the show, the Angels rushed to have breakfast not far from there. Although this idyll was bequeathed to Baldelli and Mozart when Bob and Tom's contract expired, the owner decided to sell and move to Africa and the end of the Bay was eventually decreed by the occurrence of a nasty incident. A young man was found dead from an overdose in the car park and nothing was ever the same. The disco was closed and then re-opened under the name of the angel of the Bay, Nepentha and Daniele Baldelli moved to the Cosmic in Lazise on Lake Garda.

'The Bay is dead but the Angels are still alive.'

Some would say.

☺

Angels at the Bay of Angels.

The lift.

The Bay of Angels floors.

Spending an evening with friends, listening to the tales of the three vagabonds, is just great!

'We went through San Marino!'

'Awesome!'

Driving off on your Vespa or motorbike, sleeping away a few nights and then going to the Bay is an experience that changes you. That's what Claudio has just done and he has completely changed and is totally lost.

'Every time we stopped, he'd just talk a load of bullshit.' specifies Stub.

'That's right, even without using drugs,' Jake adds.

'Yeaaaaah! Who are you kidding! Who says he didn't take

something cheap and crappy,' add the others.
'What? What stuff?'
'Come oooon! The stuff you make by just throwing an aspirin into the cooooke!'
'No! No! No! Don't talk bullshit! He just took a sip of Martini.'
'Okay! Now we got it!'
'He shot bullshit, he shot bullshit, shot, shot, shot, just like Zeb Macahan.'
'Zeb who?'
'Zeb Macahan! The one from the TV show that kept shooting.'
'Hey! Hey! Now I feel like you're talking bullshit.'
'Come on, Zeb! Tell us one!'
'Oh, yessss! I'm going to get some Fryes!'

Frye is one of the oldest footwear brands in the United States. John Frye created his brand in the mid-1800s and carried it on successfully until the time of the Angels. Many American soldiers wore Frye boots during World War II, including General Patton. They cost a heap of money, weigh a ton and are thermal suicide, but even in summer, the dream of owning a pair is almost a "must". Besides the different colours, there are two types, those with a buckle and those without.

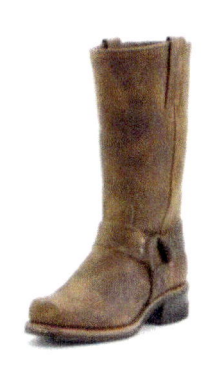

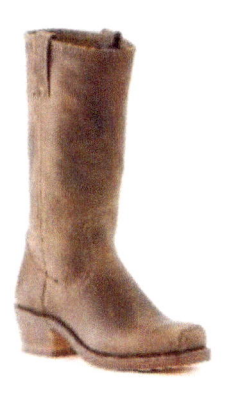

The boys prefer those without. But, where can you get them? At the Madras store in the city centre. The one and only place. They are right there in the window and every time you go for a stroll down the main street, you just look, stare and drool, captured by the hypnotic power of those much-coveted boots. A magnetic force deflects the boys' direction and pulls them to the store. But once their noses are glued to the window, their eyes are drawn to the price tickets. They will have to fork out ten high denomination banknotes to buy them, so finding ways to spend less becomes imperative.

'What do you say, Zeb? Shall we buy them? Shall we go in?'
'Calm down! Don't paaaanic!'
'And, so? What're you gonna do?'
'I have an idea! What if we change city?'
'What do you mean?'
'If we went to another city, they might cost less than here.'
'Mmmmmmm, for example?'
'What about Vicenza? It's a little smaller and, maybe...'
'That's right! It's a great idea!'

The morning is promising. Even though they don't wake up early, Vicenza is not so far away so it makes no difference. Stub, Angie and Zeb are ready for the Frye expedition.

'So? What's the plan?'
'Well, we'll go into the centre of Vicenza and walk around until we find a shop that sells them.'
'Good, let's goooooo!'

Either one in front of the other or side by side, the two PXs drive along the main road to Vicenza and the boot shop. Their speed is intermittent. If they could average 70km/h, the journey would not take so long. Stories of the expedition to the Bay of Angels are the main topic of conversation.

'And, on the way back, we also went through San Marino...'
'Yeah, yeah, thanks for the postcard! In any case, since our expedition to the Bay, we have practically earned the title of International Vagabonds, so, I 'm beginning to think that we need to give our group a new name.'
'What?'
'We need an international name for the gang of... out of their minds.'
'Ha! Ha! I can tell you're out of yours!'
'I'm not kidding, old man! Look, since 'lost' is more a state of mind than the loss of something physical, like a wallet, for example. It's actually our brains that we are missing so, I've come up with The Loss.'
'The what?'
'The Loss, it's cool, come on!'

The Vespas continue one in front of the other and pair up again a few minutes later.
'Well, what about chicks? How's it goin'?'
'I'm still going out with her, and you?'
'She dumped me.'
'How come?'
'I think I know why. We were goin' around the city on the Vespa, at night. I was travelling by the curb when I saw a tree branch sticking out of a garden and invading the whole path right into the street.'
'Did you slam the brakes on? Did you have your usual accident?'
'Nooo! Not this time! I lowered my head to avoid it, too bad she caught it in the face.'
'Ooookayyy! But, don't tell everybody!'
'Sorry?'
'Come on! Come on! You know! Like that "cocksucker" that you recorded after the three beeps, in the middle of Cosmic C8 when you were with Volt...'

Bip, bip, bip ... cocksuuuukeeeer ...
(Codek - Demo)

'So?'
'Well! She got so much piss taken out of her for listening to that tape.'
'So what? I still see that Theodelinda always comes along with Cleopatra to visit us at the steps.'
'There's a reason for that. I think Cleopatra has Jake in her sights.'
The Vespas go back to single file only to pair up again a little later.
'Yeah! They are also invited to the New Year's Eve party.'
'By the way, we'll need to suss out Volt's house, it's at our complete disposal.'
'It's a bit early! Let's wait for summer to end first and then there's Lamp's party.'
Back in single file, it's a few more minutes before the Vespas pair up again.
'Heeeere weeee aaaare, Here weeee aaaare Fryeeeee!'

Once infiltrated into the city's boutique streets, they begin to scan the windows and signs. Following a spiral technique, they start from a point and spread out unless they see the store that sells the boots. The Princess, the 5M. No luck. They stop at every show store to ask if they have Frye's until they realise that they have gone beyond the perimeter of downtown stores.

'I'm sick of it!'
'I'm fed up, for fuck's sake!'
'I'm sick and tired!'
'What shall we do?'
'Let's go home!'
'What if we went to sit on Mount Berico for a smoke? Maybe we can come up with a solution?'
'Yeah! Good thinking! Maybe we'll get a bright idea.'

Mount Berico offers a wonderful view. It overlooks the sanctuary and stately houses and the surrounding greenery is a positive stimulus to concentration. Stub has a flash of inspiration.

'Let's go to the store in our town and ask where they stock up.'
'That's riiiight! If we go directly to the factory, they will surely cost less.'
'You did it again! You're such a smart arse!'

☺

The evening sees them on the steps as usual exchanging all the adventures, events and episodes that happened during the day or on the previous days. They can't wait to tell the rest of the gang about their Frye expedition.

'So, we've decided to name the gang, The Loss.'
'That's right! And I've even made a flag!'
'Then we need to get to know each other better.'
'Nothing like throwing a party to do that!'
'Great idea! We'll have it in Lamp's basement.'
'And we also have to go to Madras in the old town to ask where the Frye factory is.'

Lamp's party seems well organised. More than fifty people are expected to come from the city as well as the province. It all starts in the best possible way.

They was dancin' and singin' and movin' to the groovin'...
(Average White Band - Play that funky music white boy)

But, like at any party, something always happens to spoil the fun. Firstly, because the spare wheel on Angie's PX is stolen, and this happens at parties because the friends of friends of friends join the guests and you never know who is coming and going; secondly, because there is always someone who gets drunk and starts to act like a looney. Apart from Hugo and Water, this time Zeb is the one to do the dishonours by hunting for a chick with a fishing net. After a few hours, almost all of them run away and the rest of the people are out on the street. The party is taking a turn for the worse. It isn't the fact that the music is mediocre... but that someone, drunk as a skunk, is acting like a prick.

'Hey! Hey! Hey! Look what Water is doing...'

Water, for example, is running around with a bucket of ice cubes trying to pour them on the boys' balls, on the girls' tits and everyone's arses by pulling at their clothes.

'Hey! Hey! Hey! Listen to what that guy is singing...'

'Long live the pussy and the rainbow, the asshole in the sky is an innuendo, the cock that stands up, the hairy pussy, the buttocks of the bride that go clap clap clap!'

Say everybody is running. Say everybody is working. Say everything is money. Say all your trust are nothing... (Barabbas - Wild Safari)

'Hey! Hey! Hey! Look at Pepper, look what he's doin'...'

'Shit! Pepper is celebrating because he got through his driving test! Besides, every time you have to say something to someone, you can't keep saying hey hey hey!'

That's how Stefan created Heyhey as a nickname for himself.

☺

The summer, which for Angels lasts from summer to summer, is drawing to a close. They are well aware that Vespa or Cagiva trips will become a little more problematic. For this reason, a party is not a priority. It doesn't even enter their heads at that moment. What is essential, before the mists prevail and the days become short, is always and only one thing: the obsession with boots.

They all gather at Tacky's bar to make decisions between a Martini, a Prosecco, a beer and Tacky's famous Pinot. Tacky's white wine has something special. You don't know if it's Sauvignon, Chardonnay or Pinot, though the latter is the most probable, but it has something special about the display on the counter. You don't order ten or twenty glasses of white, but one metre of white! A white metre.

'Tacky! One white metre for the Loss!'

'What! You order by metre?'

'Yeaaah! It's the drinkable system!'

The glasses are positioned on the bar in a straight line. Tacky is a true artist and the pouring master. He fills all the glasses without stopping, pouring the wine without ever raising the neck of the bottle. He starts by pouring the white into the first glass and, one millimetre before it overflows, with a lightning move and a click, he moves the neck over the next glass without spilling a drop. In the end, the level of nectar inside the goblets is precisely the same.

'I'm the best in the world!'

He keeps repeating.

'So! Hugo! Go to the Madras shop in town and ask where the factory is.'

'Yes! Go! We'll join you in a bit...'

Hugo leaves and they stay there to exchange the last bullshit with Tacky.

'Well, so you did the flag!'

'Yes, indeed! One for our expeditions and one for parties...'

'One for parties?'

'Sure! It stands out with a bottle in the middle of The Loss...'

'The Loss?'

'Yeah! The Loss, because loss means something lost...'

'Have you got it here?'

'Uhmmmm no! We just hoisted it on the flagpole outside!'

'Ha! Ha! You really are missing something. It's your brains that have suffered a loss!'

'Okay, come on! Let's go and get Hugo...'

A horde of youngsters has invaded the city due to the coolest event of summer: Festivalbar[19]. Finding Hugo in the middle of this confusion is an ordeal. The only safe way to catch sight of someone is to stay stock-still at the pedestrian traffic light between the square and the high street of the old town, a sort of bottleneck where everyone has to walk for sure. Time goes by but Hugo is nowhere to be seen. They wait so long that they are tempted to go to the Madras shop themselves. As soon as they voice the thought, they

---

19 The equivalent of Glastonbury or the Isle of Wight festival.

glimpse an individual who particularly stands out among the crowds in the middle of the square. With arms raised alternately, almost as if they were intent on picking something invisible out of the air, and legs slightly bent at the knees, the familiar shape staggers forward, step by step, in a zig-zag manner. It's Hugo. They go closer and realise he's off his head with booze.

'Fuckin' hell! How much did you drink at Tacky's?'
'100!'
'100? 100 what?'
'Siiiir, siree...'
'What! What the fuck is he talkin' about!'
'S, sirup...'
'Hugo! Hugo! Did you go to Madras?'

They sort themselves out and discover that the factory is in Bassano del Grappa.

It is getting late and now they have the task of taking Hugo home without raising concern. They don't want to do what they did with Jake last time when they just leant him against the door and then ran away. They want to physically take him into the house so that he can get the rest he deserves. Luckily, he has the house keys in his pocket because his parents will be out and won't be returning until late. When they finally get to his house, they are relieved to note that his parents are still out. It's better that way, they think to themselves in the twilight with happy faces. They open the door, drag Hugo in and get him into his bedroom.

'On three! One, twooo, threeeee! Aaaand, oops!'

After three swings, they throw him on the bed on his stomach, his head turned to one side and his arms along his body with the palms of his hands turned upwards, fully dressed.

☺

The distance is double that of the trip to Vicenza and so they decide to leave in the morning. This time the three expeditioners are joined by Finger, another gang member eager to buy the boots.

Zippin' up my boots goin' back to my roots yeah!
(Odyssey - Going back to my Roots)

The two PXs set off and the day is once again, spectacular. They take it as a good sign. They are sure that luck is on their side.

'Hey! Finger! A pal of yours joined us...'

'Who! Fish?'
'Yeah! The one with the black Cagiva...'
'Why is he called Fish?'
'His name is Leo but he's a queer fish!'
'Ha! Ha! He drinks like a fish!'
The Vespas return to single file and pair up again after a few minutes.
'Did you bring sandwiches?'
'No, I have nothing to eat...'
'No! No! I didn't mean that. I meant that with all the flies, we can have a nice sandwich filling...'
'Ha! Ha! Ha! As usual! An open sandwich in front as you drive and it fills itself!'
The Vespas travel in single file again and then pair up a few minutes later.
'Did you hear "2" has changed DJ?'
'Isn't Rudy there anymore?'
'It doesn't look like it. There's a guy named DJ Jenny. Rubbish!'
'Wish Rudy would come back, aaand, speaking of music; did you know Hugo is composing the Loss song?'
'Ha! Ha! He's a 100% Loss! If it's good, it's because it's full...'
'Yeeeeah, full of, spirit, ha! Ha! Ha!'
The Vespas travel in single file again and then pair up a few minutes later.
'Here, we are! Frye, here we aaaare!'
They park in front of the warehouse and, feeling a little nervous, go inside. Much to their surprise, they find a company store that looks very similar to a boutique. Instead of them wandering among the shelves with interest, it is the shelves themselves that revolve around them as if they were inside a rotating cylinder. It's a kaleidoscope of footwear. The Frye boots they are looking for are there but that's where the shoe merry-go-round stops.
'I'm awfully sorry but we don't have your size at the moment. If you want to come back another day...'
Zeb, who was the one with his heart set on it the most, goes back open-mouthed and empty-handed. For the other three, the boots become a hallucination. The only thing left to do is buy them in town. Every time one of them manages to buy a pair, another exclaims:

STONED ANGELS

'Hallucination! I must have taken a hallucinogen!'

Bit by bit, after enormous sacrifice, the Madras store sets them back ten high denomination banknotes each and, little by little, the Loss gang appear in the boots they so fervently adore.

The boots need to be worn in. The problem lies in the fact that Frye's are wide at the pull straps and shrink towards the ankle. Therefore, it would not be wise to put your trousers on first because they would end up inside the boots. An Angel would look like an outsider if he were walking around with his trousers inside his footwear. On the other hand, it would need considerable effort to pull up your second-hand Levis or Fiorucci jeans once you'd got your Frye boots on. The obvious solution? You put your trousers over the boots before you put them on and then slip into the whole combination.

☺

After the big change in name for the company of Angels, there is another waiting at the door. The evening begins very quietly as usual. A handful of friends sit on the steps, waiting for the others, exchanging any bullshit that comes into their minds, often in answer or addition to bullshit from the others.

'You know Fish got himself a chick from the stadium?'

'Oh, yes? Aaand, when will he introduce her to us?'

'I don't know, maybe he'll bring her tonight...'

'Instead, Stub didn't manage to dump his...'

'How come?'

'She burst into tears...'

'Mmmmm, we need a reshuffle...'

'What do you mean?'

'Remember when Stub sent that perfumed letter and made it look like the chick was still gasping for him?'

'Yeah! So?'

'Well! It was a fantastically nasty trick; he believed that she still had a crush on him, and she believed that he had...'

'So?'

'Since we have a boatload of addresses, if we send postcards or letters to all of them, making it look like they're crazy for each other, you know, practically inventing couples, we could stir up a whole can of worms'

'Yeeeeah, buuut, what's the point?'

'Come on! If someone head over heels in love gets a postcard

from someone else declaring eternal love, it might change their mind and make dumping easier. That way, they'd be no whining. Don't you remember what happened to Stub?'
'Shit! Brilliant! Really cool!'
'Besides, those without a lovebird might have a chance...'
They hardly get down to seriously planning the idea...
'Given the number of postcards we're going to send, we could call this operation "shabby trick or treat."'
...when a white VW Golf stops in front of the steps, right in front of the handful of friends.
'We'll send one to ourselves as well aaand, the only one who won't get the trick will be Stub, so everyone will think it was him...'
Out of the corner of their eyes they see Poplar getting out. He is the first to have a car.
'The car is like your first love! You never forget it!'
Their faces light up. They turn to look, lost for words. Everybody is speechless and amazed. Poplar, smiling like a Cheshire cat, a cigarette poking out of the side of his mouth. The smoke rises over his cheek, making him blink as it passes his eye.
'Is it yours?'
'Pa gave me it.'
'Fuckin' hell! You only just got a licence!'
They all circle the car. It has four doors and a stereo system.
'Stereo system by Volt?'
'Of course! He's the only one doing them, car radio with cassette player...'
'Awesome! You can listen to tapes without carrying radios, woofers...'
'That's rrrrright! And you know what the most important thing is?'
'Which?'
'Inside, I can push, push in the bush!'
One by one, all the Loss members arrive.
'Do the seats recline?'
'Easy! Inside we can push, push in the bush!'
The last to arrive is Fish who manages to take their attention from the car by introducing his new flame.
'Can we push, push in the bush with her? In the car?'
'No! But, I'll tell you a secret...'
Everybody goes quiet. The seconds tick by but he's playing

hard to get.
'So? At "2"? At Cosmic? Bay? Lem?'
Fish is not the type to shout his news to the four winds. No, he sneaks up instead, inviting his listeners to get closer by repeatedly curling his hooked index finger. When all the guys form a circle around him in curiosity, bowing slightly towards him with ears outstretched, eager to hear what he has to say, he finally comes up with 'What a bore, bein' so handsome.'
The "fuck yous" echo from the steps to Tacky's bar.
But they have to celebrate and what better occasion than to go to said bar.
The unmistakable tread of Frye boots descends the steps to Tacky's bar.
'Wow! The Loss are here!'
'Big change, Tacky! Poplar got a car!'
'One white metre!'
'Do two!'
'So, Poplar! With the car, you fuck more!'
'Oh yeah! Sure! And then there's always the petrol trick...'
'Oh yeah? Hold your horses! What trick is that?'
'Well! It's simple! You drive around aaand, when you see that you're in a quiet, lonely, slightly dark area, you furtively turn off the ignition and the car stops, aaand, in this case, you tell her that it's out of petrol. Perfect chance to try!'
'Fifteen men on a dead man's chest... yo-ho-ho, and a bottle of wine!'
'Come on! Go! Everyone out to make the record!'
The usual record of how many people can get in a car. With the Cosmic's C13 in the Golf's cassette player, one by one they get in, twisting, curling, crumbling, gathering, forming a tangle of boots and hair. A couple of cigars also pop up to add to the Pinot Grigio breath and the aromatic tobacco smoke mix.
'Hugo! How you doin'?'
'Aaaand a fart! It's warm! Thaaaat tickles! Thaaaat tickles! Aaaand a fart! It's warm! Thaaaat tickles! Up the arse!'
'Oh Christ! He's drunk again!'
Once again, there is no lack of volunteers to take him home.
'Shall we take Hugo home and then go to the disco?'

Tonight. All right. You have a strong way. To get me. I never realize. I guarantee. (Narada Michael Walden - Tonight I'm Alright)

It only needs two volunteers. One to take the brother's PX home and another to get him sorted behind the driver. No problem, but there's still one important thing to think about. The driver must try not to lose Hugo on the way home. With the Vespa ready to leave, the drunk passenger is installed on the seat, taking him by the armpits. The driver has to sit on the tip of the seat and Hugo as far back as possible behind. After that, they bend his body forward so that his head rests on the driver's back. Dangling legs and arms don't matter, the important thing is that he doesn't lean back while the Vespa is in motion and that the driver doesn't accelerate. Luckily, he has the house keys in his pocket because his parents wanted to go out and will be late back. Once they reach his house, they are happy to see that the parents are still out. Fantastic, they seem to say themselves in the twilight with happy faces. They open the gate, but this time doesn't go like the last. From the pitch black of the night, they hear something wheezing. Two luminescent points embedded in a black outline appear from the darkness of the garage. Initially staring, the eyes suddenly stand up and begin to bound towards them at speed. The sudden reaction causes them to drop Hugo who, almost kneeling, still has his arms around them.
'Shit! What the f...?'
'Aaaa, ttttilaaaa...,' mumbles Hugo.
It's Attila, Hugo's beast.

Warf! Warf!
(Cat Stevens - Was Dog A Doughnut)

A big, huge, giant black dog.
'Attila? So, this stuff would be Attila?'
A big, black dog with a tennis ball in its mouth.
They open the door, drag Hugo in and go to his bedroom.
'On three! One, twoo, threeee! Aaaand oops a daisy!'
After swinging him to gain momentum, they throw him on the bed on his stomach, his head turned to one side and his arms along his body with the palms of his hands turned upwards, still fully dressed.
After throwing a few balls to Attila, they set off for the disco.

The appointment is with the others and with the girls' bathroom.
'They're so fucking hard!'
'Couldn't they make them softer?'
'Wet them! Wetting them helps!'
The Frye boots are eating their feet and the idea of hiding in the ladies' bathroom in the disco to lighten the leather grip, is to avoid being taken the piss of by the rest of the Angels. First, they strut about in heels that make them 3 inches taller, then, they sneak into the toilets to lick their blisters. Rather than give them a look of solidarity, the girls eye them pitifully.

Hey everybody everybody gonna have a good time tonight. Just shakin' the soles of your feet. (Queen - Fun It)

The evenings are starting to get nippy but that doesn't stop them from wanting to be in the square. The days are getting shorter and the dimness of the city lights, as well as the feeble light that comes from the shop window, alter the faces of the Loss gang, despite the long hair covering them. While it was previously clear to see who was coming, even at a distance, now, it's deciphered from the reflections of the Vespa's spoiler or the roar of the Cagiva engine. The black PX belongs to Stub, for example, while Zeb's is metallic blue, if it comes from the crossroads at the bottom left, it's Jeep's or Giby's, if it comes from the right. The same goes for an ET3 or Ciao. Every movement that approaches the square is noticed, including the girls who often pop by on foot. But, on this particular evening, two new headlights emerge from the crossroads at the end of the street. They are a pair but not of any motorcycle. Indeed, they are lower. The moment they realise that a car is approaching and that it can't belong to some of their friends, they don't take their eyes off it. The unmistakable white silhouette, the wide window, the gurgle of the engine, the sound of the horn removes any doubt. It's a Shark. With great surprise, it slows down, heads towards them and, sporting a huge sticker on the bonnet, stops right in front of the steps.

It's Pepper.
Pepper gets out.
Silence reigns. The mouths that were previously open in laughter, song and chat about everything and everyone, clamp shut in amazement but immediately after, all lips turn upwards in a smile

of complacency.
'Come on, look at the spheres, see? A car with balls!' Pepper says, a smile printed on his face.
A Shark in the gang! Unbelievable! Pepper lights a cigarette and moves away slowly, as if wanting to feed it to a fatal attraction. Those present begin to revolve randomly around the car, each with his own curiosity.
'Is it yours?'
'Yes!'
The questions are few, but the compliments are many.
'We'll be wanderin' around a lot, won't we?'
'Why not! When the Shark comes out from the Bay, the city is full of Carabinieri!'
'Come on! Show us how it lifts its arse!'
'Come on! Turn the volume up so we can hear the woofers!'
'Come on! Let's break the record! Everybody in!'
'Stop! Stop it! Get out of my Shark!'
'Come oooon, Pepper!'
'I'll just show you the blinking indicators behind aaand, the reclining seats...'
The Shark's folding seats form a king-size bed. This means that, after a disco, there is no need for a tent and sleeping bags; you can lie comfortably down when you get in. It must be celebrated, what better occasion than to go to Tacky's bar.
The unmistakable tread of Frye boots descends the steps to Tacky's bar.
'Holaaa! The Loss comin'!'
'Hi, Tacky! We've come to celebrate!'
'It seems to me that you celebrate every weekend, what's the occasion this time? A new flag?'
'Well! We also made a shirt! However, it's for something else.'
Everybody points to Pepper.
'I bought a Shark...'
'Fucking hell! Awesome! A round of beers on me!'
A lot of rounds are turning. The last one is when Hugo, on all fours, crawls to look for some small change that he claims to have dropped. This squirming between the legs of the customers begins to annoy someone, especially those who are playing pool. Upon invitation of the bar owner, Tacky's dad, Hugo is told to leave together with all the others.

The rectangle of light made by the door of the bar illuminates the wall of the grey staircase. The usual curtain of smoke puffs outwards, forming a spiral that twists and turns as if they were the ones pushing it from inside the room. Unfortunately, there is not enough light to notice a dumpster parked at the top of the slope. Using it to lean on, they involuntarily push it down the slope where it unfortunately bumps into a pole topped by a litter basket, which duly overturns. All the rubbish spills out in front of the bar door, much to the wrath of daddy Tacky and Don Falcon, the priest who sometimes indulges in the company of clients, since the church is located above it.

'No, boys! No! Not like that! Stop it!'

Despite being inebriated, some of the Loss still have enough neurons left to manage a comment.

'Whaaaat, happened?'

'What happened? Look at those two! I don't want to see them anymore!'

The two in question are Stub and Zeb who are busy trying to catch the goldfish in the fountain of the bar using the litter basket that came off the pole with the impact of the dumpster. The noise brings the people out and Don Falcon, just like Moses and the Red Sea, sees the crowd split in two when Hugo, still crawling, is the last to come out.

'No, boys! No! Not like that! I want to hear what you have to say!'

The answer comes in the form of a colossal burp from Finger, which bounces between the walls of the slope, making the curious come back out of the bar. They go back to the square and meet Fish.

'Ah! At last! Did you finally get out?'

'Your name is, afroooo!'

'Hugo! What the fuck are you singin'?'

'You! You're aaaafroooo!'

The cold air and an hour's break, help them answer Fish in a sensible fashion.

'Forget it, it's a buuuuuuullshit sooooong...'

'Buuuut, youuuuu, haven't you celebrateeed?'

'No! I didn't feel like drinking!'

'Aaaall right, let's doooo... packet!'

The "packet" is a kind of punishment. The chosen one is forced to the ground and everyone jumps on top, as if he were a

mattress, to form a human pile. The unfortunate victim survives because they leave Fish's head out so that he can breathe.
'Fuck you! Couldn't we celebrate at the disco?'
'Yeaaaah, let's goooo to "2"!'
'We'd better get Hugo home first!'
But this time Hugo doesn't want to go home, he wants to go to a disco with them and maybe he has a point. A couple of hours in the club makes every hangover go away. They decide to go to Lem disco because Pepper wants to show the car to a girl he has just met and knows that she is there right now.

Keep your eye on us, on a moving, moving. It's a breakdown. On a bad sound... (Bionic Boogie - Risky Changes)

The Lem disco doesn't have the same sacredness as the more well-known Italian dance halls although it did hold an event that was the envy of the town: Genesis performed there.
"Exclusively from England" radio and posters advertised. Then, after the band gave two concerts, it fell back into anonymity.
While Pepper is groping around for his new flame, the Loss gang starts dancing. Although they consider the disco rather sad, this evening they happen to meet many Angel friends from the city. Due to the high volume, it's not the right place to shout greetings in ears and, given their state, exchanging a look suffices. The Angels move as if they were one people, a tribe. Even changing discos, the faces don't change much.

You don't like my music. You don't have to use it.
(Brothers Johnson - Get the Funk Out Ma Face)

In the middle of photograms of constantly bumping boys and girls, it isn't surprising that they lose sight of Hugo for a moment. However, he suddenly turns up with a cigarette in his mouth, puffing away without taking it from his lips. When Hugo isn't burning the hair of the people around, the ash, reaching a certain length, falls on the dance floor. But, when it hits a person instead, the embers stay attached, compressing the tobacco and turning the cigarette downwards. He keeps acting like this until a gentleman shows up and, gesturing, invites him to stop smoking. To no avail. Hugo keeps on back and forth between dance-cigarette cigarette-dance. It's

easier to scrounge cigarettes when you're a little drunk.
'That's enough! If I find you smoking on the dance floor again, I'll throw you out!'
The bouncer has to yell at Hugo to be heard above the racket.
'You! You're aaaaaaafroooo! And you're a toooy boooy!'
The invitation to stop smoking came to nothing. Pepper's girlfriend brought the situation to a head by joining them and lighting up a cigarette. A minute later, they are thrown out and "the Shark celebration" ends in the square in front of the disco.

☺

After more changes for the Angels group, there is another at the door. An R4 shows up at the steps. Driver's licence exams are paying off. The first thing to do, since autumn evenings are getting ready to give way to the colder winter nights, is leave the Vespa at home and scrounge the parents' car. Everyone is expecting to see one of the many friends from the neighbourhood, who occasionally come to visit the Loss gang, get out of the car. However, this time Volt gets out. The reaction is no longer of surprise but abundance. First the Golf, then the Shark and now the appearance of an R4 makes it clear that the picture they saw painted in front of the discos when they, stock-still in the square, looked at the older Angels, is gradually being completed.

'We must celebrate!'
'Shall we go to Tacky's to get a must injection?'
'Chill, chill, I don't think he'll be very happy to see us...'
'That's right! And I don't want to find my brain floating in alcohol again...'
'If only!' A girl's voice pipes in.
'What do you mean Bea?'
'The last time you left the bar, someone started licking me...'
'What? Who?'
'Just you Zeb and the next time I saw you, you didn't give me the time of day. I've been thinking about it...'

These situations, combined with operation "shabby trick or treat" letters, caused trouble among the couples in the Loss gang and surely those of the other groups. Between the Loss members and others city gangs, the circle reaches many people; we can only imagine the chaos.

Vale dumps Fish, who doesn't waste time and goes with Cynthia. Bea dumps Zeb and tries with the first single bloke she

finds. Finger takes advantage of Cynthia from another group. Poplar goes out with Fish's ex. Volt ends with Cynthia from yet another neighbourhood. One big chaos.
 'And you, Stub, how's it goin'?'
 'I've dumped mine...'
 'And she started crying again?'
 'No, I heard from Volt that she took barbiturates...'
 'Noooo...'
 'No problem, Volt broke up with his chick and now wants to go out with my ex...'
 At this point, Heyhey has it away with Stub's ex, slipping in before Volt. Stub is now with Cynthia, who dumped Fish, and the plot thickens. Vale dumps Poplar to get back with Fish.

Holly Dolly. You turn me on. Holly Dolly. You turn me on. Holly Dolly. You turn me on. Come on get up! (Kano - *Holly Dolly*)

 Despite all this blowing hot and cold, there is no conflict of any kind. On the contrary, when faced with a proposal to have fun all together, any friction instantly disappears.
 'Hey! I hear Mozart's coming to the Chalet club. How about we all go and celebrate the R4 there?'
 'Uh! That club with mill sails where the smoke comes out of the floor?'
 'Good idea! It'd be better to give Tacky's a rest for a while...'
 Mozart had already been seen around and, after the closure of the Bay of Angels, was able to travel throughout the country spreading funky music and especially his Afro style, that type of non-commercial music he had invented along with Baldelli. Claudio Rispoli, aka Mozart, also left his mark at the Goody Goody in Faenza, the Vinavil in Imola and the Much More in Forlì and now he is fortunately DJing in these extraordinary surroundings.
 Funky comes from "Funk", which, in Afro-American slang, means the smell produced during sex. Consequently, funky not only stands for a mixture of dirty, sexy and attractive, it also means free from inhibitions. Therefore, with no inhibitions, even the rhythm made the songs danceable with their insistent and repetitive bass, sharp and syncopated electric guitar riffs, wind sections, instrumental pieces and solos. The forerunner of all this, of course, was James Brown.

Fellas, I'm ready to get up and do my thing. I wanna get into it, man, you know. (James Brown - Sex Machine)

    The gang's encounters, however, are not always pure fun or hanging out. One Saturday night, just as they are preparing to leave, Angie receives a phone call from a friend telling him that Jake has smashed himself up on his way to their meeting place on the steps in Sector C. It's the topic of the evening and the first time any of the friends has ever had such a bad accident that they need to go to hospital. Most of them have suffered bumps and bruises but have survived with just a few whacks and dents to the motorbike's bodywork. Besides, these minor incidents give them a good excuse to take the piss out of each other when describing the sequence of events. They unanimously decide to visit Jake in the hospital the following Sunday. It will be the first time that a good number of them have ever visited someone in hospital.

    The unmistakable tread of Frye boots echoes through the hospital corridors. The Angels tribe knows which ward they have to go to but are not so sure about the room Jake is in. The orthopaedic ward is quite large and the staff tend to sneak away at the sight of the gang. The smell of the air soaked with alcohol and disinfectant is new to many of them but soon ignored and replaced by the need to find out where the personnel department has put Jake. Someone pops their head into the rooms, someone else stretches their neck from the corridor and they go through the ward in this way until they find him. There he is, his bandaged leg held high, looking reasonably quiet. The room has two beds and a boy reading a copy of Tex[20] from a whole bunch of comics is keeping him company.

    'Heeeereee heeee is!'
    'Hi, Jaaaake!'
    'What's up? What happened?'
    'Heyyyy, nothing, nothing, I touched the brakes, front and back

---

20 Tex Willer is the main fictional character of the Italian comic series Tex, created by writer Gian Luigi Bonelli and illustrator Aurelio Galleppini. Tex is depicted as a tough guy with a strong personal sense of justice, who becomes a ranger in Arizona, defending Native Americans and any other honest character from extortion and bandits, unscrupulous merchants, corrupt politicians and tycoons.

at the same time aaaand, nothing, didn't work...'
'But, aaaand, the leg?'
'Nothing serious, four days and then I can go home, then crutches...'
'Not bad, come on! I had an accident too, you know...'
'This is not to be sneezed at, Angie! Tell us...'
'So, it was me and the punk on my PX and we were on the road to sector E, pretty much all blocked by traffic, basically a long queue of cars that took up the whole lane, you know, Saturday afternoon, all in the city, and we were in a hurry...'
'And?'
'Aaaand, nothing, we pretended that the punk was sick and I had to take him to emergency...'
'And?'
'Aaaand, so, I told him to pretend to be unconscious and to lean on my back with his mouth open and his tongue out while I, on the other side of the white line in the middle of the road, overtook all the cars in the queue...'
'And?'
'Aaaand, with my left arm up holding a white handkerchief and whizzing by making the sound of a siren at the top of my voice, at a certain point, I didn't see that someone in the queue had made room for a car coming out of a side turning, aaaand, nothing, I suddenly found its nose cutting me off, the crash was inevitable...'
'Anything serious?'
'Terrible, I'd say.'
'Did the punk get hurt?'
'Did he hell! Not so much the mudguard of the Vespa, but the flat toe of my Frye...'
'Nooooooo!'
'Noo? It was all scratched...'
'Now? What're you gonna do?'
'Already done it! So, I rushed to a cobbler who fixed the square toe cap and coloured it with a spray. I think, he gave me the can...'
'I see, but, the PX?'
'The PX is almost ready, I took the spray can to the car body shop and asked him to repaint the Vespa in the same colour, a sandy colour, Frye and PX the same colour! Awesome!'
It's noon. They leave Jake and his roommate "Tex" with a smile on their faces. The promise is to get him back in shape asap

for a ride in Pepper's Shark and maybe go to Les Cigales. Their stories have hit the target because Jake and his roommate's morale is back on track. But there is little time. They have to meet friends from other gangs because they have planned to go to the Cosmic that same day. Ready, set, go, all together. Those madly in love and those that aren't, single guys and babes, and especially Angels. It's the first time that so many set off with only one purpose, living in friendship, solidarity and without a care in the world. A few of them pop home for a bite and then leave again while their parents beg them to sit at the table a little longer. The rendezvous time is half past one in the afternoon, no later. The Cosmic opens at three. The line of 125ccs leaves sharply on time. They absolutely don't want to miss the opening signature tune. Everyone is familiar with the road to the lake but close to Lazise, they prefer to take the one that arrives at the disco from the hills behind. The abundance of car roofs that have already invaded the car park and the number of people roaming all around is an impressive sight. Before driving up to look for a space for the motorbikes, they have the bright idea of finding a safe place to hide the PXs' side panels. They have been stolen "like hot cakes" recently and is yet another good reason for deciding to take the narrow, slightly hilly road in the middle of the fields. The same one they used before to change their clothes.

Perhaps solidarity and carefreeness ought to be questioned! They go inside at last where the two legendary DJs are ready in the spaceship. Claudio TBC, who is well known alongside Baldelli after his experience at the Papillon club in Riccione, is intent on tweaking an electronic keyboard installed in the booth. There's no time to take a sip from the drink served in cardboard glasses with the Cosmic logo or fart around since the dry ice is already swirling in. The columns of lights fill up, the chessboard on the ceiling and the dance floor light up and the notes of Michel Magne's "Signaux codes non identifiés", tremble in the bodies of the Angels. Despite the smoke layer on the dance floor which covers the lower part of the legs, there is always a bit of hesitation before jumping onto that parallelepiped of light. Initially reluctant to get onto the dance floor's rectangle and display their style of movement, many decide to wait. Some people, on the other hand, plonk themselves down side by side, close to a corner, dance with their legs slightly apart, tapping their feet alternately. Then, several Angels take the plunge and begin to move loosely, not caring a fig about the looks they might get. But there is also that stoned someone who starts to wander around, looking up as if waiting for that one song that would fulfil his expectation of who knows what. But it's the rhythm that finally makes the decision. With the notes of "Jaws" by Lalo Schifrin and those of "Let there be drums" by The Incredible Bongo Band, the dance floor is now heaving and a dancing tribe totally saturates the Cosmic. After a wild hour, it's time-out. With a stamp on the back of the hand, the show continues in the parking lot. The autumn air has not discouraged anyone from coming to the Cosmic. The number plates on the motorcycles and cars are proof of patrons arriving from all over Italy and abroad, from Belgium, Austria and Germany in particular.

Do the hustle, do the hustle. Do the hustle. Oh, do it. Oh, do it
Do the hustle, do the hustle.   (Van McCoy - The Hustle)

'Did you find the place right away from Padua?'
'No problem! We're here almost every Sunday...'
'Wow! Every Sunday at the disco...'
'On Saturday too!'
'On Saturday and Sunday at the Cosmic?'
'No! No! Just a sec, on Sunday at the Cosmic and Saturday around the clubs in Padua...'
'Not bad! You've got it good! A Dyane, discos...'
'No! No! We don't spend anything...'
'What? How can you do it!'
'We come here on Sundays to buy Cosmic stickers aaand, aaand and then the following Saturday, we resell them in front of the discos in Padua at double the price!'

They go back in for another wild hour. To join those who are still dancing, you have to move like a chess piece from one colourful box on the dance floor to another until you find the friend with whom to release energy. Wanting to catch the moment of aspiring DJs, Jeep or Giby head to Baldelli's position and glue themselves to the spaceship trying to memorise Larry Page, the performer of the song of the moment: "Erotic soul". It's already time to take another break outside. The usual stamp, this time on the other wrist, and here they are already wandering around the "campsite". They are struck by a group of Angels who appear to be leaning forward squeezing their hair. Intrigued, they close in and notice a new type of sticker with the inscription "Nepentha" glued on their 2CV with a TO (Turin) number plate.

'Hiiii, excuse us, have you been to the Bay of Angels by any chance?'

One of them turns his eyes towards Zeb while leaning over. His hair covers half his face with a side bang that almost makes him look like Captain Harlock. The palms of his hands are squashing the dangling hair as if to make it smooth but the real reason is to squeeze out water.

'Of course! Time ago, though!'

'Well! It's just that we saw the Angel of the Bay sticker and we thought...'

'Noooo! The story is that the owner of the Bay of Angels opened this club in Turin...'

These Angels tell them that the Nepentha is the freakiest disco in Turin. In true Bay of Angels' style, palm trees have been placed around the edge of the dance floor, light walls have been erected and the DJ booth goes up and down on the dance floor. Citroen DSs and Dyanes surround it every weekend, and the Piedmont Angels have made the disco a vital meeting point. They wear clothes from a couple of stores that stock their type of gear: The Shiny Goddess of Paradise and Crazy Horse, and are never without drugs. In fact, they are also known as "STONED ANGELS".

Afro sound has also swooped in there because the club has seen the great masters, Mozart and Rubens, playing there since the opening day. Some say that Mozart recorded his first tape there, calling it "Mozart's holy mass" because, in the middle of the evening, much to everyone's surprise, he put on an "Indian mass".

'Excuse me, why are you wetting your hair aaaand then squeezing it?'

'It's chamomile! Damping our hair with chamomile, makes us blonde, ha! Ha! Ha!'

A scrounged cigarette and then back through the starry tunnel for the last crazy dance before Brian Briggs closes with "Aeo".

Big Nepentha with palms trees brought from Baia (left corner).

On the way back, they recover the PX side panels, all except Pepper, of course, who is the only one to have a car. It goes without saying that girls have priority for a ride back to the city in the Shark while the others, when their parents don't lend them their cars, have to wait their turn. Every evening, when Pepper stops at the steps of sector C, those present are ready to dive into the seats designed for galactic fucks. Zeb, Angie, Heyhey, it's their turn. Maybe the ride is always the same. Now they know all the spots in the neighbourhoods where the Angels gather. They are also running out of time for finding people, in the sense that the days are getting shorter, the evenings are getting colder and colder and, as if by some natural law, the chicks are disappearing from circulation. They head to the sectors where they are sure to find the Angels of GolosAngeles and the Wall gang. A quick stop, some bullshit, and then off on the tour again. The tape in the stereo is by New York, a nightclub in Miramare, but they don't know if it belonged to DJ Yano or Pery.

Before going to the New York club, Verona-born Yano was the DJ at the Papillon in his home town. He travelled in a windowless R4 and he loved football even more than music and eventually joined the national team. Flanked by DJ Pery, together they consecrated the discotheque in Miramare, which, according to all the Angels, is one of the coolest on the Romagna Riviera.

A couple of cigars and a few cigarettes labelled "More", are all that is needed to complete the charming scene: "Shark", "Afro", "Angels", "grass": a perfect evening.

The Shark snakes through the dark streets of the industrial zone with the cabin muffled with smoke.

'Look, it's late here, there's no one around. Shall we go back to base?'

'Mmmmm, why don't we do a whore tour first?'

'Industrial area?'

The Shark snakes through the dark streets of the industrial zone in search of prey.

'Hi! Look, we're not here to fuck, we only have a fiver. Can't we just touch your tits for that?'

I'm hot on the heels of love. Waiting for help from above. (Throbbing Gristle - Hot On The Heels Of Love)

The Shark snakes through the streets of the neighbourhoods. This time they head towards the base, to the steps but, suddenly, the green light coming from the dashboard is overwhelmed by an intermittent blue. Their faces, which are tenuously reflected on the side window, have a stroboscopic effect. An Alfa complete with Carabinieri draws up alongside the DS sporting a signalling disk inviting them to pull over. The Shark obeys, grazing the wide pavement bordered by a long, high wall. They never usually speed. On the contrary, they have to go slow enough to notice anything interesting around and it therefore seems odd to be flagged down by the "cops".

'Your ID card!'

'I haven't got...'

'You! ID!'

'I haven't got mine either...'

'You too, uh? You! Your ID card!'

'Me neither! I haven't got...'

Fortunately, Pepper has his documents but even so, the smoke-filled Shark only adds to the military policemen's suspicions.

'Get out! Everybody oooout! Tell me your names!'

They get out very calmly. Fortunately, the smoke coming out of the car is not the usual "smoke".
'Faces against the wall! Come on! Hands up and lean against the wall! Legs apart!'
While the two military policemen are busy checking Pepper's documents and inquiring about any precedents over the radio, Angie detaches from the wall. He leans with his arm on the open door of the Alfa, looking at the officer who is intent on communicating with headquarters.
'Excuse meeee, what are you plannin' on doin', anyway?'
'Back to the wallllll!'
When the Shark is thoroughly searched, the seats removed and nothing found, the "armed forces" finally realise that nothing big is going down and leave the scene of the crime. The boys put the Shark back together and are free to go home at last.

☺

It's time to think about the New Year's Eve party. The idea is to organise a mega party that will include The Loss and other gangs. To do this, however, they have to re-kindle their relationship with Tacky's bar because it's the ideal place to meet a lot of kids and give out invitations.
'Hiiii, Tackyyyyyy...'
'Hi, blockheads, I warn you, eh?'
'Chill, chill, we came here to ask you something. Can you do a metre of Prosecco?'
'What're you up to?'
'A mega party, Volt has a big, empty house with two floors. We plan to hold a New Year's Eve party there and want to invite all the Angels that come to the bar or hang around the neighbourhood. And, just to get to know each other a little more, maybe we could go to a disco all together first...'
'Wow! Fabulous! Fabulouuuus! Tomorrow the whole Pope gang is going to Les Cigales. We could go too! It might be a good start.'
Between a glass of Valpolicella on one side and a Prosecco on the other, they leave the bar without any fuss. However, the evening doesn't end there. The problem is that Hugo has disappeared. Everyone scatters around the bar looking for Hugo. But just as they were about to give up and start to worry, a curly head of hair comes out of the deep darkness of the night. It's Hugo and his bush of hair,

like the "woman with pot", running towards them. He's holding a piece of transparent plastic in his hands large enough to almost to cover his face and, on reaching them, stops that mumbling noise that sounded like an engine.

'Hugo! Where...., what the fuck are you doin'!'

'Whaaaaat? Can't you seeeeeeee? IIIII, got, myyyy, PX, with the windscreeeen!'

Tacky's bar closes immediately.

☺

Les Cigales, which was once an unsuccessful expedition, this time could have the chance to redeem itself. Just past noon, Angie goes to pick up Hugo and joins Tacky and Jeep who, with their PXs, are at the head of the line. They are very familiar with the road and getting to the disco by three in the afternoon is not a problem. Jeep is the most enthusiastic because his father has rented a caravan he saw in the campsite a long time ago to use at the weekends, which could become a strategic base in case they got stoned at the disco.

Les Cigales originally opened as a gay nightclub with a manager who had a vast experience in the first gay clubs in Milan. However, the quiet province of Brescia was soon shocked by the coming and going of eccentric and colourful characters. But the real innovation was the shift to a disco that expanded the catchment area by inviting DJs Rubens and Ebreo to perform on the "transition" day. Les Cigales immediately became a place of worship. Thousands of Angels flock there on Saturdays to listen to music ranging from funky to soul, from disco to tribal sounds.

Makossa akeela mama. Ko mama sa maka makoosa mama ko mama sa maka makoosa mama...(Mano Dibango - Soul makossa)

Les Cigales is a post-hippy place at a distance from the "paninaros" in Milan and therefore a direct competitor of the Cosmic. The cicada girl stickers can be seen everywhere, on cars, motorcycles and are even sported by those who don't go to the club very often. They have become groovy. An interesting detail is the dance hall furnishings: two circular dance floors and practically nothing else. There are very few seats, in Les Cigales you go only to dance. Upon their arrival, DJ Ebreo had been replaced by DJ Meo because the former had gone to help DJ Loda spread the history of Afro and Electronics music in another disco that had just arisen from the ashes of a cinema: the Typhoon. One more word about Rubens, which, incidentally, is his real name. The municipality was uninclined to register it at first since it was a foreign name, but, charmed in life as in work, his parents managed it.

They begin to dance. It must be said that the pieces being played tend very much towards tribal music.

In a place of fire. Have took place my desire. In a nightmare of confusion. You are unveiled my illusion... (Kongas - Anikana O)

Jeep is particularly interested in these sounds and remains practically glued to the DJs' console to make a note of all the songs. It's quite easy to see the labels on the records because the booth is transparent and at the same level as the floor. Jeep wants to become a DJ and has already bought the amp and turntables. Although the DJs come from the same strain, the music at Les Cigales is slightly different from that of Cosmic. The cosmic sound, even if the tracks are practically the same, are slowed down or accelerated and mixed with electronic pieces. At Les Cigales, however, there is less manipulation and more "groove", we might say.

Uh, oooh sucky sucky now. Hey, ooh, come on baby. Hey there sugar dumpling... (Fern Kinney - Groove me)

After all, if someone wanted to set up a DJ console at home without going to huge expense and wanted to try to do the first mix, it would be better to use a genre quite similar to today's: tribal, Afro, African. An example could be Timmy Thomas, "Africano" mixed with "Afroamerica" by Continent n.6.

Pra apagar o candeeiro parana veja voce. Pai o pai acenda o lampião eu so menor de idade. (Airto moreira - Parana')

They have so much fun at Les Cigales. They brag about it almost every night with friends. They vow to go back soon but with a big group this time. But there is another binding commitment to be faced and sorted in a short time, the New Year's Eve party. Volt confirms the availability of an entirely free house, but it has to be cleaned and kitted out, the stereo system needs setting up, the shopping list made and a million other things done to make the occasion unforgettable. As organisers, The Loss members decide to meet at Hugo's house at midnight.

'How many guests are we expecting?'

'More than fifty, about sixty...'

Hugo's speciality is spaghetti with tuna so when a huge bowlful lands on the table, any serious intentions to organise the New Year's Eve party vanish into thin air, or rather, drown in wine and smoke.

'Hey! Since Jake isn't here, did you give the present to his new chick?'

'Yeah! Done!'

'Eeeexuse meeee, what kind of present was it?'

'Nothing, we took a container and filled it with milk, accompanied by a greeting card...'

'And?'

'Aaaand, nothing, just that the greeting card said "this is full of all the handjobs I did for you!"'

To make sure the party is unforgettable, they need to take a look at the empty house and decide what to do at the next meeting, so Angie asks for the keys. The first inspection is done along with Stub, Hugo and Jake. The house is located in a village slightly out of town and easy for everyone to get to. It is grey on the outside and the entrance is straight onto the street. It has two floors. The ground floor features an open porch that gives direct access into the house, or rather, into the kitchen-living room, where there are still food and cleaning supplies, a sign of recent occupiers. A staircase divides the kitchen and the bathroom and leads to the upper floor where the

bedrooms are located. The good thing is that it is bigger than Lamp's basement, but the bad thing is that they will have to roll up their sleeves to make it look like a "party house". The Loss gang decides to meet again at Hugo's house at midnight.
'OK guys! Let's talk about serious things!'
'That's right! Did you hear someone killed John Lennon today?'
'And Paul McCartney dedicated a song to Yoko Ono.'
'What song?'
'Frozen Jap.'
'Stoooop it! So! This weekend we have to go to the house and clean it. The stuff to do it with is already there but the biggest work is to do some touching up and then we have to decide where to put the benz, the food, the stereo system, the fuck-area and various embellishments.'
'We might need a van to take everything we need. The more we are, the sooner we'll finish the work and the better everything will be.'
'Yeah, that's right! If those who go to school start on Friday afternoon and those who go to work continue on Saturday morning, we can do it...'
'I say that if we finish by Saturday lunchtime, there'll even be time to take a stroll in the city to break the balls of all the shop girls...'
'Is the list for benz okay? Then, we'll think about the quality...'
'So! Usual stuff! Martini, white, dry, rosè, then, Cinzano, President Reserve Riccadonna, sparkling Gancia, brut and top brut, sparkling Asti, Vodka, Zabov, Prosecco aaaand, last but not least, the usual bunch of poor sparkling wines...'
'I'll bring a bottle with me!'
'Stub willll briiiing aaaa bottle! Grub?'
'Okayyyy! We add coke, Fanta, plates, glasses, paper napkins and Genny the bitch will bring grass, aaaand, Jeep and Giby will provide disco music...'
'Okay, but, for a complete list we need to go back to Les Cigales to take a peek at the pieces...'
'Do you know how to wipe your bum after a shit with a piece of foil? That piece you take out first when you open a pack of Marlboro?'
'Let's hear the bullshit, go on Poplar!'
'Take the foil and rip off a little piece of the corner so you get

a little triangle, then put the rest of the paper on a fingertip and wipe your shithole...'
Silent moment.
'Well, aaaand, with the little triangle?'
'You use it to clean under the nail!'
That put an end to the night but where was Hugo? They find him out cold in the garage, drunk as a skunk wearing a diving mask with a broken lens, a plastic helmet for children on his head, a rubber hose in his hand and a tyre on his shoulders. The most perplexed of the onlookers is Attila the dog, who continues to stand, fixed to the spot, staring at his master, the tennis ball dropping from his mouth. However, one step forward has been taken – at least they have a shopping list.

They make a further step forward by returning to Les Cigales to add to the music list. In this period, trips are rather freezing but Stub, Zeb, Heyhey, Angie, Volt, Jeep and Hugo, together with some of the local girls, namely Antonella, Sony and Nadia are all ready to go to the club in Bedizzole. It's Sunday afternoon and they arrive punctually at three in the afternoon. The music starts immediately with Afro tracks that glue Jeep to the DJ booth.

Twenty-four hours a day. It's early, early Afro Music.
(Tantra - Sukuleu, Mother Africa, Hallelujah)

He notes down a bunch of bands as well as other pieces that include the words Boogie and Groove. Boogie is a faster, more rhythmic type of music than Blues so its birth corresponds better with the early twentieth century. Thanks to this genre, a boom in record sales soon led it to outstrip jazz music. A veritable frenzy that influenced many musicians ensued. It also led to a type of dance, the Boogie-Woogie, which became hugely popular in all the American dance halls and was imported to Europe during World War II to boost the morale of the troops. The term was coined by a certain Clarence Smith. However, nobody ever knew why he called it Boogie because he was killed by a stray bullet in a shooting.

Get on up, on the floor. 'Cause were gonna boogie oogie oogie. (Boogie Oogie Oogie - A Taste of Honey)

Groove, on the other hand, refers to the incision on vinyl

records. However, it is also a popular term used in the sixties to identify a rhythmic genre which repeats on a loop. Earth Wind and Fire, in addition to writing their famous piece "Boogie Wonderland" in Boogie theme, turned the term "Groove" into a verb meaning "to have fun dancing" and the proof is in the famous song "Let's groove".

Come on people. Dance on the brain. Come on people. I don't want to repeat now. (Hamilton Bohannon - The Groove Machine)

At six o'clock, the music and lights stop. Everybody goes home, DJ Meo has gone on strike, so the rumour says.

☺

Luckily, the Christmas holidays have arrived and so, on one Saturday, several members of The Loss gang can be found setting up a kind of "disco-club" at Volt's empty house. They have already been shopping because, from invitation replies, they know that at least fifty Angels will definitely be at the party and anyway, since it's all packaged stuff, nothing they have bought will go off. Given the enormous amount of cleaning and arranging that they have to do, they have also included time for some spaghetti with tuna. They immediately agree on how the rooms are to be used. The living room-kitchen will house the benz and food, the large porch will be the disco area and the upper floors will be for fucking. The biggest problem, however, turns out to be the porch with its open sides as dancing in the open air on New Year's Eve is unthinkable. They decide to close it with transparent nylon used to cover crops in the fields. They do a good job and, in the following days, the stereo system is also installed. The lights seen from the outside as they filter through the tarp make the house cosmic. Everything goes without a hitch. Stub and Hugo are in charge of cleaning the top floor while Pepper and Zeb, since Pepper has the Shark, are available to go around making the last purchases or transporting material. Angie and Jake write "The Loss" on one wall. And so it continues until the final touches.

'Hey! It's almost noon, aaaand I'd like to go into town this afternoon...'

'Jake! What the fuck are you gonna do today in town if all the rest of us are here! Aaaand there's still a lot to do...'

'I wanna break the salesgirls' balls.'

'Come oooon! I understand that salesgirls are hot...'
'Nooo! Not just that! I've finished my Drakkar!'

Angels, paninaros, punks and even hippies before them, want to highlight their lifestyles, differences and the messages they want to transmit and they do so through music, art, clothing, and so on. Perfume, like clothes, is another way to stand out and is therefore used as a means to diversify and communicate. While women use it to affirm and consolidate their conquests, men have separated it from the ritual of shaving in order to enhance their physiques. It's a way to send a message. Two people are saying two different things if one of them is wearing a splash of lavender and the other has used four drops of Drakkar. In addition to Drakkar perfume, the Angels also use "pasciulì", taken from the hippie experience. Patchouli is an Asian plant whose leaves contain aromatic properties. Asian silk merchants used it to protect their precious commodities from moths and to repel insects. When the hippie movement, which saw the promised land in the East, broke out in America and Europe, it brought with it the seductive aroma of shawls imbibed with "Flower Power". In aromatherapy, patchouli is considered an aphrodisiac able to produce an endorphin useful to those who find it hard to let themselves go or have lost their libido. The fact that it can arouse, stimulate and awaken sexual energy, made it a perfect match for the hippies' belief in free love.

In 1989, Madonna made the album "Like a Prayer" impregnating the cover with essential patchouli oil. Today, this ingredient can be found in at least one-third of perfumes for men.

'At least stay here and eat with us pals, Hugoooo, come down and make spaghetti with tuna! Jake, go up!'

It's an excellent opportunity to literally keep Jake stuck to them even during the afternoon. While Jake is upstairs, they grab a tube of Bostik and smear it on a chair. The smell of the glue blends with that of the detergents and paints used to restore the house and therefore raises no suspicion. At "dinner's ready", Jake comes down and, finding the others already seated with a plate of spaghetti in front of them, sits on the only vacant chair. The Bostik, now slightly dried, is ready to do its task at maximum power. They laugh, joke, eat, drink and finally all stand to make a toast with the last drop of Vodka.

'Jake! Now go into town and buy your Drakkar!'

Due to the Vodka rather than the full bellies, the afternoon lacks the rhythm of the morning but luckily, there's not so much to do. Pepper, Zeb and Finger are immediately charged with replacing the missing Vodka and leave in the Shark to go in search of supermarkets. Stub and Hugo, the most stoned, go back upstairs to mop the floor one last time. Angie and Jake clean up the kitchen while Volt sorts out the stereo system. A final look around and one more exchange of mutual satisfaction, this time with a smug smile in the awareness that nothing is missing, and everything is hunky dory. But one small problem arises as they are loading the work tools into Volt's R4. They notice passers-by shifting to the other side of the road in an attempt to dodge buckets of dirty water flying from the upstairs window. One of these is even full of shit, but Stub and Hugo, drunk as lords, have the perfect excuse.

'We didn't waaaant to mess up the boooog you just cleeeeaned...'

The other three, Pepper, Zeb and Finger, don't have an excuse. They, instead, are glimpsed at a petrol station, intent in a bullshit conversation and looking pleased and cheerful about it too, with about twenty cars lined up behind them.

☺

New Year's Eve arrives. The organisers are already at the house at half past seven in the evening preparing to welcome their friends. Something quiet, like "Rocks pebbles and Sand" by Stanley Clarke, is playing in the background. Parents disembarking their daughters feel more reassured this way. In a matter of an hour, they are all there. The cold entrance area overheats, the music changes into something to incubate movement, "Stone Fox Chase" by Area Code 615 is the perfect choice, it's like being at Les Cigales. Many are already in the kitchen tasting the pastries they bought that morning; others are projecting their shadows on the nylon cloth as the disco lights come on.

When I look around some shadows in the sky. I forget what I'm doing with you, lover... (Black Devil - H Friend)

The kilowatts start to flow. They are a dancing tribe. The lovers, those who came with their guy or babe, are not glued to each other for the moment and everyone is doing their own thing. The Vodka they drank on Saturday has been replaced by Cointreau and brandy.

Making up for extra time. Trying not to lose all that I thought was mine. Spell it to you black and white.   (The Motels - Careful)

In a matter of minutes, some folks are already dead drunk, including Hugo. The most dangerous situation is that Vale and Cynthia feel sick. The latter immediately falls asleep, but the former becomes dull and unconscious. Worried, some Angels take her to the hospital and the others will later find out that she had her stomach pumped.

Found a cure. Ooh, for your heartache. Before you wake. Before you wake.   (Ashford Simpson - Found a cure)

The party resumes or, if some didn't even notice anything, then we can say the party continues. Midnight approaches quickly and the couples go upstairs to suck and touch up a little before attending the New Year's celebrations.

Every night when I'm dreaming. My body comes alive, oh. Hot sweet sensations. (Debbie Jacobs - Hot Hot Give It All You Got)

The bathroom, however, is the place for full sex but it is a crowded place. Sitting on the toilet in the Kamasutra face-off position is a problem since everything is wet. Going on the floor in doggy style is, besides being cold, also a problem because the floor is a vomit patch. The only option is to stand and deliver, but it's a problem for those who have a drink-numbed mouth.

'IIIII put twooo, condommmms just to beeee sure...'

Aaaaaaahhhh, mmmmmm mmhhh... mmm mmm mmm hahhh hahhhh. (Tony Silvester - Pazuzu)

Everyone gets the feeling that midnight is nigh, even those who have skulked away come down from the fuck zone. The problem is that nobody synchronised their watch with a TV before coming to the party and so the questions "Are we there? Is it time?" hover in the air for those who are still alive. No one seems willing to take charge of the radio on the stereo system for the countdown and in any case, the strobe light makes finding the right knobs complicated because you can't see your fucking hand.

I got my mind made up. Come on you can get it. Get it, girl, any time. Say what? (Instant Funk - Got My Mind Made Up)

Finger takes the initiative, goes to the devastated kitchen and begins to hand out low-quality sparkling wines that were locked in the cupboard. They knew perfectly well when they bought them that they would all evaporate so they decided that they might as well spend as little as possible. While everyone gets ready to uncork their bottles, some think about the stereo system and Jeep, Giby, Tacky and Volt cover the records, turntables and connections with nylon to stop them getting sprinkled with a foam the flavour of oxidised apple as it spurts from those disgusting sparkling wines. At the same time Stub and Zeb, left empty-handed, decide to take part in the big splash by emptying bottles of the stuff into the buckets used for cleaning and throwing them over the partygoers.

One one! Two two! Three three! Four four!
(Lectric Funk - Shanghaied)

As the minutes tick by, the situation returns to pre-midnight mode. The lovers go back upstairs, the wild people stay downstairs. Within a few hours, however, people are beginning to dwindle and it's almost time for the organisers to get out the sleeping bags. Sleeping away from home this time is not only a matter of adventure but also due to a promise made to Volt that they would give the house back the way they had found it. The two hours left of the night give them no rest at all: Poplar goes around like a zombie photographer, breaking balls as usual. So, there they are, up again, with their faces illuminated by the same light that they had no chance to say goodnight to earlier. Pepper, Zeb, Stub, Jake, Heyhey, Angie, Volt and Finger take the empty discarded bottles away to a dumpster a hundred metres away from the house. There they are, degreasing the floors of vomit and dirty black footprints resulting from trampled liquids and solids. There they are, working hard without a break until three in the afternoon to get rid of the smell of vomit and rotten apple and then, finally, go to the disco.

The Vrrr2000, in this case, has two purposes: the first, to bivouac on the sofas, the second, to watch Heyhey fuck all the chicks in his mind's eye.

'Hey! You know you still have Giby's bowler hat on your head?'

'Uhmmmm, well, how do you think the party went?'

'Uhmmmm, need a barman!'

'The party was a real blast! We have to do more...'

'That's right! Tonight, after the "2", we'll go to the bar and talk about it.'

The evening comes at last. Over a few pints at the bar, they plan future parties and expeditions but nothing is definite. Pepper then offers to take them home but with a lot of effort. This time his hallucinations have got so bad that he has to stop the car and get out every hundred metres. Imaginary people are sitting menacingly on the roof, replacing those of the Shark's fixa.

☺

One might think that winter would be a time of containment for the Angels. Going to faraway discos, riding in adverse weather conditions for kilometres and kilometres on a motorbike could create a few problems. But, when it comes to private parties, meet-ups in the squares and going to the same discos within a short-range, nothing changes at all and there is no slowing down. Besides, there are also those Angels who own a car, either because they can afford one or because they can scrounge one from their parents. However, for company's sake, the goal of the season is to stay in touch with those who don't have the possibility of going far. The discos in the nearby area are popping up like mushrooms and, among other things, don't even need to advertise given the constant reshuffling of news among the Angels. The latest one to open is in a former cinema. It's called the Typhoon club. But there are lots of them: the Manhattan in Cervia, the Goody Goody in Faenza, the Much More and the legendary Papillon Club, the Arlecchino and the New York. However, they seem to die at the same speed as they are born. We are not talking about the Bay of Angels, which has just closed, and which, in any case, did last a few years, but about the New York, which, for reasons of public order, was only open for a year, just when The Loss and their friends celebrated New Year's Eve. Closures that do nothing more than move, in this case, the Angels from Miramare beach in Rimini to Columbus beach in Riccione. Some, however, are reborn from the ashes by merely changing their name, such as Cap Creus, which reopened as Vinavil. Apart from drugs, the other main reason for these closures is the Angels' bivouacs. Try to imagine a village of two thousand inhabitants invaded day and night by four thousand Angels grouping and sleeping on pavements, in flowerbeds and parks and parking vehicles right up to the disco door. The newly-opened Vinavil closed for exactly the same problems as before.

The Loss gang, however, spend their winter time in carefree style remaining faithful to the Cosmic, Les Cigales, Les Pois and some other local discos within range and, on occasion, go to the odd organised party. And so, on this particular Sunday, Tacky suggests that he and Angie should go to the Cosmic, while the others, due to the weather being so bloody cold, are more inclined to go somewhere closer. Then there are also those who have a sweetheart and therefore have other things to do.

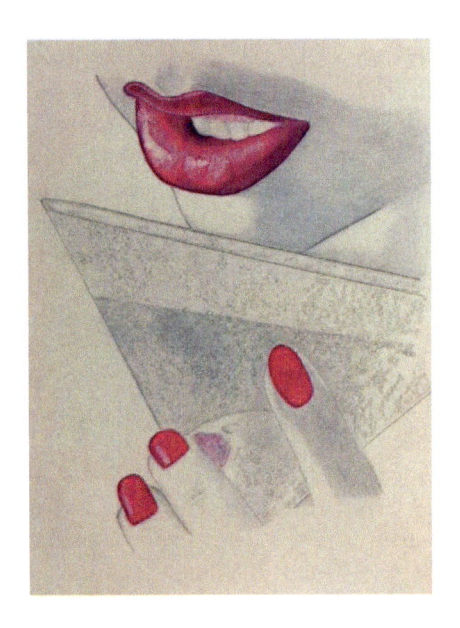

Parties at the Cosmic club.

'Angie! I heard the C24 came out and it's cool!'
'Do you want to buy it? The forecast is for snow, I don't want to be like other Angels who ride around with a blanket on their legs...'

'No worries! I've got a bottle of cognac from the bar, just in case we need a few shots along the way...'

'Mmmmm, all right! If we get the tape, we can lend it to Hugo's brother who is now able to copy them too, with the logo...'

And so, while the others are scattered between the Vrrr2000 and the Chalet, Angie and Tacky drive to the Cosmic in fourth gear practically all the way with the minimum of engine revolutions.

The patrons are always the same, a disco of freaks. Some complain about the shitty music, others say that the place is magic. Some think that the music is unique but touched up while others, instead of arguing, sell bootleg tapes. The boys find these things particularly striking but, when they think about it, it's also logical. They aren't the only ones copying the tapes. For the time being, they go inside to stomp on the dance floor and see if there is any news about the recordings, especially the release of the C24. The disco begins and the difference compared to traditional discos is once again immediately obvious. The Angels have already filled the dance floor before the "intro". The initial trepidation has totally disappeared at the Cosmic. Peter Green's "Tribal Dance" notes begin their afternoon. It's strange to call it afternoon because, once you identify with this reality, the dimension of time disappears.

State of the nation. A room you never use. See yourself in power. That sweet sick enemy.   (Fad Gadget - State of the nation)

Tapes are sold "under the table" at the spaceship and cost a vital ten. Angie and Tacky decide to pop out and learn more about Cosmic's releases.

'Hey! Hi! I see you have tapes of the various discos...'

'Oh yeah! Excellent quality on Fuji C90...'

'Even the one that just came out of the Cosmic?'

'Why not, bro! What do you want?'

'C24, but, does Baldelli know about this?'

Baldelli has always had problems with producing tapes. What is important for the Cosmic is that every Saturday, Angels buy tons of stickers and tapes. Every Saturday, Daniele and Claudio sell about 150 of them and then these tapes turn into thousands and thousands.

'You know, once I drove up to Baldelli to show him my car and I told him, see this? It's my new, brown Citroen Pallas. I bought it by selling your tapes!'

☺

The evening offers something new. Poplar declares that everybody has been invited to a party organised by the same girls who had come to the party at Lamp's over a year ago. One thing better than going to a party with hot chicks is going with snobby ones so they willingly accept.

The house is charming, cosy and well furnished. The girls' welcome is the warmest they have ever received and the party room is large and extremely tidy. There is a plentiful variety of food. It was obvious that they didn't often go to freaky parties with quiet and well-to-do girls. A stereo system has been set up in one corner and there are soft drinks on a table against the wall opposite the food. The party starts with some friendly "chat" and sweet songs.

Every man has a place. In his heart there's a space and the world can't erase his fantasies. (Earth Wind and Fire - Fantasy)

'But! Isn't there anything to drink?'
'Hugoooo, they're still there!'
The party has just begun, but someone is already seen sneaking away in search of benz. Volt, Angie and Hugo go to the house where they spent New Year's Eve looking for liquid residue. They board the R4 with the remaining bottles and shots and return to the party.
'I get, u...'
The party continues smoothly and the initial chats and dances move on to purring and rubbing.
'I get, e...'
Unfortunately, at a party, it isn't as if everything goes full blast with the first girl you try, so you move on to the next one you fancy.
'I get the, t...'
And, when you run out of chances, the law of Poplar's big numbers is applied. You flirt with them all.

Oo - wee, this feelin's killin' me; Ah shucks, I wouldn't stop for a million bucks. (Tony Orlando - Don't let go)

STONED ANGELS

'It'sssssssssss, iiii...'

The chicks are too sedated and the party is getting ugly. They are virtually all stoned, but Hugo, who has managed to drink a whole bottle of Cointreau stashed in Volt's house, is completely gone. He empties the bottle by looking at the consumption level on its side.

'Cccccccccccc...'

They never see those girls again.

☺

Today another gang suggests going to Les Cigales since they have not yet had the chance. The day, however, is very cold with a leaden sky. The gang scatters again. Some Loss members prefer to go to a nearby disco, Hugo stays at home nursing a hangover and some, including Jake, Angie and Jeep, join the proposal for Les Cigales. They leave for the disco on seven Vespas. Angie and Jeep, on a PX125, Rhino and Pilu on a PX200, Arse and Icy on an ET3, Pylon and his chick on his brand-new PX, Pizzy and Vange on a Vespa TS, Luc on his spick 'n span PX along with Jake, Grape and Lilly on an ET3, just for the record. Another tactic against the winter cold when two people are on one motorbike, is to constantly swap driver and take shelter behind, all the way to destination. As soon as they get to the disco, someone is already spreading the word that "Les Cigales is shooting up" but to be honest, nobody can see this great mass of Angels shooting up. This time, instead of gluing himself to DJ Meo's booth, Jeep just dances.

Les Cigales' double dancefloors.

Oh - Nye Oh - Nye Oh - Nye – Ay. Don't stop! We got keep moving. (Gene Farrow - Oh - Nye - Ay)

The dance floor atmosphere is not only overheated by the music but also by the lights.
'Jeep! Jeep! Don't you feel something special in the air?'
'Nnnnnn noo...'
'Feel it, feel it, it's the smell of ozone!'

Once there was a battle there in Zaire in Zaire. Hundred thousand people there in Zaire in Zaire. (Johnny Wakelin - In Zaire)

This time the problems occur on the way home. Grape runs out of petrol so Rhino offers to go and look for a petrol station. He is still not back after an hour so everybody scatters in search of him. Fortune smiles on the brave and they find him at a petrol station where he has been forced to stop due to a flat tyre. A helpful injection of tyre sealant solves the problem and Rhino is back on track. Then off to retrieve Grape. When they get there, Arse positions himself next to Grape's Vespa, sticking out his right elbow so that Grape can cling onto it by stretching his left arm. Thus coupled, he is towed to the pump.

At last, after wasting a couple of hours, they are ready to go home. It's eight o'clock in the evening. It's been dark since five and it's bloody freezing.

'Better to have a piece of ice on the arse than a piece of ice in the arse!'

It starts snowing.

☺

No matter what, they never give up, and yet, according to suggestions from the neighbourhood gangs, there are plenty of choices. For The Loss, those who want to go to their own chick go to their own chick, those who want to go somewhere else, go there, all under the banner of freedom and carefreeness. This time, some choose to go to the Cosmic, like Angie together with Heyhey, Jeep, Genny and his chick, Marcy. Others are attracted to DJ Mozart, who is in the province to launch a new disco club called the Small Club. Unfortunately, Les Pois has closed due to "traffic problems", and so, part of the Angels pour into the Small Club hoping not to create the usual public order problems.

In this period, Daniele and Claudio TBC, produce tapes to go. Afro music knows no limits and the C25, 26, 27 tapes are the proof. One is better than the other. Who knows why Afro DJs were inspired by the African music of Fela Kuti, the Funky of James Brown and then decided to mix it with experimental songs by Kraftwerk. At the Cosmic, an instrumental single by Depeche Mode becomes a tribal piece when put on 33 rpm and, never satisfied, Baldelli mixes it with a track by Brian Eno. The show begins, the notes of "I.B.M" by Throbbing Gristle bang away, but here is the Brian Eno track: "Regiment".

'They are sounds that come from heaven and hell! Put together at the same time!'

Someone says.

'Don't they ever put the Village People on?'

No commercial music. At all. Today the music at the Cosmic begins slowly. It acquires rhythm and ends gradually with a sweet "Tabular Bells" by The Champ's Boys Orchestra, just to give the idea of what an evening in this disco could be: anything but commercial. Hearing a few notes of "Born to be alive" by Patrick

Hernandez at low Revolutions Per Minute is already too much.

The Afro phenomenon is spreading throughout Italy and is even pushing into Germany. The German, Dutch and Austrian tourists crowding the disco initially found this kind of genre "strange", but now they are starting to appreciate it. In the Galaxy, an Innsbruck club in Austria, DJ Stefan Egger would become the driving force of the "Afro sound" outside Italy.

Kleiner Vampi! Auf unserem Friedhof liegen wir zwei in der Stille
In der Stille. (Nina Hagen - Auf'm Friedhof)

Austrian Angels.

Disco, party, disco, and now, just to keep up the pace, another party is required. Poplar organises it and, with his customary tours of villages and neighbourhoods, introduces all the gang to new chicks he has previously chatted up. The party is to be held in a private house where the Loss is sure there will only be hotties and that they will be the only guests. For the occasion, Angie has bought a cute, black, gangster hat with a black band. The only problem is that he has to hold the brim with his hand when driving his PX to the party so that it doesn't blow off. The last one to arrive at the rendezvous point is Jake because he had a problem with his hair. It takes an entire afternoon to dry his hair in the correct way for the party. Holding the hairdryer above and positioning a hairbrush on the inside, he pulls his hair down to his shoulders, turning the split ends towards his neck. In theory, the operation consumes the equivalent of a nuclear power plant and in practice, occupies the bathroom until evening, accompanied by much cursing from his sister and parents but not from his younger brother, Spit, so named because he spits every 30 seconds and is even crazier than Jake. He usually goes around the main streets of the town with his trousers down on the pretext of pulling up his socks. Fortunately, he isn't going to the party with them. However, Pack, a tall, sturdy and quiet guy that Poplar introduced them to, is going. He has a VW Golf and many other excellent qualities. But there are two further qualities that the rest of the gang particularly like and which allowed him to join The Loss with open arms. The first is that he lives in a group of enclosed houses, a residence just outside city suburbs, with a large swimming pool, the "swimming pool" being the focal point. The second is that his jeans highlight a very prominent bump between his legs. A very noticeable "pack". They let him in first at the party as if he were their battering ram. Despite the warm landlady's welcome, as soon as the frigid hotties go into the room, they sit in a row on one side, opposite an empty couch with a table in the middle topped with stuff, not saying a single word. The Loss take their positions on the other couch, looking at them and also not uttering a single word while Pack stands with his package towards them as if in a silent movie. The first problem to emerge is that the girls are what is known as 'freak hippies', more commonly referred to as 'freaks'.

Now we freak, oh what a joy. Just come on down, to fifty four. Find a spot out on the floor. Aaahh freak out!   (Chic - Le Freak)

The particularities of freaks consisted of wearing eccentric clothes, consuming soft drugs, living day to day and despising money. The phenomenon originated in Los Angeles as a way to challenge materialism and the American way of life at the time. In the musical field, freaks stood out by offering music that was a

mixture of jazz, blues, folk and country. Frank Zappa is a reference for this genre and is branded as the most eminent forerunner of the phenomenon. The party then bodes well because the Loss is convinced that freaks and Angels have a lot of things in common. Let's take a look at some.
- Sandals. At first glance, sandals seem to be a common denominator but there is actually a big difference. Freaks wear them for at least ten months a year without socks and then with socks for the remaining two months which, hygienically, cannot be watertight. Angels also wear colourful espadrilles, moccasins and boots.
- Fashion. An Angel tries to change his style as he grows while freaks, against all good sense, continue on their way.
- The house. You have trouble getting into a freak's house. Incense and scented candles fill the air to the point of having to live with the door wide open. Not every piece of furniture is in place.
- India. This country has inspired many movements and is responsible for the freaks' tattoos that they either do themselves or get a friend to do.
- Jamaica. Nobody knows why because no one's ever been there, although they will definitely have been to some reggae rally and been so impressed as to comb their dog's hair into a rasta.
- The cars. Volkswagen versus Citroen.
- Headgear. Angels don't wear caps. Freaks wear Peruvian hats and use them as bags, carrying them in summer.

Then there are wooden earrings, flared trousers, ponchos and other things in common with the Angels, such as bongos and chillums. But what they have most in common is the freaks' tits as they dance in their drooling hippie dresses or tank tops without a bra.

And so, the first problem apparently seems to dissolve but then there is a second. You don't know exactly who, but someone smells of sweat and after that, the party begins to degenerate. The first to make a move is Stub, who starts rummaging in the cabinets and the hall cupboard looking for liquor. He nicks a bottle of Martini and runs out. While Angie is busy chasing an olive that has fallen off the table using a spoon, Pepper has the brilliant idea of going to get a 5 of grass. The plazas where pushers sell grass are well-known and the party house is right next to one of them. To get a good price, Pepper has the brilliant idea of dropping his trousers, getting out of the house and, in this "irretrievably lost" state, heading clumsily towards the trees, the shadiest place in the square. There are rumours that the people under the trees are far from saintly.

Quite the opposite. You can sometimes actually meet real criminals there who let off steam by punching each other in front of the discos. For that reason, Poplar, Finger and Fish accompany Pepper to oversee his negotiations. The others, meanwhile, under the carefree notes of Happiness by Führs & Fröhling, put on a dance display to try to prise the incredulous chicks off the wall.

Hold your horses. Hold your horses. Looking for fire.
(First Choice - Hold your horses)

But now that everything is about to unravel. Here comes Pepper and the other mental cripples with a joint in their mouths.
'Where's Poplar?'
'Uhmmmm, outside, climbing a streetlight.'
'Stub?'
'Uhmmmm, went home to get daddy's Ford.'
'Heyhey?'
'Heyhey, went home to get the brandy.'
'Holy shit! They've smoked themselves brainless!'
'Let's go to the pizzeria instead!'
'No! Because you eat pizza from the middle and leave all the crust and I feel dorky when the waiter comes to get the plate and sees the whole circle intact.'

When everyone is back at the party – with three extra they picked up on the street -, they decide to have some spaghetti at Hugo's, since there is nothing left on the table and no more liquor in the cabinet. Pauline, who lives in the house, dramatically declares:
'Do you know that my mum and dad are in bed?'
Those girls would never see them again.
The Loss converges in dribs and drabs at Hugo's until all of them are there. The party is already forgotten and the time to make plans resurfaces. They really need to make some expeditions to new discos when the weather gets a little warmer. The names of the discos are those that the chicks at the Picchio Verde club had suggested. However, actually getting to the heart of the matter and

deciding on the next club to try out is put on hold for two reasons. Firstly, they're hungry.
'Hugoooo! Is the spaghetti ready?'
'Ready! And it's time to celebrate!'
'Again! Aaaand, why?'
'I got my PX! Spick'n span!'
'Heyhey! Come on! Get the brandy!'
Secondly, Stub is about to go out for the first time in his car, which sees all of them outside unveiling the car and, like a ship being launched, baptising it with one colossal piss on the bodywork. It's the middle of the night, maybe three o'clock, when they leave Hugo's house with the canary's water dish full of brandy, Attila open-mouthed and Stub with hose in hand to wash the car.

☺

The decision is made over the following days and the choice falls on the Panda club. Since the winter season is coming to an end, they agree to make the first expedition, destination Modena, far away from Bedizzole. Unfortunately, once again, several of the group drop out, preferring nearby discos and, in the end, only four leave for Carpi: Stub, Finger, Angie and Hugo on two PX 125s, proud to be able to tell their adventure on their return. They know the road and so, instead of stopping from village to village to ask for directions, they drive straight through, taking the piss out of the well-dressed people. Near Modena, however, a stop must be made and, once they get the directions to Nonantola, the journey starts again. A few kilometres before the village, one particular sight leaves them speechless. They notice an old guy wearing bell-bottom trousers, standing there with his bike on the side of the road talking with an empty box tied behind the bike saddle.
'Just look at that! He's off his head! What's he been smoking?'
'Let's ask that freak something on the fly.'
The old man worthy of note, watches them as they slowly approach.
'Hey! To Panda! The club!'
After a couple of seconds, he starts acting like a stringless puppet. The four, pointing their forefinger at him, mock him to the point of swapping the finger for the middle one.

And now get up. And shout. Cougar!
(Phill & Friends Band - This Man)

They finally arrive at Nonantola albeit slightly late. It's four o'clock but the goal has been reached. They are at the Panda Club.

As soon as they are at the ticket office, they realise that the disco has something strange. There are two clubs with two DJs. The largest room with commercial music, The Panda. The smallest room with Afro and Funky music, The little Panda. But they both have one thing in common: hotties.

Fashion! Turn to the left Fashion! Fashion! We are the goon squad and we're coming to town... (David Bowie - Fashion)

Panda Club.

A few hours of dancing and getting high on music and it's already time to go back home. The dancing has made them hot so the cold gust that hits them as they go out is unexpected. The weather has completely changed and is threatening rain. They realise that it would be useless waiting around for the storm to pass in that box-shaped entrance that would provide little shelter so they decide to head back. No sooner do they set off than it starts to rain.

'Better to have a piece of ice on the arse than a piece of ice in

the arse, someone said!'
'Better to have broken trousers on your arse than a broken arse in your trousers, I say!'
As soon as they leave the village, the rain turns to snow. Driving along, squinting sideways through half-closed eyes so as not to catch the slect directly in their faces, they notice a silhouette nearby the kerb. It's the old man from earlier who, with his arm stretched out and his index finger pointed towards them as they pass, mocks them by staging a dance like a stringless puppet, swapping his finger for the middle one.

☺

Blue sing La Lune, sing Lagoon. These visions are making me stay
The art is pretending, it's art.   (Spandau Ballet - The freeze)

Although the gang separate and scatter to various discos at the weekends, they spend their midweek evenings telling each other about their adventures at their base on the shop steps. This week the main topic of conversation is the car parade and who will be driving what since those who have a driving licence, have to scrounge them from their parents to take a ride in sector C, their neighbourhood. Whenever someone turns up in a car for the first time, instead of celebrating at Tacky's bar, they all go to Giby and Jeep's house as, with the approach of spring, their parents stay over at the campsite for chores, leaving the house free. It's the turn of Lamp in a red Alfa Giulia and then Zeb in an R4 and Genny in a Citroen CX. But, when Jeep and Giby's parents are at home and the gang doesn't want to hang about at the steps, they stage lengthy chases in the city streets. Genny plays the part of a delinquent and shoots off with tyres squealing along the city streets and the others, acting as policemen, have to hunt him down. It isn't a speed race, just a desire to be diabolic. The scene sees Genny in his CX chased by the rest of The Loss that, with windows lowered, imitate the sound of a siren. Occasionally slamming on the brakes as if realising he is "done for", he gives the pursuers the chance to arrest him by pulling him out of the car with orthodox methods and simulating handcuffing. Once they have absorbed the misbelief and amazement of the people, they close the scene and start again. Genny shoots off with a squeal of tyres, followed by the wailing of all his pursuers and away they go on a new chase. And so it continues until nightfall.

Whenever dark has fallen. You know the spirit of the party. Starts to come alive. (George Benson - Give me The Night)

But the very best news is when Jeep and Giby announce with so much joy that it practically atomises the Zibibbo[21] that the gang are merrily sipping onto the walls of the room.
'Our house is going to be permanently free!'
'Whaaaat do you mean? That nobody is living there aaaand your parents aren't going to rent it out?'
'Hold your horses, they're not renting it for the moment, I don't know about a year from now.'
'Shit! Could we use it as a new hangout?'
'That's what we've been thinking, we're gonna ask our parents and we'll let you know.'
'Awesome! Could we use it foooor a carnival party? Last year, the party at Heyhey's went the way it did so it would be better to do it in a new place.'
'Mmmmm, I don't think so, not just now at least.'
'No problem! We can wait. But I say we could go to the Cosmic because they're throwing a fancy dress party on Wednesday. What do you think Pepper?'
'A Prosecco!'
In the meantime, the night raids in the city continue but not for very long. One evening during a chase, this time on a Vespa, Genny enters a narrow, poorly lit alley between the houses of the old town. A police car stationed around a corner, stops them. The result is a hefty fine for disturbing the peace with noises that will be remembered for a long time.

☺

A fancy-dress party at the Cosmic seems an odd event seeing that the carnival period has just ended. However, it appears to be a different way to promote the discotheque and get itself known even if it would hardly seem to need it, seeing the number plates of the motorcycles and cars parked in the square. This party seems to be an extension of the Afro DJs' idea to create events such as the

---

21 Zibibbo is a Sicilian dessert wine, obtained from highly sugary musts. It was brought to Sicily by Arab conquerors and "Zibib" means grape in Arabic.

STONED ANGELS

"Marilyn Day" that Mozart organised at the Bay of Angels. There are also rumours that a particular "Moon Party" took place at Les Cigales. Surely, everybody remembers the legendary "Flower Party" organised by Rubens, Mozart, Ebreo and Spranga at Les Pois and later the fanciful "Hawaiian Party" with Ebreo, Spranga and the new DJ Daniel, again at Les Pois but this time in masks.

To honour the party but mainly to have fun, The Loss decide to wear fancy dress. Angie, because he has a black hat, is inspired by that strange character in a Van Gogh painting. Heyhey, on the other hand, plays a drunkard with classic red cheeks and nose. Finger dresses up as a shepherd. Stub goes as a mountaineer, Pepper as a nurse, and so on until Volt arrives in his bathrobe. This time nobody goes to other discos, they are all there and, after smearing Volt's cheeks with shaving foam, they go inside.

Feel like dancing. I wanna dance with you, feel like dancing. I wanna dance with you. (Emilton Bohannon - Feel like dancing)

As usual, the coolest thing is the DJs dressed as astronauts. In the middle of the dance floor, a gigantic foam rubber tree with a pile of foliage dances about awkwardly, continuously turning round.

I got up in a whirlpool of love and I rounded rounded, downed downed downed.   (Edwin Star - I get up whirlpool)

Not everyone is wearing a fancy dress but that may be justified by the fact that many have come from far away, as they find out during chats outside in the disco square when they take a break.

However, people are at least dressed as Angels.

Carnival Party. Cosmic.

'It's the first time I've seen a car with a Rome number plate!'

'Yeah! We did a big, non-stop stretch from Rome but it was worth it.'

'How did you find out about this place?'

'To be honest, this Afro genre has now reached central Italy aaaand, here we are.'

'Are there any places like this in your area? You know, for summertime, just to change seaside, to see what there is, which discos...'

'Of course! But even without coming as far down as Roman shores, you could stop first near Grosseto, Tuscany, for example...'

And so, after hearing that, they go back inside and dance until closing time. In fact, they dance so much that, at the end, they have to take off their socks and cool their feet, especially Angie, waving his black hat.

Los niños en el parquet. Son muy afortunados. Van paseando, y sueñan caramelos. (Liaisons Dangereuses - Los Niños Del Parque)

After the fancy-dress party, they meet again at Jeep and Giby's sitting round the table with a sumptuous plate of macaroni and a bottle of Mateus brought by Fish.

'Aaaand, speaking of disco parties, where did DJ Spranga go after he played at the parties in Les Pois?'

'I know! He went to Chicago.'

Chicago is that damn club they still haven't set foot in and so, there they are, ready for a new expedition.

This time Angie is accompanied by Stub, Tacky and Jeep, who also want to make up for the time when they found the disco closed. They are familiar with the road but this time they want to make an exception. They want to see where the Arlecchino is. The Arlecchino is a disco that many Angels occasionally remember. Perhaps because Meo was a resident DJ there or maybe, since it isn't very far from the Chicago, it can be an excellent alternative just for a change, although certainly not for the music. Armed with a camera for some souvenir photos, they arrive in Baricella just after three in the afternoon and this time the scene is entirely different. The square is saturated with every type of vehicle imaginable and a mass of Angels is crowded at the entrance. The dark green, metallic Shark is beautiful. The girls are sexy. Wonderful how all those guys can squeeze into a car or ride a motorbike to grind kilometres and kilometres to be there every Saturday and Sunday. A little tipsy, a little high but in love and carefree. Passing that sort of concrete enclosure that looks like interlaced branches and twigs, they head towards the entrance. Walking among Angels, they hear a variety of accents coming from north and central Italy. Chicago appears to be the centre of the Afro movement and the fulcrum of the Afro scene - Brazil - Jazz - Fusion - Funky. Before reaching the red canopy of the entrance, an Afro sound coming from among the people captures their attention. A guy sitting on the floor is playing the bongos as if to welcome the whole tribe. After a few minutes, he stops the tribal rhythm to take a drag giving them the chance to ask

him a question or two.
'Well done! Are you here to play until evening?'
'Nooooo, I'm goin' in, I'm goin' in...'
'Look, we really wanna go to the Arlecchino, is it far?'
'Nooooo, 15 kilometres, always on this road, but it isn't worth it today.'
'How come?'
'Because today, at Chicago, Spranga is here with Rubens and Mozart, you can't even imagine!'

Since the age of fifteen, even Spranga has been influenced by the music of the two American DJs from the Bay of Angels. To buy his DJ gear, he had to sell the Vespa 125 that his dad had given him. Shortly after that, he was called to play in the first clubs until his consecration at Chicago.

They go in along a short dark corridor that culminates in red neon lights and finally opens out onto the disco's vast hall. The music of happiness has already begun and they start exploring under the legendary notes of the Chicago symbol. An Afro music that no longer exists.

Now that it feels so good. Tell everybody. Tell everybody. Tell everybody... (Lee Oskar - Our Road)

Beautiful music that the DJs propose and sometimes fish out from years before. Every musical genre always has a direct line with whatever precedes it.

I can feel it. Don't you feel it, don't you feel my love, for you, for you. (George McCrae - Don't you feel my love)

It's time to pop out and there is an odd, hasty coming and going of people behind the disco. They soon find out why.
'There's a chip van parked behind the disco and since the Chicago stamp has a short time limit, we have to hurry to eat our fries.'

And now, before leaving, they deface the Chicago toilet by scribbling the date, names and signature of the gang, "The Loss" conspicuously on the walls.

This means of communication seems to catch on with nicknames, dates and dedications in all the nightclubs they go to. During these weekends, the presence of The Loss is stylized not only in Chicago but also in Les Cigales, Small, Vrrr2000 and Cosmic, helping to tell the story of all the passing Angels. But these walls talk more than they do at the club. These walls tell of the adventures that the Angels have experienced up to that moment. From there you get the idea of the coolest places they have been, new towns, cities, discos, streets, loves and adventures. The beauty is finding that an Angel, who passed by there before someone else, can still see his name written there but it is now accompanied by a reply to the dedication that he had left some time ago. For example, the boys find out by reading the toilet tiles that a new Afro club has opened in the province of Mantua.

The Melamara disco opens with DJ Rudy proposing alternative music. In addition to the afore-mentioned Funky, he mixes music and sounds from all over the world. Brazilian funk carioca from the favelas of Rio de Janeiro with the typically electronic sound from Northern Europe. The meditative atmospheres of Californian new age up to Arabic, Indian, Reggae and general Latin-American musical influences.

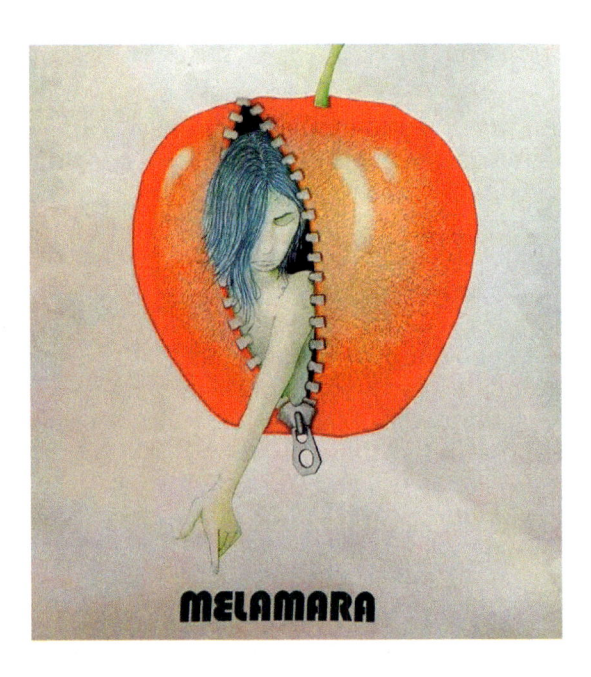

MELAMARA

☺

At Tacky's bar, once the stories of their adventures have been milked enough, they go back to talking about appointments that cannot be missed and, what's more, they agree not to split into small groups as they had during the previous weekend.

'Well! The house is free for us to use but we have to agree on what we wanna do.'

'A new base, we set up a new base there. The steps are getting really messy...'

'Anyway, come on, we all have to take turns cleaning up that house, sort out the usual...'

'Mmmmmmm, it's Marina's birthday first.'

'Hey! Hey! April 4th! It's the Star party at the Cosmic!'

With the promise of another meeting at Giby's to compare ideas about what they will do with the house, thoughts go to the Star party.

It's a mild Saturday, they feel good. The Cosmic opens at nine o'clock but before going inside, they enjoy watching the commotion of the tangled mass of Angels outside. It's an exercise in trying to memorise faces in case you meet them again somewhere else and want to flirt, or just to talk about them among friends by bringing up the strangest comments. Did you see what he did? Do you remember that guy? And those triplets with the long blond hair, wearing white blouses, light straps, tight, ultra-short white shorts and ankle boots! Inevitably, nobody has forgotten them, especially inside the Cosmic where they danced with spectacular synergy. Among all these faces, even the face of the Cosmic has changed. Daniele Baldelli and Claudio TBC have come up with the idea of installing a computer-sequencer and other electronic devices. They now have four turntables with two mixers where, within a single half-hour, they can play a bunch of tunes, all equalized.

Moreover, Tosi Brandi now has an electric battery to accompany DB mega-mixing, all strictly live. The evening marks a moment in the passage from funky disco music to electronic. The "disco" sound is beginning to decline and become obsolete. The discos are playing another type of music to dance to that, while in direct line with the previous genre, is made with electronic instruments in an attempt to evoke a futuristic feeling. On this particular night, the show is doing exactly that and opens with a few notes of "Electric Garden" by Conrad Schnitzler, proceeds with "Joyo can you hear me" by

STONED ANGELS

Visitors and then "Countdown" by Lee Ritenour. Besides these composer pieces, it is worth remembering that the precursors of electronic music were Kraftwerk for Germany, Jarre Michel Jarre for France and Giorgio Moroder for Italy. But it's already time to see what's going on in the square so, a quick stamp on the hand "and thence we come forth to see again the stars[22]", those bright ones surrounding the word Cosmic on the sign. Smoking cigarettes with some other boys, the number plates on of their Vespas catch their attention and they are intrigued by where they come from. Bozen.
'Hang about! Is there a good disco in Bolzano to have fun in? Where's the best place there?'
'You want to come up to Bolzano? Go to the Witches club. It isn't exactly in Bolzano town but when you get to Trento, ask for Canazei. In any case, that's where the buzz is...'
'Have you ever been to Bay?'
'To the Bay? It was our home. But it's going to be commemorated here again...'
'What do you mean?'
'Don't you know? On April 16th, here at the Cosmic, they're throwing a party called "Remember Bay 78". We'll be coming...'
'Cool!'
They go back in where "R.E.R.B" by Shock get them straight back on the dance floor to enjoy this cosmic, even stellar, evening. Opening hours at the Cosmic are shorter compared to Italian Riviera discos, and those of the Riviera nightclubs are shorter than those at the Bay of Angels. At the Cosmic, the evening starts at nine and ends at one, on Riviera, it ends at three and at Bay of Angels, at four. But when they hold parties, closing time is extended for an hour or an hour and a half. At two, or half past two, Stub, Angie, Zeb and all the others are reflected in the mirror at the far end of the dance hall because a lot of people have already left and the dance floor has emptied. The Star party is coming to an end and, on Mike Oldfield's notes of "Incantation", they go back home. Before they go inside to bed, their ears still ringing, the celestial canopy calls them to witness its true enchantment. They look up at the Milky Way. It looks like the side bang of an Angel. The Star party is not yet over.

---

22 *The Divine Comedy, Dante Alighieri, Canto XXXIV.*

Stepping out, the weekend's open wide. Fill it up, let's blast. The jams and ride. Stomp! All night! (The Brothers Johnson - Stomp!)

Since daylight-saving time gives them a little bit of light towards evening, the works begin at Jeep and Giby's house, which is located outside the city suburbs, in a small village almost in the countryside. There is only one road into this hamlet and it leads to a square surrounded by terraced houses. The house has two floors and is a distance from the rest of the houses, perfect for not busting anybody's balls. There is parking space directly in the square in front of the door, which is bordered by rows of half-dry roses, whose roots are choked by weeds, a prelude to what they would find inside. The facade is entirely faded and crumbled plaster has left patches. A better name for the door would be "board" and the four window shutters, two on the ground floor and the others on the first floor, would be good for a barbecue. Fortunately, once inside, the stale, grandma-house smell is covered by that of crushed stink beetles. The good thing is that the water and electricity supplies are working, even if the number of kilowatts is the most critical issue. Good thing they have a van to take all the rubbish away from the house and to bring in everything they need to clean it up.

'Tacky comin' today?'

'Mmmm, no! He's at Vinitaly[23].'

The only justification for Vinitaly is on Monday, the last day of the event. At around seven o'clock in the evening, when the visitors have left and the wineries start to pack up their stands, that's when you can get in free of charge. You go in with extra bags and a backpack on your shoulder since the companies give bottles and bottles of wine away because it's easier than taking them home.

'So! The sockets are here so we can put the stereo system there...'

'And here, where the sink is, we can set up the bar and this time, we can even have a barman.'

'Since we're going to use this place for parties and our hangout, I say we call it The Loss Club!'

'Awesome! Cooool! Aaaand, of course upstairs there is always the other room, the fuck zone...'

---

23 *Vinitaly is an International Wine and Spirits Fair held every year in Verona since 1967.*

'Mmmmmm, noooo, let's change the name, something more, more... what d'ya say to... incantation?'

'Yeeeeah, yeeeeah, the incantation room!'

In fits and starts and with many hours of work, The Loss Club is ready for opening. The HI-FI system, the lights and mattresses have all found peace. They are sure the place will be there for a very long time and so they imagine putting up signs along the road indicating "The Loss Club" and eventually even their own banner on the facade. However, before meeting to organise the first party, they all decide, guys, babes, but especially Angels, to go dancing together in a completely unknown disco, the Witches Club, near Bolzano. So, there they are again, all ready to go. They are joined by others from the neighbourhood who are relying on their road knowledge seeing as they had made the trip once before to Caldonazzo lake, which, they presume, is close to their destination. The mild spring day promises good weather but, since they have often been caught out, this time they are well equipped and have bought a front luggage rack for the PX to store all eventual necessities. The goal is to reach Trento by noon and then ask for directions. Some minor news is that Jake no longer has the Cagiva. He has destroyed it with countless accidents. He now has a red Vespa ET3 with beautiful white luggage racks in front and behind in which to transport backpacks and bags, bags, bags, something that he couldn't do on his old motorbike. Sunday mornings see a lot of guys lying in, snoring with bubbles coming out of their noses, but if you want to eat up three or four hundred kilometres, you have to spring into action early. This Sunday is the perfect day for it and, on about ten Vespas, they leave at around 10 am heading for South Tyrol. Taking the main road and staying close together all the way to the destination seems the most natural thing in the world, but they realise it isn't quite like that. In fact, as they ground out the kilometres, those who are more or less in the middle of the group realise that the pace is not the same for everyone. Those in front have raced on ahead while those at the back are moving more slowly. Not far out of the city on the road that follows the Adige valley, the tribe has already stretched out so much that they don't know how far ahead the leaders are and how far behind the last one is. They lose the conception of where the others are very early on. It's easy to do because you move up alongside another Vespa to exchange some bullshit, or rev up for exhibitionist reasons or to overtake

everyone, or you get lost to snog your sweetheart and other stupid things like that. But then the sheepdog instinct sets in and someone decides to gather the flock by speeding up at full throttle to reach whoever might be leading the expedition.
'Sheep! Is there anyone ahead?'
'Dunnoooooo!'
'Stop at Saint Leonard! At the stall, on the road!'
'Good! I'll have a flask!'
'We'll stop to do a count and see who's last!'
As the riders regroup, the same question resounds.
'Have you seen Jake?'
'Yesssss, he's dropped behind!'
'How come?'
'His chick, Lipgloss, she lost her safiiii[24]...'
Saint Leonard makes the best sandwich in the world: speck[25], cheese, mushrooms, wine and bikers. Tiny but characteristic, the bar is located on the roadside and therefore easy to spot and a mandatory stop-off for travellers. Unfortunately, they have lost sight of Lamp and his chick. Nobody knows if he is in front or behind. At this point, they think that Sheep was wrong. They wait in vain for half an hour and then decide to set off again, Lamp is sure to catch up with them later, if worse comes to worst, at the Trento city sign at least. The journey resumes at the same pace but still with the odd problem. Lace runs out of petrol and only those behind him stop. Unfortunately, the petrol stations on this main road are few and far between and mostly closed. Luckily, a rubber hose, just right for decanting, pops out. Positioning Lace's Vespa on the roadside and Angie's next to it but slightly higher due to the lay of the land, they begin the rite of transfer. Bearing in mind that you have to suck the petrol from tank to tank and that the hose is not transparent, the first hint of liquid in the mouth needs to be spat out but then, after successfully decanting, they are ready to go again.

Better get the Breakdown squad out. Get me rolling on.
(Manfred Mann's Earth Band-Stranded in Iowa)

At last, they reach the first Trento city sign but there are only

---

24 *Safi is an Indian fashion colourful scarf made of 100% cotton or silk.*
25 *Speck is a type of cured, lightly smoked ham typically made in South Tyrol.*

two of them and it's already one o'clock.'
'And the others?'
'Dunno, some got fed up and turned off at Rovereto to go to the lake...'
'Fuckin' hell! Anyway! Let's ask around in the town for directions to the Witches!'
Bad situation. After endless wandering, they get the information they were looking for.
'The Witches disco? Sixty, seventy kilometres away from here...'
Too late. They go back to the lakeside. By now, resignation replaces any hope of recompiling the group. To hell with it, they think among themselves, the others will catch us up at Marina's birthday.

☺

The first Loss members to arrive at the party are Stub, Angie and Poplar. The apartment is already full of people nosing around the rooms, some with a peculiarity they have never met before: the peasants. The main occupation of a peasant is to spend their time in the fields. No evenings together, no Saturdays, Sundays, discos, smoking, Martini. Their only true God is not Afro music, but the plough. Their sacred vehicle is not a Shark but a tractor. They find worldliness, city life, the city and apartments repulsive. They give you a bad look if you say things like: "Shall we go to the seaside?", "To the lake?", "Hello!".
'Poplar! Did you invite the hillbillies?'
'Weeeell, I met Friar at agriculture school aaaand, I told him about this party...'
'Good! So, he brought this music with him!'

Everyone. Everyone here. Here from different towns. For just one purpose. Dance for only one. (Instant Funk - Everybody)

'Yeah! Plus, he's got his gang with him, nice impression for Marina!'
Fortunately, there are no hillbilly girls at this party, only bay girls. Bay girls, at a birthday party, in front of a disco or hitchhiking, just capture your eyes and soul. With that flamboyant air and their simple gestures, they bewitch you from the very first moment. They walk in small groups, showing their faces as fresh as the dew. Side

STONED ANGELS

by side, they smile merrily and when a breeze moves their hair, their eyes enchant you even further. So, at parties, when you notice one that you particularly like, you are immediately stuck. A strange feeling, like a circle of ice running through your body, brings to mind similar situations, but with a higher intensity. You thought you were invincible, but you daren't tell her you are having a heart attack. You begin to brood over sentences that could sweep away this obstacle between you and her, the obstacle of embarrassment, of being awkward and maybe ridiculous. But before you can say anything to her, you have to overcome her lack of interest in you and then try to smile at her, even just to make sure that her disinterest isn't real. Maybe it works. She smiles at you. Your eyes meet and, in hers, you see the reflection of your summer story, every day, every night with her. It's time to wear your heart on your sleeve and say something.

'Batida de Coco!'

Hugo and Giby emerge with their heads through the front door followed by their torsos, legs, arms and finally the bottles of Batida de Coco they are holding in their hands behind their backs. The birthday party takes a detour. The idyllic dreams of those who are trying to get laid burst with the arrival of the two latecomers swaying among the guests. The bottles of Batida de Coco are empty.

'How old are you today?'

'18!'

If you ask her, she tells you she is 18, but she is actually only 16. Forcing maturity among the Angels makes no sense. The age gap between the Angels is of no importance. There can be an age-gap of ten years between those on foot and those with a motor of some kind. The reason this gap disappears is that all Angels are merely simple, kind, in love with life and the same lifestyle, regardless of any age. And apart from age, to celebrate a birthday all together, you even have to socialise with the hillbilly boys. What can the common denominator be?

Across the crowded disco-room. You're amazed of dancing people
Eye to eye contact. Eye to eye contact.   (Edwin Starr – Contact)

Marina emerges from under a blanket of smoke with several bottles of brandy because hillbilly boys are allergic to water and so, they have found their way to socialise and the party takes flight.

☺

Parties are a unique opportunity to be together. The atmosphere creates itself and makes them all euphoric and beautiful. The Loss gang make the last touches to the Loss Club. They have a burning desire to organise a party but, as the Easter holidays approach, interests turn in favour of the first outings outdoors. The period is unusually warm and could play in favour of a trip to the Bay of Sirens at Lake Garda or even to the sea along the Riviera to dip their feet into the cool water. Since there is a risk that few people will show up and that a party at the club would turn sour, they decide to postpone but are determined to invent something else. Something that will make Easter unforgettable. Sitting in Tacky's bar, the ideas flow from the most classic, like a picnic in a meadow or a walk along the lake to a hike in the hills, a fuck in the incantation room, smoking and drinking in company. Since all these ideas have one thing in common, that is, the availability of parental cars, they agree on doing a long journey. So, they decide to go to Bologna and then see what they feel like doing when they get there.

Six cars! This morning they have six splendid cars to load everyone into. More than twenty of them. Before forming a convoy behind Tacky's VW Passat, Lamp has the fantastic idea of taking a camera, while Tacky is firmly intent on taking a stadium trumpet. Wild moments in the neighbourhood square block the traffic until group photos exhaust their interest. They set off heading towards Rovigo taking the road towards the "foggy lands". In Cerea, a blow on the trumpet while going by the Small Studios is an obligation even though today's destination is not the disco. The journey seems to proceed well. At least it does until, lost in the countryside Zeb, in his R4, swerves and collides with Volt's R4 that in turn buggers Genny's CX. In these cases, the only thing to do is to stand up with morale and some bullshit.

'Easyyyy, old man, easyyyy, just fill the dent with plaster, like Angie did with the mudguard of his PX...'

'Nooooo! Just buy stickers like everyone else and cover it ...'

'Do you know how to tell if a chick will still be pretty when she gets older?'

'Go on!'

'Take a look at her mum!'

Nothing serious. Accident over, they leave again. At last, the long and narrow main road ends and they take the motorway to

Bologna. The most marked difference between a main road and a motorway is the latter's monotony so they shake the dust off an old game and play cops and robbers, chase and capture.

You can hit and run. I've got to be. Number one. Gotta make up your mind.'Cause you'll never... (Loleatta Holloway - Hit and Run)

This time it's Tacky in his WV Passat who must try to escape with Poplar in a Golf, Stub in a Ford Fiesta and gradually all the others giving chase. The distance between the cars mustn't be too large because they have to stay within the sound of the trumpet which is the signal to stop the race on the emergency lane so that Tacky, Pope and Finger can be 'caught'. The scene sees the cars parked in a line in the emergency lane, with everyone jumping out to surround Tacky's vehicle, forcing the passengers out with their hands up, turning them around, putting their hands on the roof, legs apart and arse out. The search simulation goes on for several minutes so that other unsuspecting motorists notice what's going on and slow down due to the gestures and hustle of all the friends. The game continues all the way to Bologna.

Just the other side of the city, sullen clouds begin to gather here and there and it starts spitting with rain. They decide to stop for a moment to decide whether to continue towards the Riviera or go somewhere else.

'It's already half past one, we left at 9:30, and in four hours we've only just passed through Bologna and the weather is looking shitty...'

'If you ask a woman from Bologna the difference between blow jobs and tortellini, do you know what she says?'

'What?'

'What are tortellini?'

'Oooookayyyyy, shall we go to a disco?'

'Arlecchino!'

They get back on the road and, after a while, stop for a sandwich. The bar is run by two strange guys who pay no particular attention to their potential customers as the gang goes in. At the request for sandwiches, they get up from their old chairs, bordered by round rubber thread, leaving the shapes of their roundness imprinted in the seats due to their weight being very much different to the Angels' average seventy kilos and, with the speed of two sloths, eventually serve them. To bridge the gap between the gang's vivaciousness and their lethargy, the friends begin to exchange some sarcastic jokes about the day's events.

'What did you say to that old lady who ran away when we were stuck at the village sign?'

'Run away, old bitch! We're on the rampage!'

Santa Maria Codifiume. They finally arrive at the Arlecchino club, the disco made famous by DJ Meo.

'Excuse me. How come there are so few people around?'

'Mmmmmm, I think they're all at the Chicago.'

'At Chicago? Aaaand, what's goin' on...'

'A party, moon party, or, second moon party, with Mozart, Rubens, Ebreo and Spranga, all together, at least...'

'That's right! The moon is full at the moment!'

'But, sorry, is it a sort of Sand party like they threw at the Bay of Angels?'

'Yeaaaah, just like the Night of Angels, something like that...'

At 3:45 pm they are in Baricella in front of Chicago. The square itself is a sight for sore eyes and worthy of delaying entry into the disco. It looks like an Afro gathering. Wrecked cars, full of stickers on every dent, with the most unlikely adornments: curtains, lights and Arabesque patterned bodywork.

Chicago club.

'I'll wear my Pallas out going back and forth from Venice.'
'There are two hot tapes to buy today.'
They can already hear them.
Brothers and sisters have come from all over. Those wearing Indian slippers, someone else is flaunting a reindeer jacket and, despite the most disparate clothing, bay girls don't wear tons of makeup.
'All yesterday afternoon braiding hair.'
They overhear the conversation.
'Then, when you take them out, your hair is wavy...'
They approach the entrance and the tam-tam of the bongo players in the square progressively mixes with that of the legendary DJs as they dive into the "Moon Party".
They are inside at last! The music is a brilliant super groove that only these tribal DJs are able to achieve. They are already dancing to the sound of the piece "Regenmacher" by Hans Joachim Roedelius. Those are vibrations that don't oblige you to take part in

the frenzy of pure dancing but allow room for everyone to look around, catch each other's eyes, get to know new people and try to create a fantastic friendship and, who knows, maybe experience a story of a few hours on the disco sofa.

Here comes Love. Just walking down the street. Here comes Love, and heated for me. (Stargard - Here Comes Love)

The only thing to think about is having fun. You are just part of a group, both inside and out, and seeing someone you met at some other discotheque fill you with immense joy.

'Mary Jane[26], Mary Jane, does anyone have a Mary Jane to sell me?'

Do me a favour, don't be so cool. Do me a favour, act like a fool. Do me a favour, don't be so great. (Amy Bolton - Do Me a Favour)

Friendships that become granitic over time are made and very close human relationships are established.
'We're all Aaaangels, Aaaangels...'
'Two tapes, the DJs made two tapes of the Moon party, super hot!'
'Yeah, I heard that. Let's see, meanwhile I took some stickers.'
The link with American legends, as at the Marilyn Party at the Bay of Angels, continues in Chicago with stickers of Janis Joplin.

---

[26] *Mary Jane Rathbun, the woman who invented marijuana brownies.*

In addition to the characters, the names of the discos also recall the United States. Chicago, the city where disco music was born, and New York, Manhattan, for example. However, since the latter arise from the ashes of discotheques with another name, such as Pap or Belfagor, they unfortunately die due to problems of drug or public order in general. Outside, in the square for the usual break, the Angels confirm the news that leaked a short time ago: New York closed and the Much More and Goody Goody, one of Mozart and Rubens discos, have come to the same end.

'Goody Goody? Did you know that they're a band and made a piece called Bio-rhythms?'

But it's time to detach Jeep from the DJ console and make their way home.

Motel to Motel. New start to new start. People to people. A flashback to my destination. (The Quick - Young Men Drive Fast)

The event at The Chicago after the "Second Moon Party" and Marina's birthday party urge Jeep and Giby to encourage the Loss to inaugurate the Loss Club. Since Finger is meeting a couple of hotties from the Wall gang in a local snack bar, they decide to join him to make final decisions. And so, over some crisps and a few

beers, they at last begin to discuss the programme, seriously.
'Ohhhhhhh! Here comes Giby too.'
'Jamboooo! Don't you know? I'm 17 today...'
What is supposed to be a quiet evening to work out how to start organising the Loss Party, now turns into something totally different. Since Finger was the one who suggested the meeting in this bar, he feels it's his responsibility to take the initiative towards a minimum of celebration.
'Barman! Bring the beer!'
'Weee r the chaaampions .... my frieeends...'
All together.
'Yeeeeeeah!'
'No time for losers ...'
'Yeeeeeeah!'
The other Loss members arrive in dribs and drabs and after Jake, Zeb also shows up and gives them the fantastic news.
'Helloooo, gaaaang, have you heard the latest? I've been discharged! I don't have to do my military service!'
Since Finger was the one who suggested the meeting in this bar, he feels it's his responsibility to take the initiative to celebrate this news too.
'Barman! Bring Martini!'
'No! No! I've brought Prosecco!'
'Barman! Bring glasses!'
'Aaaand, we quaff, quaff and quaff!'
Despite the absence of Jeep and Stub, who popped by the campsite, they take the first decisions on how the party should be communicated with the okay from the campers that every choice will undoubtedly be excellent.
'So! We decided that we'll go to the fashion show first, which is next Saturday at Vrrr2000, then we'll go to the party... remember Paul the punk? Well, his brother is organising a party at Zibri's house, and then we throw ours...'
'Good! So, after the party at Zibri's, since they have fantastic stroboscopes, we could borrow them in exchange for inviting them to our party...'
'Shiiiit! Great idea! But, why don't we do the same as the Chicago Moon party! The stamps! Jeep and I will take care of printing the invitations and we can also make a stamp for going in and out of the Club during the party!'

'Woooow, that's cool! Barman! Bring Martini!'
'Oops! Watch out, Martini at the bar! We'll get fleeced...'
'Barman! Take away the Martini, bring the Prosecco!'
Meanwhile, two guys sitting behind two pints of beer in the corner of the bar stand up and walk towards them. One is tall, the other short and thin. It's Tex and his friend. It's good to see that Jake's hospital roommate has recovered and then congratulations turn into friendship.
'Barman! Bring the beer! Aaaand, you are?'
'Suri, I'm Suri, hu! Hu!'
Suri is a skinny guy with long, straight, fair hair, who works as a bricklayer. He looks just like the "vagabond" sticker but, instead of walking around with a guitar and sleeping bag, he goes around in a blue Dyane with a sunroof. Tex, on the other hand, is always on foot. He walked so much once that he lost an Indian sandal at Lake Garda and walked all along the lakefront and back home with one bare foot. When he realised he was missing a sandal, he went back, again on foot, to look for it.
'We hear you're having a party, can we come?'
'Why not!'
'Besides the party at Chicago, we think you go to private parties too. We know Zibri for example...'
'Wow, gooood! See you again then! Hopefully, it will be as good as Marina's...'
'Ha! Ha! That's right, a real sleazy joint!'
'How'd it go? Nice people? Hot chicks?'
'We trashed the apartment, broke the springs of the bed in the master bedroom, smoked all the weed, drained the cellar and shoved our hands everywhere and, in my opinion, even in the pussy and on the tits of Marina! Ha! Ha!'
A bit more bullshit and then the bartender comes up.
'Excuse me, but are you the guys who went to that birthday party in the apartment up there?'
'Barmaaaan, yeeeesss, whyyyy?'
Now Finger is legless and Giby isn't far behind with Hugo in third place and all the others following on.
'I'm Marina's father!'
Finger's two girlfriends disappeared and refused to go to that bar anymore.
The other guys drag Finger and Giby out but big steps forward

in the Loss party organisation have been proudly accomplished.
☺
The Match Ball fashion show is a not-to-be-missed opportunity to have fun and maybe make new friends to invite to private parties. As soon as you go into the discotheque, the air is already electrifying. The sapphire blue and UV lamps enhance white trousers and teeth and the dance floor is practically full, while older men surround the two bars in the corners. A typical commercial disco. The Loss gang reserve a prime position for themselves by sitting on the floor closest to the stage in a central area where there are still a few places. The music is not loud so they are able to exchange a few words about what promises to be a beautiful Saturday night. The programme includes the new summer line which they are most excited about seeing.
'So, Fingeeeer! You got your PX, at last...'
'Yeaaah, shit! I've been waitin' for almost six months!'
'Hey, hey, hey...'
'What's the matter, Heyhey?'
'Me too! Yesterday I got a brand-new, spick 'n span PX, bright orange, red...'
'Awesome! And, how did you find one like that?'
'It's from Germany!'

It's Saturday night. My hits still in live. I'm going to disco. Night and day with my baby. (Kinsman Dazz Band - Saturday Night)

The presenter appears and rants on about the shops that are sponsoring the event and new entries that, according to her, will be explosive summer trends. The show begins. Hyper-coloured models, colourful shoes, mesh knits but it's the leggings that throw the audience into raptures.

I can feel the heat, no one has to tell me. It's so good, once it starts I'll never let go. (Steve Winwood - Spanish Dancer)

'Yesterday, Lamp popped over. He was very sad. He told me his chick dumped him.'
'And why isn't he here now? Did you tell him to come here?'
'Oh yeah! I told him, but he showed up in the morning and told me they're back together.'

Gigantic gold necklaces, metal hoop earrings, high-waisted belts with huge buckles, bracelets with beads of all shapes and sizes. One might say that there is no sense in wearing all that bijoux but the watchword is: dare. Huge sunglasses with geometric and multi-coloured details and handbags with chains. The accessories are just a reminder to exaggerate.

Tokyo, fly away to the rising sun, Tokyo, fly away to the rising sun.
(The Rah Band - Tokyo flyer)

While Ray-Bans with their thin, silver or gold-coloured frames make some of the audience drool, they are not Angie and Hugo's cup of tea. After spending almost all the time of the parade scrounging small change from people, especially at the bars, it's time to go out to find their own dimension at Tacky's bar to spend their fortune in beers.

☺

In anticipation of the next fun event, namely Zibri's party, Reggae lovers are shocked by the news that Bob Marley has passed away due to a mole under his big toe. All the various genres of music that intertwine in this period include Reggae. The songs Rastaman and Jammin' are always played in discos, much to the appreciation of the druggies. It is also much appreciated by Finger, who invites Angie to go for a ride on his new PX to a record shop to buy a Bob Marley LP, the one that includes his favourite songs: "Is this love", "You could be loved". Going in a record shop is like being at home. You are engulfed by a particular warmth that embraces you and makes you feel relaxed. Mountains and mountains of colourful covers where you spend your time rummaging through hundreds and hundreds of unknown singers and bands that you may have unconsciously listened to. It's like being in your personalized bedroom with all the icons you care about. Shops like these are not only places where you breathe the air of music but are, first and foremost, places of encounter and passion. The staff is always accommodating and friendly and does its utmost to satisfy your every need, even when strange people show up.

'Helloooo, I have this tape, can you tell me the name of the track at the 23rd minute?'

'Ahhhh! That's Body to Body Boogie by Orlando Riva Sound...'

There are four beautiful shops, all very close to each other, in the city but, strangely enough, they don't seem to compete. Each one specialises in something of its own. One imports from England and the United States, another makes DIY productions... In short, each shop has its own soul. Angie and Finger go to Memories shop and the seven notes of Peter Tosh and Bob Marley are playing in the background. It's the beginning of the "Rasta" culture. Rasta is a religious faith founded by the Ethiopian emperor, Ras, aka Haile Selassie I. He was practically the umpteenth "God incarnate" who demanded the restoration of the cultural and national dignity of Africans, suppressed by deportation and slavery in America and, in the case of Bob Marley, the Caribbean. In Jamaica, in particular, the Rastafarian movement developed mainly to actively support the return of the black population to the African homeland. Members of the movement characteristically wear their hair in "Rasta" style, similar to the mane of the lion that appeared on the imperial flag of Ethiopia, an animal that symbolised the emperor's family. To have this hairstyle, you have to cotton your hair and then crochet it until you get a weave that is impossible to undo. There is one last peculiarity about the hairstyle. The hair must be long because it expresses divine strength. Just think, for example, about the story of Samson. The vehicle that transmits this faith in Jamaica is the musical genre known as Reggae, a type of popular music featuring a strongly syncopated rhythm. Its name derives from a mockery of the English who called it "ragged", in other words, poorly dressed like a "peasant". One last thing, the clothes and hats worn by Reggae musicians are the colours of the Ethiopian flag, not those of Jamaica.

Much to Finger's joy, he and Angie find the albums "Rastaman vibration" and "Babylon by bus" and go home to enjoy a good dose of Reggae.

Reggae was also the background for an idea of two Angels from Brescia, Majo and Gil. They were classmates at an art school, cartoonists for Tex and Vampyr published by Bonelli, and also collaborated with several publishing houses in France. They listened to Bob Marley and, in an hour of free drawing, wanted to create something that embodied the ideals of freedom and carefreeness of that period: wide trousers, belt latched around the waist, Indian sandals, long hair, sleeping bag and guitar. That was how the character of the "Vagabond" came about. The design, cut and plasticised by hand, ended up on Gil's Vespa ET3. Like all the

Angels who went to the America shop in Verona, Brescia also had a second-hand clothes store and fancy oriental goods shop that Majo and Gil used to visit from time to time. On seeing that sticker on Gil's Vespa, the owner liked it so much he asked the two students to make more copies. It was a big mistake. The young, idealistic and naïve boys, saw their character spring up everywhere within a few weeks. Despite consulting a copyright lawyer, there was nothing they could do about it and for many years to come, that vagabond appeared on the Sharks, Citroen 2CVs, Dyanes, Vespas of all Italian Angels. It was so successful that it was even seen outside Spanish clubs, on German Angels' cars at Lake Garda and the T-shirts of Cologne markets next to those of Led Zeppelin and The Beatles. "Vagabond in motion", "Vagabond with friends around the fire", "Vagabond with crossed legs", "Vagabond in Mecca" are just some of the drawings that appeared, all based on the original.

Vagabond became a business. Another shop, trying to compete with the stolen idea, asked them to draw "Vagabond seen from the front" in order to show his face, but the two refused. The train had already left.

Several Reggae pieces are also heard at Zibri and Rudolf's party. However, this time, it isn't so much the music that interests the Loss but the spectacular stroboscopic system they have installed, and, of course, saying farewell to Bert, Paul the punk's brother who is leaving to serve in the army. Zibri owns a hotel and, for the occasion, has reserved it exclusively for party guests. The whole lot, from the bedrooms on the upper floors to the restaurant on the ground floor. The party entrance is from the dining room where all the tables have been moved to the sides to make room for a dance floor. Coloured lights and strobes have been installed on bars fixed to the ceiling and cover the perimeter of the dance area perpendicularly. The inevitable mirror ball, the symbol of a disco, hangs above the dance floor of what is expected to be an unforgettable party. That is the scene that greets Stub, Poplar, Giby, Zeb, Jeep, Hugo, Fish, Jake, Angie, Finger and Volt as they appear at the entrance after being received aristocratically by Gray, a guy with a Napoleon hat on his head.

One, Two, Three, Four! How you doing? Woop! Hello Everybody!
(Gary's Gang - Showtime)

'Jake, How're you?'
'Great, great, I crashed in GolosAngeles doin' a wheelie but, nothin', everything's fine...'
'How come Pepper isn't here?'
'He crashed his Shark against a green Renault R4 in GolosAngeles...'
The tables overflow with sandwiches and bottles of wine. The first to bear the brunt is Jeep who, a few minutes after they arrive at the party, is seen sitting on the floor, with his back leaning against a wall, a bottle of Brut between his legs by way of a penis, with the foam still coming out of the bottleneck. He's smashed.

Savage! Savage lover! Oh! Savage Savage lover. Savage!
(The Ring - Savage)

In a short time, everyone is completely plastered, even the chicks as they come down from the upper floor, intent on using their thumbs to sort out their panties that have taken refuge in the middle of their buttocks.

When you're lovin' me lady, spank. That's how I want it to be baby, spank!
(Jimmy Bo Horne - Spank)

After throwing the sandwiches, Stub is also on the road to destruction and goes out to find a bike, which he crashes and so he comes back and heads for the dance floor.

From the park I hear rhythms. Marley's hot on the box. Tonight there will be a party.   (Stevie Wonder - Master Blaster)

Every time they come across Gray emerging from the smoke curtain, they see more and more Loss Club stamps appearing on his forehead acting as the first invitations to their upcoming party. And, speaking of invitations, Angie and Zeb go through all the chicks to invite them to the newly-established Loss Club, telling them several times, not because of Marijuana fumes floating around in the air, nor the alcohol. They simply don't remember whether they have already invited them or not.

Mercy. Baby you know, I ain't hard to please. But when you come around, you play the big tease..(Jimmy Bo Horne - You get me hot)

Jake is the first Loss member to leave, subsequently falling off his Vespa again in the same street, in the same place and with the same modality: by doing a wheelie in GolosAngeles.

☺

The Loss's club.

The day of the party at the club is fast approaching. Practically everything is ready. The last details are discussed on the pillows of the incantation room. In the end, everyone agrees on how each task will be subdivided.

'So! Volt and Heyhey will go to take down the strobes from Zibri and bring them here.'

'I'll tell Lamp to mount the psyche.'

'We had no barman last year. Finger can do it this time.'

'Angie and Zeb will go to hand out the invitations in the city. Did we print out the invitations?'

'Yeah, buuut, which sectors?'

'Do sector G where the Wall gang hangs out and sector D.'

'Pepper will pick those without transport up in his car.'

'Well! Anyway, let's say that we'll do not one, but two, parties in a row! We have to do something new and unforgettable...'

'Two days in a row?'

'Eeeeeexactly! Those who want to bring a sleeping bag, can sleep in the incantation room.'

'Jake! What time do you call this? Where the fuck have you been?'

'I'm on foot. When I left Zibri's party, I crashed again on the same street and in the same spot as last time.'

'Don't tell me. You were doin' another wheelie!'

'Yeeeeeah!'

'And maybe because you saw Frog's wide mouth and wanted to be cool...'

They even invited the old women they met on the street, but Giby, stationed at the entrance with the stamp, hasn't stamped one yet. Jeep, who wanted to be called DJ Moses, is ready with his DJ set. Angie made him buy "Hotta" by Sky and persuaded him to open the evening with this song even if Jeep, with his immense knowledge of albums having spied on all the DJs' turntables, is definitely more inclined towards the genre played at Les Cigales rather than electronic Afro. But they also have an equalizer, just like at the Cosmic. The first to arrive are the organisers.

'Tacky! You sort out the psyches!'

Unfortunately, to make the psyches work, you have to turn them off and on using a switch.

Heyhey arrives with his old motorbike, which is known as the "boiler".

'Heyhey! Aaaand, the red PX?'
'My brother's got it!'
'Come on! Come on! Hide the bike back there. Are you taking the piss out of us?'
Pope, Pizzi, Arse, Vange, Rod Stewart and their friends are coming.

How do you do. What you do to me. How do you do. What you do to me. (Brass Construction - How Do You Do)

Zibri, George, Drug, Chicken, Twin, Pepper. Come in.

We never give it up. Even the funky stuff. I like funky music babe...
(Uncle Louie - I Like Funky Music)

Bea, Susy, the Gipsies, Vale, Mary "the disgrace". Dance.

Ehi mister, i like your staff, i know you do. It's so sophisticated mister!
(Rafael Cameron - Together)

Mila, Anna, Filly, Birdie, Fiore, Patty, Bitch. In and out.

We will wait. We will watch. What we would have done...
(Sea level - We will wait)

'Who the fuck invited the one with the moustache?'
The party is going well. Since the DJ's console has been placed on a platform so as to avoid any objects being thrown on it like at the last New Year's Eve party, it's from below that the guests see Tacky spending the evening flipping the light switch and DJ Moses intent on mixing his vinyl. With a single earpad held tight between his shoulder and his ear and the rest of the headphones straddling his blond hair, Jeep plays dance music: Soul, Electronic Dance, Groove, Funky-Jazz, Pop, Hip-Hop, Rap, all genres of the moment. In addition to peering at the LP covers, he also saw how Claudio TBC uses the equalizer. When the instrument is turned off, he intervenes on the cursors to prepare the frequency, then, rhythmically, turns it on and off to accentuate the voice or the bass. DJ Moses, aka Jeep, does the same.
A Jamaican DJ, on emigrating to the Bronx, noticed that New

Yorkers did not particularly like Reggae. During his evenings in the discos, he also noticed that those who danced preferred the accelerated parts with steady percussion. He quickly developed mixing techniques to keep the participants active and excited. Two things resulted from that. The first, two turntables were used to promptly mix the Reggae with more beat genres. The second was hip-hop. The name for this type of "mixed music" was coined during a competition with another DJ. One was called "hip", the other "hop". In Jamaica, this genre was often accompanied by a singer who spoke about it, known as the ceremony head or "master". The repetition of "master" "master", "master" led to coining the word "rapper" and hence the music and term "rap".

The party continues to go well. The piece "Rapper Dapper Snapper" by Edwin Birdsong is perfect for all tastes. Those who want to chat go out into the courtyard with the club stamp slapped on their bare skin at the entrance door by Giby the "watchdog". Those who want to dance come in subject to Giby's careful stamp check. Those who go upstairs to fuck are not checked at all. However, sooner or later something has to go wrong. At the request of something to eat, the Loss staff realise that they only brought a few packets of crisps and popcorn and, at the request of something to drink:

'We got beer, go to the bar and ask the barman.'

'Excuse me, where? Which barman?'

Finger is not in his place. They find him behind the counter, sitting on the floor, with his back against the wall, holding a can by way of a limp penis between his legs, surrounded by empties. He's totally plastered.

'Finger! You drank all the beers?'

The answer is an equalized belch. The party is not going well. No benz, no smokes, no crisps and the incantation room is occupied by the usual head-over-heels in love couples. Since the chances of having fun have suddenly diminished, some people leave or stump about on the dance floor, get pissed off and then leave. At around ten o'clock, the dance room at the entrance empties and almost everyone is in the courtyard chitchatting. The party is not going at all well. Close to midnight, Stub, having drunk all the beers along with Finger, begins to uproot all the roses in the courtyard. The others, frightened by his weird behaviour, decide to leave, reducing attendance even further.

'Fuuuuck, watch oooout, can't you see you hit the scooooter...'
'Shiiiit!'
'Ah! We know who you are! You're the ones who came down the hill and hit us...'
'Shiiiit! The ones we twisted the wheeeel of!'
In the end, only a few slept over on the promiscuous mattresses in the incantation room. The remaining hours of the night are spent in a state of catalepsy, impossible to remember anything.

I don't want your love any longer. 'Cause you're just easing it for yourself. (Supermax - As Long As There Is You)

On opening the window shutters, they notice that the only two girls left with the Loss gang are the gipsies. Opening the windows, a light breeze and the intoxicating scent of late spring enter the incantation room, replacing the stale, cum-filled air of the first day of celebration. The front of the club faces north and so, the rays of the early morning sun don't disturb any eye-bogeys. Jeep, Giby, Tacky and Poplar sit on the mattresses and look around while the others peek out and take a look down into the courtyard. The only person still crucified between the electric blue cushions is Finger, who probably wasn't conscious enough to stick two fingers down his throat before collapsing in bed. They go downstairs in single file and realise that it's already lunchtime and time to prepare for the second day of the party. Sticking to the plan means earning some notoriety so that they get invited to other parties. Rummaging behind the bar, the guardian angel of the bay has already fixed himself something to eat: a bag of crisps, a bag of popcorn, a can of beer. There is barely time for Poplar to light up a cigarette, Jeep to walk over to the console to check the instruments and the others to start tidying up than they are disturbed by the sound of a motorbike pulling up in front of the club. It's Heyhey's "boiler".
'Heyhey! Where's the red PX?'
'My brother's got it!'
'Come on! Come on! Hide the bike back there. Are you taking the piss out of us?'
The party starts again, but never really gets off the ground. Only a few have answered the Afro call. The situation sees Jeep and Giby go to get laid in incantation, Angie is on the equalizer, Tacky on the console. Although someone has come back and some, who didn't

come the day before, have arrived for the first time, there is still a bad feeling. A Sunday afternoon is probably not like a Saturday night. Maybe there aren't as many around today; maybe the organisers forgot the drinks again. At a certain point, Angie dumps the equalizer, takes his PX and starts driving around with the hotties that the Loss gang met for the first time.

'Why do you keep coming and going?'
'Just to reach 30,000 Km on the speedo.'

Everyone agrees that a two-day party will never happen again, but they also agree that a lot of parties will be thrown at the club. The fact of not having to depend on others is just too cool. Now they can leave everything set up without having to dismantle and reassemble the equipment every time. But, after that party, they also all agree to take a break, no discos and indoor parties.

☺

It's spring and the evenings are particularly warm, a sure invitation to all and sundry to take a trip to the lake and maybe even go for a splash at San Vigilio. After all, German visitors have already been dipping their bellies in the "Garda See" for a couple of months. And so, they decide to spend the coming Saturday night in Lazise.

'Genny! Why don't you come with us?'
'I wanna go to Les Cigales!'
'Come oooon, shit! For once, your chick wants to go to the lake!'
'No sweat! Take her with you. What's the problem?'

Apart from the odd defection, they get together a friendly group and so with Hugo, Volt, Heyhey, Zeb, Stub, Fish, Sony, Marcy and a few others, Angie leaves with his time-honoured PX. Like a caravan of camels in the desert, they proceed at the speed of an unsouped-up Ciao, also because they enjoy bumping each other in the rear of the motorbike just to make their presence felt to whoever is driving in front and make them smile.

Tunisian ride! Tunisian ride!
(Sticky Jones Band - Tunisian ride)

Beaches at Lake Garda turn into open-air clubs in the evening. Numerous kiosks, from the beginning of spring to late summer, organise themed evenings, outdoor concerts, barbecues and cocktails to suit all tastes. From North to South, on both sides, you can meet new people and have fun. The Krauts break free from their Teutonic canons, become affable and, after several mugs of beer, even speak Italian. Fireworks are set off village by village around the lake as if signalling a new place waiting to be discovered. However, one place attracts like a comet. After a couple of hours sitting on boulders along the shore, someone hears the call, a tam-tam from just over there.

'Shall we raid the Cosmic?'

As usual, the parking lot in front of the Cosmic is overcrowded with people of all kinds and from different parts of the planet. Besides the Dutch and the Belgians, what strikes them this time is a motorcycle with a "Roma" number plate, "Bet his arse is the same shape as the seat now!", they thought amongst themselves. Tonight, however, seeing that it's almost midnight, they decide not to go in. In any case, the comings and goings in the square provide plenty of entertainment. After half an hour, everyone leaves for home and only Zeb, Angie and Stub remain inside the entrance tunnel. Leaning against the curved walls, close to the cash desk, you can still enjoy the sound of electronic pieces such as "The Theme for Great Cities" by Simple Minds. It's the "Cosmic Sound".

Their sound? Otherworldly. Dislocated. Unreal. Cosmic. It was as if their music had a different history to the one you knew, like they'd been shopping for records on a parallel planet. Dunny funk, jazzy electronics, spacey rolling drums, nodding, warping weirdness, all pushed endlessly forward by lazy, overweight basslines. There was little sense of individual tracks; you lost any firm ground as elements shifted and merged, as you entered tunnels of EQ and phasing, as songs exchanged sides with each other and back. It was put together like film music, as if every tiny shift in sound and feeling was accounted for. Wildly eclectic, but not sunny like Ibiza, not gothic like Belgium, in Italy the music was channelled straight from the moons of Jupiter.

(Bill Brewster, Frank Broughton - Italian afro-cosmic)

'Thank you! Thank you for being born at this time!'
Someone invokes.
Going back outside in the square, a blue Shark with all the

windows lowered goes by slowly, almost touching them. The driver is a guy with long, greasy hair, white shirt, elbow out the window. He looks at them and nods, smiles and nods. Albeit strange, some of the most fantastic music they have ever heard is coming from the Shark.

'Heyyyy! How're you? Piacenza?' they ask curiously.
'I feel great, my afro pal, great! Yeah, Piacenza...'
'Nice trip and beautiful music...'
'Travelling is the most beautiful thing in the world, travelling with music is even better...'

He drives slowly straight to the end of the parking lot while they, dodging the Shark's arse, notice the Ohm sticker.

'Keep an eye on him! He's got the ohm symbol!'

Buddhists and Hindus recite "ohmmmmm" at the beginning of sentences or mantras that wish for happiness and peace. Ohm for weed smokers is a joint, their own particular mantra for achieving peace and happiness. The graphic symbol looks like two lips with a joint and a little cloud.

I'll fly with you to the mystic hills of Katmandu. Pack my case gonna leave behind this human race.   (Tantra - Hills of Katmandu)

Angels with Ohm.

'Well! Well, well, from the stuff he listens to, he must be a Buddhist in my opinion...'

They finish their cigarettes and go back to the tunnel to take another shower in "Cosmic Sound".

Someone singing in the shower.
(Simple Minds - This fear of God)

'I'm dyin' to get in!'
'If you give me money!'
'I've got an idea!'
'Come on! I'm all ears!'
'Let's search the car park. We might find a wallet on the ground or some small change people have dropped. With all the mess there's bound to be...'

Going back outside, the Blue Shark, returning from the bottom of the yard, is just passing by again at 2 km an hour, almost touching them. The guy looks at them and, by way of greeting, smiles and nods.

'Heyyyy Piacenza! Excuse meeee buuut, what kind of music is that?'

'Anambra, Ozo...'

Om mani padme hum. Om mani padme hum. Om mani padme hum. Om mani padme hum. (Anambra - Ozo)

OM *generosity, abandonment of greed, mind that benefits others, abandonment of anger.*
MA *morality, do not harm other sentient beings.*
Ni *patience, abandonment of anger, jealousy, abandonment of ego and self-attachment.*
PE *enthusiastic effort, eliminates laziness and is directed to study to eliminate suffering.*
ME *concentration, meditation, concentration on virtues without distraction.*
Om *wisdom, knowledge of all phenomena. Trust in the Master.*

He slowly drives by towards the car park exit and they, dodging the Shark's arse, begin their patrol. Although it is dark, the illuminated stars on the disco's sign, the car headlights and the light from the lamppost give off enough light to see every object around. They come across a pile of blankets next to the gigantic hedge that surrounds the Cosmic's car park. Convinced that some Angel or other has left them there, they tug at them to see if there is anything else worth taking.

'Ouch! Ouch! Easy uh? Eaaaasyyyy...'
'Ah, fuck! Sorryyyy, we didn't see that someone was under...' exclaims Stub.
'But! Were you sleepin' down here?' adds Zeb.
'Yeeeeah, sure, whatever. I'm an easy-going guy, I...'
'What?'
'A happy-go-lucky kinda dude, I'm just gonna sleep heeeere.'

The Cosmic disco is about to close and in this makeshift campsite, they have come up empty-handed. They decide to take the Vespas and have a beer in a bar run by two pretty cool chicks. They know the bar because they once saw the owner of the Cosmic go in for a drink and they'd love to meet him for a chat. As they were leaving the car park and about to drive onto the road, they come across the Blue Shark again as it turns back in. It passes by, almost touching them, doing 2 km an hour. The guy looks at them and, by way of greeting, smiles, nods and continues to drive by for another stroll around the parking lot.

Unfortunately, the two chicks at the bar have been replaced by a guy. The boys are the only customers so the man wastes no time serving them with three small beers and an attitude as if inviting them, given the late hour, to consume the drink quickly and piss off. They drain their beers silently within a few minutes without looking at each other, their eyes focused on the mug. On the point of getting up, the silence of the room is suddenly broken by the slamming the door. A long-haired blonde comes staggering in, barefoot, holding an almost empty bottle of Valpolicella from the neck. She walks towards them muttering something unintelligible:

'Drinke dranke cruket craket, what the fuck does this chick say?'

The ranting girl keeps pointing her finger at something outside but they, fascinated by her moves and words, just stand and stare at her from top to toe and smile while still sitting at the table.

'Yeaaaah, yeah! Bitte ein bit!'
'Hey! Hey! Hey! Kraut! Look, we're here for the two bitches at the bar...'

At this point, the bartender approaches, takes the three mugs by the handles in one hand and makes a sign to stay calm with the other, saying something in Kraut language.

'So, boys! Well, bitte ein bit doesn't mean anything. She's just asking for a ride to the city station because she wants to go to Germany by train...'

'Oh, if that's the case, I'll give her a lift...'

'Zeb! Fuck! Let her take a taxi!'

'Jà! Jà! Taxi!' Suddenly the Kraut lights up.

'Jà jà, my arse! Look, we're here for the two tarts at the bar!'

'I'll take her! There's no taxi now, is there, barman?'

'Right, there are no taxis at two thirty at night. Let me give you some advice. Take her with you, you won't regret...'

So, a little on Zeb's insistence and a little on the bartender's assurance, they accompany the chick to the Vespas and invite her to sit on Zeb's blue PX metallic seat, which is already in motion and ready to go. Angie and Stub only have time to take the bottle away from the Kraut and set the PX in motion when two more Krauts, each holding an almost empty bottle of Valpolicella from the bottleneck, jump out of the twilight. They are drunk. They are obviously the girl's friends and the boys realise they've been fucked.

'And by the way,' said the bartender from the door of the bar, 'the two girls in the bar are my daughters!'

For the entire twenty-kilometre drive from the bar to the central station, the Germans writhe, wiggle and rant incomprehensibly to the shadows of the night. Even the whores in the industrial zone have gone by now but they still keep waving and shouting to non-existent people. They finally reach the station and, fortunately, Angie's passenger understands English. At the word "station", he understands that they have arrived at their destination and, pleased, all three Germans get off the Vespas.

'Very good! Very good! Drink, drink, restaurant...'

They would now like the boys to go with them to a restaurant to drink and it takes a while to make them understand that there are no restaurants open at this time of night. The ordeal appears to be over and hopefully, they are about to get rid of their undesirable passengers when the girl holds Zeb's arm for a moment. The three Germans gather and a few moments later, put their hands in their pockets. Angie gets seven 10,000 Lire banknotes, as do Stubs and Zeb, except that the latter also gets a tip in German Marks from the blonde "corn cob". Astonished, Angie, Stub and Zeb take the road back home and, as soon as they enter Verona, when the night seems about to end, they see a girl cleaning the steps of the restaurant under the skyscraper. And so, the night finally draws to an end inside the restaurant with three pints of beer.

I'm happy and satisfy, and now I wanna have some fun
(Sharon Bailey - Cosmic Dust)

The summer is coming and, unlike last year, midweek evenings are spent between meeting at the steps and The Loss club. The weekends are usually freer from commitments. The most popular destinations are the Ferrara Riviera and the Small Studios, which is increasingly home to DJs of a certain calibre. It's hard to make a group with all these choices but it's always a pleasure to tell each other their adventures every time they meet. However, there is one deadline that must be honoured: the Loss's first birthday! Everyone feels the duty to celebrate the occasion together. Jeep and Giby's idea to celebrate at the Loss Club is a "given" but this time there is no intention of inviting half the city.

'We won't print anything this time but we will still call the party, The Loss' birthday...'

'Ooookayyyy! And we'll only invite those who move around in our square...'

'Jeep! You put some funky disco stuff on but we won't bother getting the amp from Zibri this time...'

'Two cases of beer, a case of Martini aaaand, pickles, canapés?'

'Don't forget Prosecco!'

The fast and furious decision was made just a couple of days before the party they want to throw on that following Saturday. Inviting people is not a problem. They only have to mention it to three or four guys and then let word of mouth do all the work. Shopping at the supermarket, on the other hand, is a pain in the arse because they don't want to waste a whole afternoon buying stuff.

'Take the cakes from the trolley of that old woman!'

'But she's shopping!'

'Fuck off! Do you want us to spend two hours in here looking for stuff among the shelves?'

It actually took them very little time to organise the birthday, helped by the fact that the stereo system and lights were still permanently installed so they didn't have to go back and forth to Volt's and Zibri's to pick up all the bits and also didn't need to run around the city to invite everybody. The meeting point is to be at the steps and not directly at the club. That way, the Vespas can all be lined up as, little by little, all the Loss members join the group. This is sure to attract the attention of anyone passing by and is seen as a wish for a happy birthday. The only eyesore is Fish's mismatched Cagiva. After much cheering and clapping, they shout "The Loss" in unison and off they go towards the club. The party is about to start.

Get up of that stuff! Dance, what are you waiting for. Going to the move. Come on girl let's groove. (Raydio - What are you waitin' for)

This time, instead of heading straight upstairs to the incantation room, the lovers, like Fish and Biby, his latest chick, stay on the ground floor to dance with everyone else. But, Giby is suffering, he has a crush on a girl and she still hasn't shown up.

'Hasn't Vanna arrived yet?'

'No, hmmm, no, I can't see her...'

'Listen, Angie, can you go and see if she's still there with her pals? Can you ask her if she likes me?'

'Gibyyyy, we all know that with chicks you're like a Selzer. After the bubbles, everything's back to normal...'

'Nooo nooo, go and ask. Please. Come on!'

Knowing how famous Giby is for falling hopelessly in love with a girl in five seconds flat and then getting bored with her at the same speed, Angie still concedes and, taking Tollbridge with him, goes to the small square where Vanna usually hangs out with friends. Luckily, she is still there and Angie gets straight to the point.

'Why didn't you come to the party? Giby's waiting for you...'

'Giby?'

'Yeah, He said he really likes you...'

'Ahhh nooo! I'm going out with Nick. Tell him I don't care...'

They go back to the party to tell Giby, who, not surprisingly, is already smashed. Interestingly though, one of Vanna's friends has followed them and, without giving them time to report the bad news to Giby, spurts out desperately:

'Wait, wait, wait a sec. Vanna has changed her mind. She told me that she does like Giby...'

'Gibyyyy! She said she likes you! She wants to go out with you...'

Giby, however, in a drunken, yet calm voice, manages to piece together one sentence.

'Ahhh nooo! Tell her I don't care anymoooore...'

Never could believe the things you do to me. Never could believe the way you are.   (Hot Chocolate - Every 1's a winner)

The biggest problem of the evening though, is that even Jeep gets drunk. Without a fully functional DJ, the needles start to screech and, at around midnight, the party loses bite. The situation doesn't bode well for the Club's continual existence when the gang realises that taking Jeep and Giby home to their parents, who live in the same court of houses, in their present condition would only make his mum and dad even less inclined to look kindly on them, especially after the mess at the previous "Loss Party".

'Hey! I hear Pope got dumped by his chick. Let's go over there so that I can try to bang her?'

'Finger! Fuck off! We have to take Jeep and Giby somewhere to get some air!'

Together, they decide to take them to the lake but before leaving, there is yet another problem. The throttle wire on Jake's ET3 breaks, or rather, it comes off the grip. At this point, Jake has a brainwave. He opens the seat and removes the throttle wire from the sheath on the carburettor side and links it up to the front brake lever.

'This way, when I pull on the front brake, I'll speed up! If I need to brake, I'll use the foot brake.'

He goes ten metres and smashes against the wall of the building adjacent to the club. One Loss less. Fish can't help but laugh and lay into Jake with some first-class piss-taking, and when he finally sets off, having forgotten to unlock the steering lock, he also crashes to the ground with Jake within a couple of metres, only to have Jake return the favour. Two Loss less.

'But, where will we fuckin' go at this time of night at the lake!'

'Let's try... the Caneva?'

The Caneva is a disco in Lazise located inside a new water park of the same name. Once they get there, they realise something is wrong. The cars are all good quality, clean, well-kept and neatly

parked. The people are calm and collected, quiet and well-dressed.
'Ahhhh! Fuckin' hell! They're paninaros!'
'Go, go, come on! Shall we go to the Cosmic?'
They hang out in the square outside the Cosmic long enough for Jeep and Giby to clear their heads and listen to some new wave-post punk pieces coming out of the tunnel.

And you may find yourself. Living in a shotgun shack, and you may find yourself...   (Talking Heads - Ones in a lifetime)

After a while, they head home but soon realise that something is wrong. Vale and one of the gypsies are missing. They have left them behind at the Cosmic. They turn back and find the two wandering around the square in front of the disco. While not at all upset by being abandoned, they are filthy and extremely annoyed by something else.
'What happened to you?'
'We had to pee so we went behind the Cosmic and slipped into the ditch!'
They head home again but, on the way back, they decide to go to the bar where the "two not-bad chicks" are. They park the PXs in the courtyard in front of the entrance and climb the two of three steps to the door where they can already see who is behind the counter. Unfortunately, the girls are not there. They can't decide whether going in and thanking their father for the large tip the kraut eaters had given them last time would be a good idea seeing that they had also spoken ill of his daughters. In the end they go back to the Vespas and start them up. Just as they turn towards the main road, two guys jump out of the twilight.
'Heyyyy! Heyyyy, caaaan youuuu give us a lift...'
'Bloody hell! Does everyone hide in there? Stoned and smashed?'
'Easyyyy, old man, easyyyy, we're two easy-going guyyyys...'
'What?'
'Bro! broooo, whatever! Just happy-go-lucky dudes, man...'
'Hey! Aren't you the guy who was sleeping under the blankets in front of the Cosmic?'
It certainly is him except now there are two of them. For the entire twenty-kilometre drive from the bar to the Croce Bianca area of Verona, the Angels writhe, wiggle and rant incomprehensibly to

the shadows of the night. Even the whores in the industrial zone have gone by now but they still keep waving and shouting to non-existent people. They finally reach the suburbs of the city and leave them to their fate. The remaining Loss members go back to the club with Jeep and Giby, who have now sobered up.

To their surprise, a blue Dyane is parked in front of the club door.

'Suri! Tex! What the fuuuuck are you doin' here?'

'Uh! We came to the party, late...'

But they are not alone. The door of the club, faintly lit by the beams of light from the Vespas, opens. Their attention is caught by the movement and in order to see what's happening, Volt revs up his PX. The revolutions of the engine make the scooter's beam of light strong enough to clearly make out the contours of the door. The light, which alternatively loses its vigour and revives again in rhythm with the revs, is more than enough to frame Poplar, who stayed at the house to continue partying with Mara, leaving behind a smell of cum.

☺

Summer is not all fun; it also means study and work. Those who work already have their responsibilities and duties. Students, on the other hand, try to earn a little extra cash wherever they can before returning to their books. Angels, whose parents own a shop, lend a helping hand while others find seasonal work in a store or something similar. Those with strong arms offer their services to agriculture, picking fruit or carrying out some heavier activity. Jeep, for example, helps his parents in their own cleaning company and Angie is happy to join him. Their job is to clean the new BMW warehouses at Lake Garda and, although they leave at dawn to get there and spend the day cleaning baseboards with solvents, plans for the weekend are never far from their minds.

'Hey, you two! Are you working? Oooor...'

'We were just thinking of going camping for the weekend...'

This year, Jeep and Giby's parents are spending the whole summer at the Val Verde resort near Brescia, a few kilometres from the lake and a few kilometres from Bedizzole and Les Cigales club. While the first Loss members' postcards begin to arrive either from the sea or mountains, at 4 pm on a fantastic summer Saturday, armed with sleeping bags, Tacky, Angie, Jeep and Giby, together with Bert, Tacky's brother, are already on four PXs riding towards

Val Verde. This time, not wanting to waste time in bullshit along the way, they speed towards the campsite so they can spend as much time as possible in that oasis. After about thirty minutes, however, Tacky signals a stop and asks for a break. In the parking lot of the Thucana club, a bottle of Prosecco pops out from the glovebox of Jeep's PX, and the stop ends up in a game of cops and robbers with the 'crime' being possession of hashish. However, after only half an hour, a familiar figure emerges from the side of the building with an even more acidic look than before and, as they depart, the Sweeper just picks up the empty bottle of Prosecco. At half past five, they are already in the neighbourhood of Bedizzole when Jeep and Giby signal another stop. According to them, a Vespa-cross in the gravel pit is an absolute must. By now the terraces on this man-made mountain have been battered by bulldozers and actually go quite high. The fear of being on the edge of a precipice messes with the Prosecco bubbles but curiosity wins the day and they climb to the top, even if they have to dismount and push the bikes on the last stretch.

The excursion ends classically with their trousers round their ankles and bare arses kissed by the valley air.

They drive into the holiday village without being asked for identification. The chick in charge of check-in was on duty in the cage at the entrance but she doesn't turn a hair as they pass her by. Looking from the little window with her elbows on the wooden windowsill, she follows them with her eyes as they advance at walking pace. She's trying to figure out what is under that layer of dust and mud covering them from head to toe and from front to back rack. It's like a scene from a western when the sheriff, sitting in a rocking chair, sees five bandits coming into town, including the black hat. The PXs proceed in first gear at the minimum speed allowed, which causes the motorbikes to advance by small hiccups, surprising the passengers every time. They switch off their engines in front of Giby's tent and lean their motorbikes on their stands. While Jeep sits on the seat, cleaning his glasses with his shirt, Angie gets off and starts banging his black hat on his thigh. Tacky and Bert, on the other hand, start flogging their shirt and trousers with their hands. Faced with this scene, Jeep and Giby parents, who were just finishing setting the table with the final details, stop in mid-air for a moment as if turned to stone. It's about eight o'clock in the evening. The table erases every care and every defect.

STONED ANGELS

CICADAS, SISTERS, IN THE SUN WITH YOU I HIDE IN THE THICK OF THE POPLARS AND WAIT FOR THE STARS.
(SALVATORE QUASIMODO[27])

The singing of the cicadas accompanies them from the campsite to Les Cigales. Jeep and Giby plan to have a mega party at the club since it would provide the best opportunity to enrich the baggage of Moses' records. The night in the disco has already begun and the notes of "Super Kumba" by Manu Dibango make them dance from the ticket box all the way to the dance floors. With this Afro music, you could dance all night and that's what they intend to do.

Everybody run, run, run, yeah. Everybody scatter scatter, yeah. Some people lost some bread. (Fela Kuti- Sorrow, tears and blood)

'Afroooo, you don't listen to it! You live it!'

Les Cigales. The booth.

---

27 *Nobel prize for literature and translator of the works of Moliere and William Shakespeare.*

Suddenly the music stops and, although disoriented, everyone stays on the dance floor waiting for it to start up again so they can back to dancing. But the spotlights turn up toward the ceiling and everyone looks around in dismay. A big question swirls around the room. Is it only an ephemeral encounter? An encounter between night and day? No one has ever seen Les Cigales fully illuminated by day and to be sure, only very few among the Angels have ever seen a club "dead". Dogs on leashes come in making a considerable effort to pull the carabinieri policemen holding them. Their paws grope on the smooth floor without finding a precise direction. It's a drug raid. They are forced to remain in and out of the club while the search takes place. The last police cars pull away at half past one in the night, too late to start again. When all seems lost and the evening ruined with only a sad tent awaiting them, their ever-faithful companion, the summer night, comes to their aid. "Summer night" is the most beautiful combination of words ever, a catalyst of good mood. From above, the stars tickle your hair, from below, the fresh grass tickles your bare feet and your tent fills with laughter until it bursts.

'Up with vulvaaaas!' Screams Giby.

'Up with vaginaaaas!' Shouts Jeep.

Let's groove tonight. Share the spice of life. Baby slice it right. We're gonna groove tonight.   (Earth, Wind & Fire - Let's Groove)

To speak of "awakening" is rather risky and should be followed by "out of a vegetative state". The idea is to go back to meet the others and start discussing the party that Jeep and Giby want to throw at the club. The village bar is a well-stocked establishment offering delicious confectionery. A cappuccino and four doughnuts fill the hole in the brain and around noon, they are already on their Vespas, destination Vrrr2000.

The entrance to Vrrr2000 has a cloakroom on one side and a babe in a ticket office on the other. A few metres ahead along a slightly curve corridor, another chick snatches the tickets under a wide, shadow-filled arch that is the real entrance. The twilight plays in the favour of needy, penniless Angels. Two people can get in with a single ticket and split the cost. The ticket has two sections and the girl at the entrance tears the shorter part.

By holding the ticket in your hand, almost covering it entirely

with your thumb so that only the bottom of the coupon is visible, in the complicit safety of the penumbra and with a friendly smirk aimed at the girl, she tears the other part, the piece that isn't valid.
'Will you give me a kiss?' you might say to mislead her.
After five minutes, you go out, get stamped and hand the ticket to your friend. Needless to say, the Angel with the ticket goes in getting the right part of the ticket torn while the other friend displays his stamp.
'How about a quick lick?' just to mislead her again.
The whole Loss gang all together at last, happily making decisions about the next party at the club.
☺
A week of work goes by quickly in the BMW warehouses and Saturday morning soon rolls round again. Angie and Jeep are proud to have done all their work. They can now look forward to meeting Jeep's mother, the owner of the cleaning company, at the campsite to get their pay. Around 11:30, after having finished emptying the baskets in the offices, they dash off on Jeep's PX towards Brescia. A few kilometres from the village, at the crossroads for Bedizzole, Jeep stops and turns off the Vespa. Intending to set the motorbike on its stand, Angie gets off, as does Jeep and, before Angie can ask "why?", the answer appears. Jeep opens the glovebox and, this time, there are two bottles of Prosecco.
'Are we on the bubble?'
They celebrate the end of their work by emptying one of the bottles, saving the other one for the evening. They arrive at the campsite at about one o'clock where Jeep's parents are waiting for them with two plates of delicious pasta and their pay. It's the first time in their lives that Angie and Jeep have ever seen a whole one hundred thousand Lire banknote and, quite frankly, they have no idea how to spend it wisely.

Gimme money. Gimme yours. It's all depends on your choice.
(Bill Summers & Summers Heat - Straight to the Bank)

However, they soon come up with some. Jeep wants to spend the afternoon in Brescia city centre to buy new records for the next party. Angie, on the other hand, wants to find something to wear and so, following the indications of Brescia Angels, nobody is going to do him out of a nice pair of Levis from "Strawberry field", "Moon

Strass" or "Casbah". After shopping, Jeep has another wish to fulfil: he wants to meet DJ Meo in person so, a lovely evening at Les Cigales is imminent.

After leaving the records in the camp and dining with the parents, the boys head out to take a look at The Typhoon club, a disco recommended by the Brescia Angels. Once they arrive, they take one look at the Angels wandering around and instinctively express their judgment.

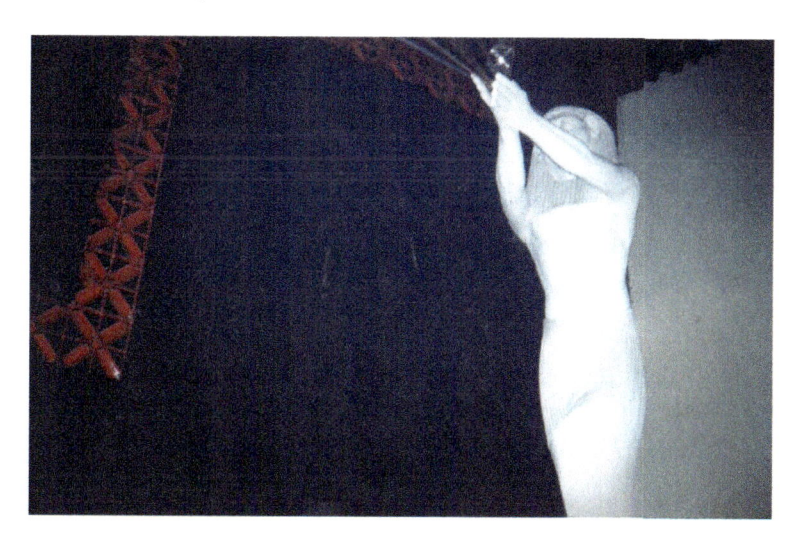

Typhoon club. An Egyptian statue fired a laser beam.

'What vulvas! Up with vulvaaaas!'

The second bottle of Prosecco further enlivens the evening.

'The vagina! The vagina!'

'So, Jeep! What do you want to call the next party? Have you already thought about it?'

'Summer party! Yes, summer party aaaand, with two DJs, this time...'

'Two? Who?'

'Yeah, two, just like at the disco. My pal Sygno is coming. Just wait and see what a show!'

The agglomeration of Angels in front of the Typhoon is getting awesome.

'Are you two talking about a party?'

Jeep and Angie want to appear innocent as if they don't know what they were talking about.

'Yyyyeeeesssss?'

'Sorry, it isn't today. DJ Beppe Loda, the Sun party, here at the Typhoon. He did it in March, too late, I'm sorry...'

'Oh, nnnnnnnooooo!'

A thousand people at least, but they have Les Cigales in mind and so, away they ride again to Bedizzole.

Jeep's wish comes true. The end of the evening finds him waiting for Meo outside his booth and, in addition to exchanging a thousand jokes with the DJ, he also gets to meet his colleague, Daniele. To their delight, they discover that he too is part of the group of DJs who hold the banner for "alternative music". The career of DJ Daniele started at the Titos discotheque in Verona following which, he went on to become the DJ at Les Pois. He was the one who, having Rubens as his reference, immortalised stratospheric "Hawaiian" and "Flower" parties in every Angel.

In the morning, advancing on their elbows and crawling for about half a metre, they poke their heads out of the tent. With one eye closed and the other half open, they look at their surroundings which, from such a problematic awakening, still appear foggy. Today they plan to laze by the edge of the pool but, as the oxygen reaches their brains, they realise that something is about to make them change their minds. Jeep's uncle is standing there looking at them, his legs and arms crossed, leaning his arse against his fairy tale chassis, a light ivory convertible Mercedes Pagoda.

'Rabbit Island Bay?'

How do you get super-hot in 15 minutes? Just take the road that links the holiday village to Rabbit Island, a mere ten kilometres in a light ivory convertible Mercedes Pagoda. In an astronomical car like this, your sub-communication changes. Your body language is different and you acquire such confidence that movements slow down and gestures are no longer hectic. The wind in your hair, mirrored sunglasses, printed smile.

'Fuckin' hell! Should we walk to the island?'

'What if the radio gets wet?'

The island is nothing more than a natural extension of the mainland. A headland that starts from Manerba and submerges for a metre or so until it reaches San Biagio Island. They carry the radio high above their heads in the same way as the soldiers in Apocalypse

Now held their rifles to keep them out of the mud. But here the waters are crystal clear and despite a few cuts on their feet, the day goes by quietly between diving, sun and some quiet funky songs.

You come in numbers to feel a groove. I have a groove to make you act a fool.The night feels funky, the Sun is here.(Sun - Sun is here)

Everything is ready for the party and everyone is wandering about the neighbourhood inviting people. Angie and Zeb are in charge of attracting new people and going to collect the money for the coming "high party" after the others have been round to ask the gangs they already know. Riding either Angie's or Zeb's PX, they wander through the local streets where they think they will arouse particular interest. While stationary at a give-way sign, they see two hotties sitting on their Ciao in the distance. Angie engages the first gear and, with a sharp acceleration, heads in the direction of the two girls. The front-wheel lifts slightly and the motorbike leaves a cloud of smoke behind due to exhaust accumulation when the Vespa has been idle with minimum revs of the engine. Zeb already has his arm outstretched with the invitation in hand but the two chicks, seeing their menacing silhouette approaching, move off and drive away. It doesn't take long to catch them up but it does take a little longer to flank them due to the neighbourhood's narrow network of streets.
'Heyyyy, it's just a partyyyy...'
'An invitatioooon...'
The girls give in at last.
'But, aren't you Pope's girlfriend?' asks Zeb.
'Nnnnnoooo, not anymore, I've...' the girl replies curtly.
'Sorry! Sorry! I remember now. Finger goes out with you...'
'Nnnnnoooo, I'm going out with a guy from the same crowd. The one who goes cycling...'
'Shit! Heyhey is fucking Finger's chick!'
The guy/girl scene is certainly spectacular! Sony dumps Stub, who doesn't care and goes out with Birdie and so on. A girl's ex-boyfriend goes out with another boy's ex-girlfriend. Finger goes out with Vale, who then dumps him and goes out with Zeb, but since Birdie dumps Stub, Finger goes out with Birdie. A certain Niki asks Angie if he wants to go out with her but he says no, then he changes his mind and she sends him a definite "fuck you". He's currently going out with Monica after Sony also sent him a "fuck you". They

are all "exes" going out with "exes" but, despite that, all the neighbourhood gangs are invited to the same party: the sector A gang, the GolosAngeles gang, the Wall gang... with bags of money in the kitty. For example, at the wall, while the Loss are handing out invitations, they receive an unexpected visit. Suri's Dyane with Tex poking out of the sunroof and Suri himself, joint in mouth, stops at the Wall gang gathering. A tinkling sound coming from under the front seats is so loud that it attracts everyone's attention. Suri's sudden braking as he drew up has caused bottles and bottles to collide with each other on the floor of the car. Sitting in the passenger seat next to Suri is a new character. Height - not very tall; hair - not very long; eyes - not very big; face - not very square; look - not very Angel. The name says it all.

'My pleasure! I'm Vinitaly!'

The open door of the Dyane reveals bottles of beer and wine tumbling under the seats.

'Fancy a beer?'

Vinitaly doesn't have a corkscrew and neither does he place the crown of the cap on a ledge and, using the Mount of Venus part of his hand, try to open it with a single blow. Nor does he use a car key to uncork a bottle. Vinitaly uses his molars! Vinitaly can uncork any bottle by clenching the tin cap between his teeth as if they were the bottle-opener slot on a Pepsi-Cola vending machine.

'Fuckin' hell! We've got a new barman for the club!'

People start arriving at 9.30 pm as instructed by the organisers. Pepper, in his Shark, continues to pick anyone without their own transport up. It's a fantastic scene. Arrivals are met with beams of light and music coming out of the club, several Loss members dancing, PXs, ET3s and Ciaos parked all around and Pepper's Shark dropping people off in a constant coming and going. The entire scene is embraced by the twilight and the DJs accompany it with Herbie Hancock's fantastic "The Twilight Clone". There are people from Milan and Brescia that the gang had met in Les Cigales or at the campsite. There are people that nobody has ever seen before, like Bulgaria and Chicken. Nobody knows who invited them and if they paid but at this point, the situation is already out of control and it hardly matters. At midnight, everybody is still there. Nobody has left at all, a sure sign that, this time, the party is a real bomb. A time bomb. They dance.

You're just sixteen. You're all I got. Feel up, but don't give up, don't give up. (Grace Jones - Feel up)

They drink. After giving out beer bottles, Vinitaly takes out the empties and stacks them in the square, sucking the last few drops out of each one before adding it to the heap. The pile soon takes the shape of a 1.5-metre-high pyramid. The width is uncertain.

They fuck. But not upstairs in the crowded incantation room because seventy mostly curious people, are going up and down the stairs to look around and join the smokers. Volt is the first victim when sees his R4 rocking in its parking space.

'Who the fuck is fuckin' in my car?'

The door is locked but he insists so much that he gets an answer from the inside. The window opens just enough for him to recognise Finger inside. But instead of an apologetic voice coming from within, a condom full of cum is placed over the pane of glass and then the window is wound up and closed so that the used condom is left dangling on the outside.

Do lovers ever need to hide? The things they really feel inside. If you won't show your heart to me. (Level 42 - Love games)

In this turmoil of freaky people, the toilet bowl is uprooted from the bathroom and placed in the middle of the room. Too bad that everything is broken. As if it were a Juju[28], people dance around it to the notes of a wild DJ Moses with one of his favourite African songs.

Remember! I was fire! Yeah! Yeah! Usted!
(Usted Del Fuego - Usted)

As if that were not enough, all the nearby road and location signs have been removed and piled up in the bathroom. Only The Loss Club signs have been left up so people can find the way. Despite everything, the chicks are having such a good time that one of them asks the Loss to come over to the campsite.

'What do you want Filly? Do you want to give me a hand job?'

'No wayyyy, I'm inviting you to the campsite because I'm giving

---

[28] *Juju man (by Passport) was an important track at Baia degli Angeli.*

a party in August?'
'Oh, Holy cow! Why not!'
It's time to break ranks. Zeb goes on holiday to France, Giby goes to Belgium, Poplar slinks off to Venice and many more disappear to who knows where. The coolest expedition is won by Stub, Pepper, Volt, Tacky and Zeb who decide to go to Florence on their Vespas. Those who stay at home always find a place to spend the long summer evenings. Riding downtown with Suri, Tex and Vinitaly in the Dyane is a sure way to piss oneself laughing. Every night, whenever Suri sees some chick on a balcony, in a window or just on the street, he stops.
'Hiiii, Come for a little ride with us?'
'Bugger off!'
Then Suri, with his usual foolish smile, gets back in the car, drives away, goes around the neighbourhood and comes back after half an hour to the place where the chick rejected him.
'By the way! You don't know what you missed!'
And off he drives again. And the scene repeats itself over and over again in similar situations.
'Suriiiii! Won't we run out of petrol?'
Suri never worries about such things. He gets out, unscrews the cap of the tank and invites everyone else to pile out.
'Come on! Everybody on one side and shake the car!'
With one ear leaning against the fuel vent, he gives his verdict.
'Five kilometres!'
When Suri is thirsty, he has two options. Either he asks old ladies for a glass of wine, or he goes to a melon field in the countryside during the night.
'Where the fuck do you wanna go Suri? To Pablo 3? To Melamara? We're getting close to Mantua!'
'Shush, shush, fuckin' hell!'
Suri takes them to a pitch-black country road. The only lights come from distant farms, otherwise there is total darkness and the harvested crops give a minimum sense of civilization. He comes to a halt, turns off the engine, gets out, jumps across the narrow ditch that runs along the gravel road and sinks into the darkness into surreal silence. Minutes go by when, all of a sudden, growls can be heard coming from the field he disappeared into. The snarls turn into threatening barks, getting louder and louder until the others imagine their friend is being mauled to pieces. A few seconds go by

and they hear muffled blows. The barks turn into whimpers that gradually recede further and further away. Suri comes out of the field with two melons in his hands.
'Christ! What the fuck, did you...'
'I kicked it in the balls a couple of times!'

Dancing in the city. You got to be hot, to be cool. Volume is so pretty. (Vicki Sue Robinson - Hot Summer Night)

The holidays around the world don't last an eternity. To forget the sadness of homecomings, Giby proposes spending the mid-August bank holiday, which falls on a Saturday this year, at the Valverde Campsite. Like Jeep's, Giby's parents also own a caravan on a permanent plot now and, seeing how many agree, Giby books a tent where they can all sleep as of Friday. And so, Suri, Vinitaly, Poplar, Pack, Tacky, Volt and Pepper, to name but a few, seize the chance and go to the holiday village on the same day. Towards evening, when Zeb finishes his shift at the paper factory, he and Angie leave for Bedizzole and, even though they get the umpteenth fine near Desenzano, in about an hour, they join the others. Despite the Angels' look, Jeep's father greets them with a smile at reception to authorise their entry. It wouldn't be the first time that a story might be heard of parents on holiday at a seaside hotel pretending not to know their children when they turn up for dinner unannounced because they don't want to make a bad impression in front of their friends who are sitting at the same table in the restaurant.
'Heyyyy! Hiiii Lossss...'
'Heyyyy, here comes Angie and Zeb, shit! You missed the Vinitaly aperitif!'
'Really? What?'
'He brought Clinto[29]!'
'Fuckin' hell! That's a good start, huh? But what about food?'
'Chill, he also brought that...'
'Vinitalyyy! What did you make for dinner?'
'My password! Salami, onions and Clinto!'
'Gibyyy! The tent?'
'The tent is there. That's where you'll all sleep and tomorrow night at Les Cigales, DJ Rubens will be playing a great groove!'

---

29 A type of wine. Explanation to follow.

They spend the evening telling each other about the adventures they had during their holidays and, among all the positive experiences, one makes them particularly sad. The dancer, Stefania Rotolo has passed away. She starred with Sammy Bardot, the Charlie Club's DJ in Rome, where they met and he wanted her with him on the TV show Piccolo Slam. Her dancing so enlivened evenings that even the boys had learned some moves to perform in the disco.

'What the fuck are you doing Vinitaly?'

'Nothin'! I'll show you how to open a bottle without a corkscrew with three nails stuck in the cork.'

'In my opinion, he gave himself a fix!'

'On the fly, as well...'

'Haaaaaa, that could be the right name! Flying trip!'

'What the fuck are you saying, Jeep?'

'The name of the next party at the club! Fly or, flying trip!'

Awakening out of, you could say, an unconscious state, is a risky business. Ten people sleeping in a tent meant for five and with Vinitaly, who continues to eat sweet and sour onions all night, is a severe deal. If then someone else blows off a garlic, salami and smoke mix, the smell of feet is a small concern. The main thing is to get some sleep and try not to crush Angie's black hat.

Eyelids slowly detach, leaving a horizontal fissure for the pupils and nose bubbles burst at the first facial movement. A gentle tug on the balls and a little arm stretch are the early preparations for the next moves. The first thing the eyes really focus on is the hole in the village toilet in an attempt to piss in it. The village snack bar is a well-stocked establishment offering delicious pastries. A cappuccino and four doughnuts fill the hole in the brain and the afternoon is spent by the pool waiting for sunset.

The sky finally dances with the colours of the sunset and the new vacationers, who have music under their skin, go dancing beneath it.

But something is wrong at Les Cigales. It's Saturday night, mid-August and hardly anyone is there or, at least, the crowd of Angels that is usually getting ready to go in is not there. Unfortunately, when they ask around, they are told that there is an air of crisis due to continuous raids by the Police.

'Too many toxics?'

'What shall we do? Shall we go to the Cosmic?'

Leaving Les Cigales at full speed, they reach the Cosmic in half an hour and something is different here too. People are waiting to go in because they want to see all the stars of the Cosmic inscription turned on. The lucky ones who own a camera even pose for a souvenir photo.

'We are also among the stars of the Cosmic!'
'It's like someone threw a handful of them up there!'
'Spatial times!'

Someone says. But the boys go straight in. They don't want to miss the first pieces that are usually super cool. And the Cosmic certainly doesn't disappoint them. Their feet begin to itch with "Chiropodie No. 1" by Sky and "Lescudiak" by Michael Chapman and away with "Turkey Roll" by the Rah Band. A fantastic evening made even more memorable because those who didn't come to the campsite, meet them all here. Genny, Drug, George and many others, all in chorus in the square.

'Fuuuuk! We forgot that Filly invited us tonight to her little party at the Garda Campsiiiite...'
'Shit! Nobody went...'

The final piece they listen to is Mike Oldfield's "Charleston". They leave the club and go their separate ways. While the others return to Valverde, Tacky, Angie and Giby give in to the two gipsies' desire to go back to the city. A quick word with Valvoline, the lighting man from Vrrr2000, who is also here, and they set off.

Later that night, on the way back to town, they decide to go to the bar where the two "not bad chicks" are. Switching off their PXs in the small court in front of the entrance, they peek inside. Unfortunately, the girls are not there again. To avoid a dressing-down from the father in front of the gipsies, having spoken ill of his daughters, they get back on their Vespas and go. At GolosAngeles, they drop the girls off and, just as they make their way home for what seems the last date with the night, something fishy attracts their attention. Driving calmly side by side at 40 km an hour on their PXs along the long, deserted road through the industrial zone, they notice the outline of a greenish car parked at the give-way sign of a crossroad. The nose of the car is invading the other lane. As they go round it, they cast a glance to see which fucking jerk has planted himself in the middle of the road with a greenish Renault R4 at 3.30 in the morning. A half-bald, rabid guy in a plaid shirt like a Village People worker, maybe with a beard and, beside him, a really scary figure. An old, angry, frowning and gloomy-looking black woman, staring forward as if she wants to eat the hood. She is wearing a hat, like the Queen of England, adorned with fake flowers and covered with a type of black netting that is usually lowered over the face. She is tightly clutching a black handbag to her belly. These are the only details they notice because, as soon as they overtake the car, the guy begins to rev the engine as if he were waiting for a chequered flag to drop. Grinding on the gearbox, he shoots off with a screech of tyres. Clinging to their PXs, the boys immediately realise that the two crazy fools want to run them down. The PXs speed up at full throttle. The pursuit begins through the streets of the industrial zone. All they can hear behind them is the engine turning over so high that the pistons must surely jump out. To try to shake them off, they take side roads that they know to be full of bends, but to no avail, the two spirits, bent on turning the night into Armageddon, are still on their heels. They hear the scratchings, gratings and scrapings of the gears as if the driver isn't able to change them properly. He is, however, good at keeping the throttle at full speed. Shivers. Leaning the PX into a curve, Angie scratches the asphalt with the footboard seriously risking a crash. They look back occasionally to see if they have put any distance between them but all that does, is heighten their fear at the sight of those half-mad and wild faces. Fear. Dread. Nevertheless, as soon as they reach sector C, the game turns in their favour. Relief. They know the streets and alleys like the back of their hands and it's a piece of cake to fuck their pursuers up. Comfort. Finally, the adventure ends and, to relax, they take advantage of Tacky's couch to smoke and watch an educational porn film on the Capodistria Channel.

'Angie! For the first time, I saw sparks coming out from under your PX!'

☺

The Forst pub in the city centre is the meeting place at which to dot the i's and cross the t's for the next party at the club. Given the success of the last event, there is little to change but new friends, such as Suri or Vinitaly, can be given further assignments for constant improvement. The enlightening ideas that pop up over a few beers are disarmingly brilliant. The first is that Jeep wants to start with danceable background music and then, at a certain point, play the theme song, like at a disco, and then continue with rhythmic songs. Another idea is to make a deal with a little all-night grocery store rather than buy tons of beers and keep them at the bar of the club and then Vinitaly, the bartender, can take the shuttle in case more are needed. A further suggestion is to have a similar agreement with a local chemist in case the need for more condoms arises. The last suggestion is to pay particular attention to the drinks that chicks prefer to get drunk on.

'Remember to buy Johnnie Walker because Birdie likes to dance with that...'

The invitation cards are ready and the organisational machine is in motion. While everyone more or less knows where to go to invite people, Suri's technique is quite particular. Driving his Dyane 6, he goes on patrol in the outskirts of the city and, where there are buildings, stops in the adjacent square where the local inhabitants are socialising and trying to enjoy a little fresh air.
Suri lets out a phantasmagorical shout!

'Mmmoooonicaaaaa! Monicaaa! Monica!'

If there is a Monica and she comes towards him, he gives her an invitation card. If he gets no response, he simply changes the name until someone is caught.

There are a lot of new people at the party. The club can't contain them all.

'But how many actual payers did we get?'

'Eighty-five, buuuut, there are a lot of clever arses. They sneak in and out. I've no fuckin' idea...'

Fernanda and her friend Tic are there. The old friends Panda, Mila, Sony, Cleopatra and Rissole arrive first. Paola and Irene, the last to be picked up by Poplar, also arrive. New acquaintances called Solid and Parallel Tits have also accepted the invitation and there are a lot of... Monicas.

I took my baby to Sunshine Hotel. Just walk on in. No needs ring the bell.
(Richard T Bear - Sunshine Hotel)

Vinitaly shows up with his latest flame, John Lennon, because she wears round goggles, a precious helper to go back and forth to get beers and condoms. The Padua gang also turns up and the party takes off with the theme song chosen by the DJs, "Prophecy" by Moebius followed by a pounding "Japanese Girl" by the Italian group Gaznevada. Someone also invited the Goat gang, a group of blaspheming yokels. Each sentence starts with "fuck" and ends with "shit".

*Don't stop the music. Don't stop. Uuuuu I say it again. Don't stop...
(K.I.D - Don't stop)*

The vomiting area is outside and, since the toilet is still broken from last time, there are groups on the club square that only go to piss and groups that only go to shit. Lined up like athletes in a 100-metre race, they spring forward at the "pop" of a newly uncorked bottle of Prosecco.

Hot whispers in the night. I'm captured by your spell. Oh yes I'm touched by this show of emotion... (Spider - Better be good to me)

Some say you reap what you sow, others call it karma.
'But, aren't you the one who told me you had a crush on a friend of mine?'
'Yeeeeaaaah!'
'Good! Here, she is!'
'Weeeell, what the fuck! I don't even know her! I only said it so you'd bring your pal too!'

Why don't mind mind your own business. Why don't mind mind your own business... (Sandy Steele - Mind Your Own Business)

And there are inconveniences. Intent on bringing chicks to the party, Pepper has an accident in his Shark and smashes a window.
'Shit, Pepper! What happened?'
'Noooothing! I hit a greenish R4 with two wild-eyed guys in it, aaaand, I fled the scene...'
Although the party is the best they have ever given, the desire to have another one before the end of the summer is really strong. Unfortunately, Jeep and Giby come bearing news that the residents of the hamlet have complained about the revolution that has been going on around the club and are threatening to call the police and get it closed down. This forces them to downsize the parties and pay more attention to who wants to go and have sex inside the club.

☺

The Forst pub in the city centre is once again the meeting place at which to dot the i's and cross the t's for the next party at the club to celebrate the birthdays of Vale, Volt and Vinitaly: the VVV Party! Vale is going to be sixteen while Volt and Vinitaly are turning twenty. The decision made is wise and prudent: in addition to the Loss, they intend to invite the gangs that rotate near them which would already make a large number of partygoers. They agree on no excesses this time and to let the music be the main speaker. Everything must be done to prevent someone from calling the Carabinieri.

'Angieee! I'm leaving the Shark here. Can you lend me your Vespa? I'm going to get some weed; I'll be as fast as I can...'

'Sure, go aheeeead.'

In the company of Rissole and Bea, a Shark left there with the keys in it is just too inviting. Angie and the two girls drive away on the pretext of tracking down one of their friends, Emily "four speeds", and begging her to come to the VVV Party. He drives round and round. They finally track her down, she gets in the car and, just as they are about to go back to the steps, Pepper comes out from a side road on Angie's PX and blocks the car by cutting off the road.

'Shit, Angie! You don't even have a licence! What if you get stopped?'

Taking command of the car and leaving the Vespa to Angie, Pepper hot wheels and skids angrily away with the three hotties still in the Shark. He only drives about thirty metres when a Carabinieri police car coming from the opposite direction, notices his Formula 1 style departure. They block him by cutting off the road and, guns in fist, jump out of their vehicle yelling at him to get out of the car. The scene with Pepper, hands on the car roof and three petrified chicks sitting on the back seat, soon draws a crowd. The search begins and, since the agents only find his wallet and a packet of Marlboro fags, it seems that it will end up as a routine check. But curiosity or experience induces one of the two policemen to open the packet of cigarettes where he finds a piece of foil containing hashish.

The policeman roughly turns Pepper around to face him. 'Where did you get this? Who gave it to you?' he asks, grinding the tips of Pepper's toes with the heel of his boot. After making the three chicks get out of the vehicle and taking everyone's details, they start a full search of the Shark. Even the seats are taken out but nothing else is found. The Carabinieri realise that no big sting is about to go down so they finally leave the scene of the crime but not before giving Pepper a heavy fine. Once the Shark has been put back together, they all head for the party. The VVV Party can begin.

Do you remember the 21st night of September? Love was changing the minds of pretenders...   (Earth, Wind & Fire - September)

> 'Hey! Pepper! What happened to the grass?'
> 'Carabinieri took it. By the way, did Pussycat come?'
> 'Pussycat? Oh yeah, she's in...'
> They dance to an immense "In A Gadda Vida" by Julia Keen & Pin Up Stick.
> 'Hey! Weren't we supposed to go to Tic's party at the Cisano Campsite?'
> 'Fuckery fuck! Nobody went...'

We move, in mysterious ways. We move. Slip and slide. Cut through the haze.   (Visage - We move)

    The party ends with Hugo and Giby, staggeringly drunk, going in search of Birdie who, totally stoned, is thought to be wandering around the streets of the hamlet. Although the party was contained, the pressure is on Jeep and Giby, who, since their parents own the house, are responsible for it. They decide to suspend the parties in expectation of better times and keep the club just for skulking. No sooner said than done. One night Jeep, Giby, Tacky, Suri go to the club to fuck and lock themselves in. At one point in the night, Poplar also goes there and, on finding the door closed and not being able to get in, drives his Golf round the corner to fuck in the car. When he sees the others going by, he realises that the club is empty and overturns the situation. Forcing the door open, he goes in and locks it from the inside. The others, who, for some reason, come back, now find that they can't get in. These recurrent situations cause arguments among the Loss and continuous mumbling among the inhabitants of the hamlet due to the constant, and dubious, comings and goings around the club. The club is closed until better times and one morning, an angry Stub hurls all the incantation room mattresses out of the window, onto his beloved half-dry roses, or at least what remains of them.

Five in the morning all alone in your room door locked tight private moon no faces to face no one to blame.(The Cars - A Dream away)

    Time goes back to the days when the club didn't exist and the boys went to parties organised by discos or in some tavern. To find out if there were any parties on the horizon, Angie and Finger, after buying the LP "Tattoo You" by the Rolling Stones, decide to spend an evening at the Cosmic.

And there certainly is news. Yes indeed! As soon as they go in, they notice the Cosmic's brand new and wonderfully colourful stickers and, once in the dance hall, they also find the new C42 mix tape on sale.

Cosmic stickers.

    They start to dance to Pete Shelley's cosmic "Witness the Change" even before reaching the dance floor and then, one by one, tracks mixed with that scale of growing notes in the middle of the piece "Do What You Wanna Do" by T-Connection. As usual, the time comes for a smoke break out in the square.

'You know who that guy is?'

'Dunno! Never seen him before!'

'That's Prey. When he goes into class at school, he always draws a pussy on the board with chalk and then licks it all off.'

    But the most shocking news is that they hear that Les Cigales has been closed down due to disturbance of the peace and drug dealing.

    'Les Cigales closed? And now? Ah! That's why all the freaks are here...'

Fais pas le con, passe moi tes vibrations. Moi j'ai pas vu passer l'avion.
(Plastic Bertrand - Tout petit la planete)

'And to think that there were those who went back and forth to drink wine...'
'Eaaaasyyyy, no worries. They've opened another one that they say is mind blowing! A place where there's even more Afro. Where you live Afro and celebrate...'
'What's it called?'
'The Mecca, Melodj Mecca, where you drink, smoke aaaand sin...'
They go back in to discover that the freaks are not only outside but also inside since someone has put their head into one of the disco's JVC speakers blasting at full volume.

People. Action. Faces. Fashion.
(New Musik - While you wait)

Back outside, breathing the first autumn air, their attention is captured by a guy who has opened a stall near a car with the trunk open. He is Uzo, the drug salesman.
'Gooood stuff, a lot of gooood stuuuff, blaaaack, reeeed, greeeen, Pakistaaaan, jooooiiiint, who wants a joint? Come oooon, grass makes you hungryyy...'
It's time to dance the last cosmic piece from Baldelli and TBC's repertoire.

It's the countdown. Baby. It's the countdown. Baby.
(Lee Ritenour - Countdown Captain Fingers)

As they make their way back home, they once again decide to make a stop at the bar of the two "not bad chicks" but they still aren't there. The summer season is over and they are busy with school. They will have to wait until next year.

Stickers at the cash desk.

☺

The Loss gatherings return to the steps although it seems on the verge of losing some crucial members. A shocking event disturbs the whole gang: Stub, Volt, Pepper and Vinitaly have their hair cut!

An angel told Samson to refrain from intoxicating drinks and never to cut his hair because that was where his strength lay. In this case, neither the drink nor the hair had anything to do with taking away the Angel's strengths. The boys have been called up to do their military service. They had all groped their balls in the past to see if they would be eligible for military service or not, but this time, it was the military doctors who had squeezed their testicles.

To make the departures a little cheerier, they stick together and go to the station with each of their friends as they leave.

'Where're you goin' Pepper?'

'To the Bay of Angels!'
And every time a friend leaves, it's always on a night train. And every time you walk past the station toilets, there's someone inside with an open door giving themselves a fix. And every time you come back out, you see the same person crouched, smashed and dazed.

'Zeb! Look at that blonde hottie!'

'Ahhhh, fuck, she's smashed!'

A never-ending year that is, however, interrupted every three weeks with home leave just to get a taste of the good life.

While waiting for them to come back, the others discuss organising evenings to go out and have fun. They find out, for example, that Mozart, Rubens, Ebreo and Spranga will be DJing for "The Night of the Angels" at the Chicago. And since the season is turning cold, the days are getting shorter and Les Cigales has gone, their attention turns to a discotheque that is much closer and which they have never even considered in the past: the Small Studios in Cerea. The owner, a great friend of Vittorio Salvetti, the creator of Festivalbar, has completely renewed the place, probably due to his showbiz connections, kitting it out with red leather sofas, white tables and completely redoing the dance floor in black granite. But, it's always the great DJs that make this provincial town on the plain a new Afro hub. And so, the new elixir of youth that makes the Angels forget the closure of Les Cigales begins. Sunday. Afternoon. All the Angels are here. It's hard to get in, but luckily, you can swap with someone going out to smoke something. The greatest Afro DJs take turns to perform in this club every weekend almost as if they were in some kind of race. The only difference between one and the other is their choice of tracks and the way they are mixed but, in terms of quality, they are on equal footing. The session starts with "Hand in Hand" by Phil Collins. They dance.

The disco is just one large square room with the DJ's console at one end. It only takes five minutes to realise that the venue has no architectural oddities like the other dance halls. One noticeable thing is Vinitaly and Hugo's constant going in and coming out of the Small. In fact, they spend more time out than in. The others dance. At one point, there is a procession as if a handful of undertakers were carrying a coffin on their shoulders, heading out of a church after the funeral service. Some guys are taking a totally stunned Stump outside followed by her friend, Frog "wide mouth".

Toe to toe dancing very close. Body breathing almost comatose. Wall to wall people hypnotized. *(Blondie - Rapture)*

It's not the first time Angie has seen his ex smashed. She did the same thing at the Cosmic but not quite as badly. He and Poplar decide to follow them out to make sure that it's nothing serious. Luckily, she is not in a coma and is reacting to the odd slap.
'That's good, she's pulled through again!'
'We better go to the bar across the street and have a drink...'
'Aren't we goin' back to the dance?'
'Forget it. It's total chaos in there...'
'What? Another freak?'
'No, no. They caught Stub on the dance floor bursting the soap bubbles coming down from above and spitting on them. Pity that there's spit everywhere...'
'Let's go to the little bar...'
They discover that the bar offers a whole range of forbidden things making it very clear why so many Angels are going back and forth from Small.
'No prohibitioooon! No prejudiiiice! No ruuuules! Just make yourself looooved!'
Someone says as he staggers out, unable to walk in a straight line.

They soon find out that, instead of serving the classic Prosecco, the bar sells Clinto and Bacò. Forbidden wines. The steamboats that, at the end of 1800, managed to cross the Atlantic in ten days, brought a sap-sucking bug over to Europe which, with a life-span that coincidentally lasted up to ten days, destroyed the viticultural heritage of the old continent. Many attempts were made to save what could be saved but all, unfortunately, was in vain. In a northern US town called Clinton, however, it was noted how some types of wild vines were practically immune to this parasite. The idea arose to take these American vines and cross them with the remaining European qualities. Other experiments conducted in Montpellier in France led to creating new hybrids and one of them was given the name Bacò in honour of Bacchus. The Clinto, or Clinton, or Crinto, or Grinton, has an unmistakable purple colour, so deep as to leave indelible traces in the bottles, in the glasses, on the lips and probably coats the throat and stomach red too. What makes it unique is a bitter aroma and its intense fruity perfume. Due to its rather low alcoholic content, which makes the wine hard to preserve any longer than the spring of the following year, the quality of both Clinton and Bacò is poor. Another negative aspect of this wine is the high quantity of methyl alcohol which, if taken in abundance, can cause severe damage to the nervous system if drunk frequently over a long period of time.

There's a little bit of everything inside the bar with civilians and Angels standing or sitting here and there on the typical wooden tables found in taverns. They particularly notice someone kneeling with his elbow resting on the backrest of a chair and another person sitting on the chair holding his head up with his knuckles resting on his cheeks and his elbows propped up on the table.

'Shit! Poplar! It's Hugo and Vinitaly!'

'Fuckin' hell! Hugo is smashed!'

'Vinitaly! Haven't you noticed? Hugo is smashed!'

'Saalaaamii, aaaand, clinnnntoooo...'

'Fuckin' hell! Vinitaly is smashed too!'

Since Vinitaly's face is exactly the same whether drunk or sober, they didn't immediately realise how totally pissed he is.

'Poplar, come on! Let's get them out!'

'Let's take them to the gardens nearby!'

> *I DRINK IT WHEN I'M HAPPY AND WHEN I'M SAD.*
> *SOMETIMES I DRINK IT WHEN I'M ALONE.*
> *WHEN I HAVE COMPANY, I CONSIDER IT OBLIGATORY.*
> *I TRIFLE WITH IT IF I'M NOT HUNGRY AND I DRINK IT WHEN I AM.*
> *OTHERWISE, I NEVER TOUCH IT, UNLESS I'M THIRSTY.*
> *(MADAME ELISABETH BOLLINGER)*

They are in no fit state to stand and so, taking them from under their armpits, the two boys drag them out of the forbidden bar and, not without a little difficulty, eventually reach the park. There they sit them on a bench with their arses a little apart and tilt them sideways so that they are leaning on each other at the shoulders for support. They adjust their bonces slightly so that Hugo's head is on Vinitaly's shoulder and Vinitaly's is resting on Hugo's hair. From behind, they look just like two lovebirds.

They bump into Tex later in front of the entrance to the Small during cigarette break. He has just left the bar.

'Hi, Tex! You a Clinto taster too? Just saying 'cos we found Hugo and Vinitaly earlier who...'

'No, no, no, no! I'm for Bacò. My dad makes it. Anyway, let me tell you what I saw...'

'Yeeeessss?'

'I went to the park a few minutes ago aaaand there's a guy going around with the stick aaaand, as soon as he sees a couple snogging or looking like two lovebirds, he beats them with it!'

☺

Even if a few beatings can hurt, what happened to Fish hurt a lot. While racing along a street near the steps where the Loss usually hangs out, he crashed violently into a lorry at the crossroads. He lay on the ground, while the Cagiva fell onto the asphalt and, like a bomb, slid and smashed into an Alfa Romeo parked on the side of the road. The car, due to the sparks caused by the impact, caught fire and was practically destroyed, and now, the boys are once again, for the second time, going to the hospital to visit a patient.

The unmistakable stomping of Frye boots echoes through the hospital corridors. The Angel tribe already know which ward to go to but not exactly which room Fish is in. The orthopaedic ward is quite large and the staff leans back against the walls at the sight of the gang, like the waters that DJ Moses parted. Someone pokes his head into the rooms. Someone else stretches his neck from the

corridor. They go through the ward until they find him. There he is, with his legs pulled up high and in plaster. He suffered severe facial trauma and is in a coma. It takes him several days to re-awaken and recognise his friends.
'Come on, Fish! You'll be as fit as a fiddle by the New Year's Eve party. You'll soon get well!'
He nods.
Since holding a party at the club is no longer an option, they decide to return to Heyhey's basement for their New Year's Eve do with the promise that they won't make any trouble. Obviously, inviting hundreds of Angels from all around the neighbourhoods is no longer possible, but what makes them really happy is that Fish is with them, on crutches. There are about thirty of them and the company calls Jake, DJ Fonzie, to be the DJ. The party starts in the best way. Their desire to dance is as great as their hunger so everyone dances with a delicious sandwich from an excellent deli in the city in their hand.

Listen! Can you hear me? There's somethin' in the air. Hold me, get listenin'... (John Davis & The Monster Orchestra - Love Magic)

'Hey! Who's that cow? I've never seen her before'
'That one? That's Fang because she's got big teeth!'
'Ah, yeeees? Then, why is that other one called Emily Four Speeds?'
'Ha! Ha! Becauuuuse, she often changes!'

Listen, listen to the voice, the voice is an illusion. Listen to the voice, don't let the words confuse you. (Todd Gundgren - Healing)

At a certain moment in the evening, Heyhey notices that someone is barking at his front door and makes his first mistake. He lets Prince's gang and Zambo in, all with a bottle of Prosecco in hand as if it were the entrance ticket. Heyhey has no choice but to welcome them all. After all, it isn't fair to call it a mistake since the reverse situation had happened at Lamp's New Year's Eve party.
''Scuse us for coming! We got bored at the other party, so decided to come here!'
The party takes off and things start flying. Bottles of sparkling wine are shaken, popped and sprayed around and everyone opens

their mouths wide to drink it as it lands on their tongues from above. A swamp begins to form on the floor in the same way as at the New Year's Eve in Volt's house and, since it's such fun to slide on it, Finger and Zeb start dancing barefoot. At some point, Tex is peeing in the upstairs bathroom and notices someone wandering outside through the window. He tells Heyhey, who then makes his second mistake. He lets Birdie in, dead drunk, supported by four friends of hers, who, intoxicated, claim that they also got fed up of the party they were at. They lose count of the people there and, although some start to wander around the house, the basement is constantly full. Despite the concentration of Angels, Finger finds enough space to slide and drag Zeb onto one of the stereo system's speakers and breaks it. No matter, the other one is still working, but then they fall asleep on the broken speaker. Luckily, Heyhey has a camping mattress in the garage and, after partially inflating it with the help of Tex, they lay the two stoned guys on it, side by side. They hardly have time to make it back to the basement when they find Birdie crashed out on the floor. She also ends up with Finger and Zeb, except that they lay her head to toe so that her face is right in the middle of their filthy stinking feet and, vice versa, her feet are between their heads. Hoping the stench will return them to consciousness, it's back to the dance.

The sound is on the visions move. The image dance starts once again. (Ultravox - The thin wall)

    It's almost midnight. Heyhey makes it clear that he doesn't want any sparkling wine bottles popped inside the basement so, following the little tip-tap steps of Fish's crutches, they leave the house to celebrate outside on the street. Since the bottles of sparkling wine were emptied much, much earlier, the only thing left to do is to plonk hickeys on all the chicks, one by one, swapping them around as they go. Back inside the house at about one o'clock, they discover that the lighting system has given up but, on the bright side, Finger, Zeb and Birdie are back in play. With the food all gone, the benz all gone, the smoke all gone, the lights off and the stereo system only half blaring, the party begins to have little to offer and, towards two in the morning, numbers start to drop off. At Zeb's suggestion, at around three o'clock, the veterans find themselves at the Cosmic and the party, with all its lights and a McIntosh stereo system, takes on new vigour.

From here to eternity, that's where she takes me. From here to eternity, with love love... (Giorgio Moroder - From here to eternity)

At closing time, somewhere around five o'clock, the last words are in the square addressing those Angels who need it.

'So! If you have no place to sleep in your car, go out into the countryside. Take that street, you will find barns...'

'Thaaaank youuuu, thaaanks afro broooo...'

☺

There is no shortage of exclusive opportunities to return to the Cosmic in the New Year, such as Valentine's Day, music and love.

Even if funky seems to have had its day at the Cosmic, DJs Baldelli and TBC always play pieces that, for the Angels, are timeless. Tracks like "Flash" by The Duke of Burlington. Suri, the bricklayer, is the first to offer to make a declaration of love to his Pauline.

'Come on, Suri! A declaration of love!'

'My heart beats for you like a gravel shovel inside a cement mixer!'

'Wooooowwww! You're great Suri, greaaaat!'

'Suri! Suri! Suri! Tell her another one!'

'My heart beats for you like the rocks of a landslide down a mountain!'

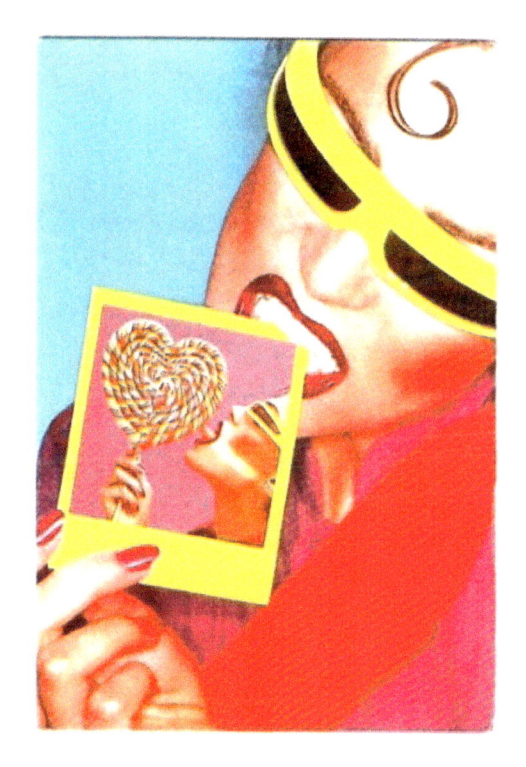

Valentine's Day party.

No! No! No! Ah! Ah! Ah!
(Kinkina - Jungle Fever)

The tour is always the same: people hallucinating and wandering about, people getting tangled watching Lucifer, the lighting man. But the music turns towards a mix of oriental, arabesque and, as the experts call it, tribal electro, such as "Tim Toum" by Codek.

'Music still makes me travel!'

Someone says. And it certainly leads to a great deal of travel since, outside, there's a car with a Zurich number plate.

'Saint Valentine's Day means having your heart in your mouth!'

Someone says.

The buzz at these parties is guaranteed but not for everyone. Unfortunately, these are the last few nights that Poplar can come because he has been called up for military service and so, to make him feel more at home, they do their best to collect a load of tapes for him to take to the barracks.

And here they are again, all together accompanying him to the railway station, walking among spaced-out people, the reason why the city has been labelled the Bangkok of Italy.

'Poplaaar! Watch out for the tapes! Someone says they get pinched in the barracks!'

I was born on the wings of the dawn. Oh I was born on the wings of the dawn. Like a thief in the night. You came to me. And stole my heart away. (Monsoon - Wings of the Dawn)

However, if the bay girls want a lift into town, especially for shopping, the boys are always ready and willing. It doesn't matter if they're going to buy something in a second-hand shop or just rummaging through a boutique at end-of-season sales, what is important, is to encourage them to try things on. That way, grey Saturday afternoons can be spent watching them parade out of the dressing rooms under the curious eyes of the salesgirls, who get grumpy when they leave without buying anything.

☺

Besides popping by the Small Club and the insipid Berfi's club, local village beer festivals pass the time on grey and blue Saturday evenings. At one of these, Loss bumps into Hugo and Tex on

Hugo's PX with a completely bent aileron and a dented side panel. The story goes that they had got smashed and raced down from a hilly village and, at the first intersection with red traffic lights, neither of them put their feet down so they ended up splattered on the asphalt.

'Just think! When we rescued them, they were still on the seat, in the same position as if they were still upright, except they were on the ground!'

'But! Hugo! Tex! How did it happen? Are you hurt?'

'Nnnnnooooooo! No! No!'

'How fucking much did you guys gulp down?'

'Guuuulp doooown? Nnnnooooo, we just listened to the muuuusiiiic...'

'Music? Was there a band?'

'Yeeeeah, the Sniff band, at goooolden Bacchussss...'

'But! Sniff? Bacchus? We got it.'

'Yeeeeah, at Bacchussss, the wine tastes of cork...'

The arrival of the good weather brings with it a turning point in their habits. Fish's parents put up a tent at Garda Campsite and the scene shifts lakeside. It's practically a repeat performance of the Valverde village near the Les Cigales disco, except this time, the nearby nightclub is the Thucana. It isn't the same thing. The music the Thucana offers is classic commercial with Chic, Sister Sledge and the Angels that make for such wonderful entertainment at the front entrance are not as funny as those at the Cosmic. They seem a bit "all there". Anyway, since there's a lot of hotties involved, they accept the new situation with a few reservations.

They finally get the chance to apologise to Filly, who is also camping with her friends in this holiday village, by taking part in her new party since they had forgotten to go to the last one. This one though was already over before it really began because Pepper is caught screwing, with his arm entirely in plaster due to an accident at work, on the camp bed inside Filly's parents' tent, heedless of the rhythmic squeaking that could be heard throughout the quiet campsite. They therefore decide to go to the Thucana, visibly disappointed at the choice due to the commercial music, a disappointment that turns into a public protest. Vinitaly shows up on board a beat-up old Simca 1000 and Suri with the ugliest, shittiest car of all time, a Talbot Horizon with a bluish colour similar to bird droppings. A general roar of laughter becomes even louder when, always wanting to prove his loyalty to the craziness of the Loss, he gets out of the car with his feet tied together, making only one person freeze, Thucana's famous sweeper.

Inside, they meet the Chilly gang and the Shanty gang, a lot of new but also familiar faces.

'See that fatty? If you give her a pack of Marlboro, she'll give you her pussy.'

'Look who's there! That's Cornflake, the one Stub wants to shag. We should tell him...'

'There are also some girls who are a little ugly..... well, forget the 'little'. They're definitely ugly!'

They go round and round around the dance floor when one calls them to her attention.

'Have you got any small change?'

'What? Bugger off! I can't stand these folks!'

Round and round the dance floor until they notice a face that isn't new to them.

'Isn't that Sweet?'

'That girl at the bar? Yeeeeah, but, who's that hot, black-haired chick wearing black next to her?'

That's a familiar face too.

'Even the other one close to the hottie seems...'

That's a familiar face too.

'Fuck you all! Bastards!'

It's Morticia, the shop girl who watches them come in every Saturday to try on a bunch of clothes and then leave without spending a penny.

'Fuck you all! Idiots!'

The other is Tic. She expresses her disappointment in the fact that they broke their promise and didn't go to her party at Cisano Campsite.

'Well, Angie and I are leaving! Because it's time!'

There's a crack in the sky and the warning's out. Don't take that dive again! (Mike Oldfield ft. Maggie Reilly - Five Miles Out)

The Thucana, however, just about manages to save itself because, at least for half of the evening, DJ Armando Jee plays Afro music, the alternative to commercial. Nevertheless, the big news going round is that the Cosmic has scheduled an evening similar to the one organised by Jeep at the old club, the Flying Trip. They have the suspicion that someone copied or suggested the name. However, what stops the Thucana campsite comings and goings is not the Flying Trip, which is to be staged later, but the invitation everyone receives to the party that Pack is giving on his birthday at his house in a real village with holiday homes and a gigantic swimming pool. The imagination immediately wanders to a film-set scenario where the protagonists are all beautiful, glitzy, smiling and sprawled along the edge of the pool holding multicoloured cocktails. Angie arrives early with Pepper and Stub. Very early, to be honest, since the party is scheduled for the evening, but deliberately because they want to get their first sunbathe of the season in. The village is located in the countryside, not far from the city outskirts. All the amenities and facilities are entirely fenced in. The kids' playground, the lawns and the pool are for the house owners' exclusive use only.

Since Pack isn't answering the intercom, they decide to climb the main gate at the entrance to the resort, lie on the lawn and have a good sleep, as if they had a big hangover. They are not, however, prepared for the sprinklers, which actually turn to their advantage since they give them the opportunity to take a shower, remove the sweat, soap their balls and foam up their cocks since Stub has some fragrant green apple shampoo in his bag. After squeezing out their costumes and getting re-dressed out of the sprinklers' reach, they realise they have become the village attraction, in a negative sense, as the pool and playground are already populated with families. However, the sunset hides them from the embarrassed faces of the mothers. Cheeks appear to be blushing but it's only the sunlight that, before painting the sky graffiti-like, points them in the direction of the fun.

All the guests have arrived. They have the house all to themselves. Pack has thought of everything for an unforgettable birthday.

'Where the fuck did that Jonny Walker bottle go?'

They float in the music interrupted occasionally by Pack's shouts.

'Hey! I warn you! You go outside to smoke!'

The front door is wide open and leads directly onto the lawn. The difference between dancing indoors and on the lawn can be felt by the coolness underfoot.

Music composed for a tropical birthday is playing.

Il l'a laissé là bas. Ses amis, pour retrouver l'amour, de sa vie.
(Antena - Bye Bye Papaye)

Then, under Pack's umpteenth recommendation not to throw anything in the water, everyone gathers on the edge of the pool.
'Everybody here! Everybody here! Synchronise your ears on the most beautiful sound in the world!'
A general hush followed by the dull sound of a cork popping and the squirt of the Prosecco spray as if the bottle had been given a handjob.
'Aaaahhhhhh!'
'Ahhh fuck! The cork is in the water!'
But sometimes, the warnings are never enough. Amy, dead drunk, drops the bottle of Jonny Walker in the beautiful blue illuminated by the lamps at the bottom of the pool.

You know you drive me crazy baby. You've got me turning to another man.
(Indeep - Last night a DJ saved my life)

Jake volunteers to stop Pack from being thrown out of the village by retrieving the bottle before too much strange liquid can be shed into the water.
'But, this is a Prosecco bottle! Amy! Did you drain this too?'
Another scuba dive.
'Fuckin' hell it's empty! Amy, you drank the whole bottle of Jonny Walker!'
Amy responds by retching and, to avoid spilling further strange liquids, Angie takes her by an arm with one hand and by a leg with the other, inviting Stub to do the same with the remaining limbs. They lift her horizontally from the ground and, holding her by her limbs, head towards a group of bushes.
'At least this way she won't throw up on herself or her feet!'
'Okay! Okay! See if she pukes near the bush!'
Nothing.
'Listen! I'm sick of it! Throw her in the bush?'
And so, swinging the body as if were a battering ram for breaking down a castle door...
'On three! Oooone, twoooo, aaaand three!'
The hustle and bustle bring in some village people.

'What's that aromatic smell, mixed straw, hay?'
'Eaaaasy missus, it's the aroma of our pal, Mary Jane.'
'But! Hold on!'
'Yes? Tell us, milady.'
'You! Weren't you the ones washing on the lawn today?'

The party ends by watching them walk towards the darkness of the night on the notes of "How Stupid Mr Bates" by The Police, without Amy.

A few days later, they hear that, strangely and inexplicably, Pack's parents are moving out of the resort. They would never see that pool again.

☺

Since they have now pulverised every possibility of ever having parties at Pack's house, the Loss returns to the nightlife on the lake, but this time, it's not for DJ Armando Jee, but the Flying Trip party at the Cosmic.

Almost everyone comes to the campsite in the morning, but Angie has arranged with Hugo to pick him up late in the afternoon. Hugo shows up with the long beard. He is fed up with razors, creams and electric machines.

'If it needs cutting, I just snip it and trim my hair with nail scissors...'

'Good! The bush and beard style is complete! Look, if you like, let's not go to the campsite and drive along the lake. Instead, I know a bar where there are two "not bad" chicks right next to the Cosmic. We could stop there and, when we feel like it, go to the Trip Party.'

By evening, the two friends are already on their way. Angie is on the seat of Hugo's PX with his bare feet resting on the side panels and his face turned in the opposite direction to where Hugo is holding his cigarette to prevent any sparks ending up in his eye. Hugo usually holds his cigarette on his right and smokes it hanging out of his mouth, since using his hand would mean removing it from the throttle grip. When they arrive at the bar, the chicks' daddy is once again working at the counter. At this point, they decide to sit at a secluded table for two in the corner of the room and wait for the two girls.

'What'll it be?'

It isn't as if, on a Saturday night, they can afford petrol, disco and booze and, in any case, they came for the daughters.

'Nnnnnothing! Mmmmm, we'll wait...'

After serving a few other customers and washing some cups and glasses, the barman comes back to them.

'Have you two come to some kind of decision?'

'Nnnnothing! We won't have anything tonight!'

At this point, without saying a word, the bartender moves away until he disappears from view and turns off the light that illuminated their table leaving them in the dark. They realise that it's in retaliation but, unperturbed, they sit at the table for at least another hour until they are sure that their chances of seeing the girls are less than zero.

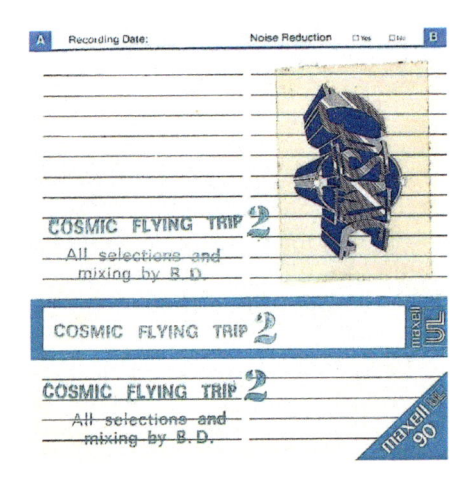

At the Flying Trip, the music, while still electronic, alludes to mystic oriental. You dance to "Chinese Revenge" by Koto, which used to be "Koto" by Chinese Revenge.

'It's the sound from another galaxy!'

Someone says.

Outside, in the middle of the chaos, you recognise some familiar faces: Joan, Ludy, Grape, Tekila, but the best known, the most popular, are a couple, Red "red hair" and Hawk "the Indian", who keep a ton of grass ready for sale in their car. He's called Hawk "the Indian" because he is the spitting image of a sticker of an Apache Indian with a headband, which can often be found glued onto an Angel's vehicle right next the vagabond sticker.

A lot of girls are walking around barefoot, either in small groups or in pairs and every now and then snippets of their

conversation can be overheard.
'Did you get Predictor at the pharmacy?'
'Hey, isn't that Mary "the frigid"?'
'Ah! What would she do with Predictor?'

A sad Antonella is also there. She's Beba's ex-chick. He recently died of a heroin overdose. But the freakiest of them all is the one who goes up to Pope and starts raining curses of suffering and death upon him.

'Because you have done this, cursed are you above all livestock and above all beasts of the field! On your belly you shall go, and dust you shall eat, all the days of your life[30].'

Her insistence begins to be a bit worrying so much so that Pope thinks she must have escaped from an asylum and he jumps on his PX, goes to the first phone box and calls an ambulance. Despite repeatedly asking her to get the fuck out of here and to fuck off somewhere else, the witch continues with her claims of black magic until the ambulance arrives and takes her away by force.

Things settle down at last and they can get back to dancing both inside and in the open space designed to look like a giant seashell, the Bay of the Lake.

Be my friend. Be my friend. Be my friend tonight.
(Monsoon-Ever So Lonely)

Seeing Angels arriving from so many different regions of Italy and abroad reminds the Loss that it's time to carry out an expedition. They remember what the boys from Rome, that they had met at the Cosmic, had suggested: Grosseto, Tuscany.

Stub and Jake's experience of going to the Bay of Angels and sleeping in the tent there proves to be very helpful for planning their trip in the direction of Rome. Luckily, Stub is able to scrounge most of the material from his scout friends. Tent, stakes, pots and pans, the only thing they have to buy is a camping stove. Stub's decision to travel at night to avoid the summer traffic also implies taking a tank of petrol, since the service stations will be closed and it's a long drive. The only thing they're not sure of is the route. They are confident about reaching Modena easily, and maybe even Formigine where the Picchio Rosso is, but after that, they will need

---

30 Genesis 3.14

a map and a good torch to cross the Apennines at night. Whatever, no problem. Everyone is invited to come along but in the end, only Stub, Jake and Angie take part in the expedition on just two Vespas since Angie's is broken due to an accident.

They set off at sunset. Angie is riding Stub's PX and Jake is on his ET3, both bikes unrecognisable due to all the stuff crammed onto the front and back racks.

THE SUNSET IS ALWAYS EXCITING, INDIGENT OR GAUDY, BUT EVEN MORE THRILLS THAT FINAL AND DESPERATE GLOW THAT RUSTS THE PLAIN WHEN THE EXTREME SUN SINKS.
(JORGE LUIS BORGE)

The journey starts off smoothly. They are familiar with the road to Modena. Even if the night paints everything at either side of the road with asphalt, making the universe around them appear all the same, they sense their progress on their faces every time they pass over a canal and the air temperature changes from hot to cool. At 10 pm, they arrive in Mirandola and take their first breather. The night gets sultry when they stop travelling and a slight gust of air takes their minds back to when they were sitting on a bench looking at the stars with their girlfriends, dreaming, making plans, telling them all the things they will do, be and hope for.

'Do you know I'm back with Mila today?'

'What! But you only just split up!?'

On reaching Modena, Jake says he would like to go to a town where he had worked, even though he hasn't a clue where is it. Fortunately, they find someone walking along the street.

'Listen, whore, the road to Maranello[31]?'

'Fuck you!'

'No! No! Pardon milady, we have to go to Maranello...'

'That way, toward Formigine...'

'Thank you, whore!'

At half-past midnight they arrive in Maranello and stop for another breather to replenish the tanks. People work nights in this town. Like Apache Indians peering from the top of the hill, the three travellers watch a wagon train of tractors crossing the prairie, the beams of their headlights illuminating the land they are ploughing as they move further and further into the distance. Which is exactly

---

31 Ferrari Headquarters.

what the boys are doing too, for that matter. With Jake's desire finally satisfied they head out of Maranello along the road to Pistoia when, at around three in the morning, they notice a flashing blue light. The Carabinieri have stopped two Angels on a Cagiva. The boys, having nothing to hide and aware of being of age, drive impassively by in front of the checkpoint, earning only a glassy stare from the agents, who watch them go without doing anything other than repeatedly tapping their signalling discs on the side of their boots. At four, they drive past Pistoia in the direction of Montecatini Terme and unfortunately, feel a few raindrops, but this doesn't stop them from taking some photos with a Polaroid snapshot. At half-past five, they arrive at Lucca and at six, they are thrilled at being in Pisa with their Vespas under the leaning tower. By seven they are in Livorno. It starts to rain and the port city, besides being disappointing, also becomes distressing. They continue south but the heavy rain stops them from continuing and, having seen a cottage in the countryside, they decide to leave the main road and take shelter in it. They sit there in silence, thinking about nothing. An imperceptible shiver descends from their shoulders. The wind caresses their hair. The pouring rain kisses the tips of their shoes. They smell of soil. It's well after noon when they leave Grosseto behind and, at last, just before Porto Santo Stefano, a campsite welcomes them, dead tired and starving hungry. It's about two in the afternoon. They find an empty plot and unload their stuff, then they go straight out of the campsite where they previously saw a sort of pizzeria van. Strangely, nobody seems to be working in it so, too hungry to care, they help themselves to pizza squares and gobble them up like turkeys. Thoroughly overfed, they still don't see anyone so leave without paying because they know their first task now, before starting their holiday, is to put up the tent. It's hilarious, to say the least, to see what camp folk do to get settled in. Since the main objective is to pitch the tent as high as possible to avoid flooding should it rain, some people actually check the ground morphology by laying a cheek on the soil in order to locate, with one eye closed, a mound. Some dig a kind of moat around the tent as if to install a drawbridge. It's all pointless because the campsite is as flat as a pancake. When the tent is up and all the Vespas' cargo is unpacked, they rush to the Jolly supermarket to buy food: hamburgers, jars of peas and Lucky Strike cigarettes will be their lunch and dinner on every day of their stay. The day draws to an end with the boys falling asleep in the company of a cloud of mosquitoes.

There's no need for an alarm clock since Jake and Angie are woken by the comings and goings of people chatting and banging pots and pans as they head towards the washbasins. Stub, however, is still dead to the world so the other two wake him by sticking a match between his big toe and the next and lighting it. To appease his anger, they offer him a wagonload of yoghurt for breakfast at a Porto Santo Stefano snack bar to remind him of his girlfriend, yoghurt Mila[32]. From there, they go straight to the beach to enjoy the sea in an alternation of swimming and sunbathing.

'Jaaaake! I told you not to sleep on the same side! You only have one tanned arm!'

'Shit! I'll soak the other in beer so it tans more quickly!'

They take great pleasure in pissing in the water. A real relief for the bladder but feeling the hot piss that initially inflates the costume and then explodes, warming the inner thigh, is particularly satisfying.

'Hey! Keep away! I don't want the current to carry your piss towards me!'

'Fuuuuckin' heeeell! There's a piece of shit floating here!'

'Shit! One's passing right in front of me!'

They look in the opposite direction of the stream, where they see a grinning Jake.

'Jake! You're a fuckin' arsehole!'

Evening comes and they have to decide how to fill it. Although villages like Porto Sant'Ercole are enchanting, what they are looking for is something with a bit more life. There are no Angels on the horizon, so they look for someone who is a bit out of the box to have a better chance of getting to know where the fun places are. A hairy blonde guy with an arabesque shirt and an iconic map of the Netherlands seems the right choice. He is a Dutchman.

'Discotheek? Albinia, Club 72!'

The Afro genre doesn't seem to have reached the disco and neither are there people outside inhaling or smoking chillums. Rather than songs like "Time warp" by Eddy Grant, "Saving Grace" by Thomas or "Reel" by Nova, they hear commercial tracks that still make for an enjoyable evening.

---

32 A Tyrolese brand.

STONED ANGELS

I hear the drums echoing tonight. But she hears only whispers of some quiet conversation. (Toto - Africa)

The shit hits the fan on the way back to camp when it starts to rain and the night gets as bad as it can. The ground at the campsite fails to drain and they begin to take on water. The tent is soon flooded, forcing them to come out although they have inflatable mattresses to float on. Morning arrives quickly seeing as they returned late from the club. First light sees them hanging all the stuff inside the tent on the branches of maritime pines accompanied by the applause of those who had pitched their tents on hillocks or had dug ditches.

'I'm sick of this fucking place! Floatin' shits, low-flying mosquitoes, floods and, and, and, and...'
'Let's leave! It's a mess!'
'Leave? What do you mean?'
'Let's go to Rimini! We could cross the Apennines and go to the Bay!'
'To the Bay of Angels?'
'Yeah! Come on! Let's go! We're going to the Bay of Angels!'

As soon as the sleeping bags, mattresses and clothes are dry and loaded onto the Vespas, they leave in the direction of Saturnia, not before quarrelling with the campsite cashier to get a good discount. Stub studies the route and keeps the map handy, guiding them towards Lake Bolsena. They take the first breather in a lay-by below the town of Pitigliano, amazed by how the houses seem to climb up the hill and the thousands of tiny windows. Not to mention a peddler selling white Pitigliano wine that turns out to be out of this world. Approaching the lake, they are engulfed by a cloud, or perhaps a mist, and drive through it for what seems hours. When it finally dissolves, they are surprised to discover that they are still by a lake. It turns out to be Lake Trasimeno and, at this point, they have to re-plot the route because they are further north of Perugia than they thought so they decide to head courageously towards Rimini instead of Ancona as previously planned. The hours go by, and they begin to feel hungry. At Sant'Angelo in Vado, they scoff a take-away pizza between them from a pizzeria that is about to close.

It's night time. The lights of the Romagna coast are still not visible. All they can see are those of the odd village perched on high among the stars. Late at night, they reach the signpost for Urbino and, not wanting to do any more calculations, they decide to lay their sleeping bags in front of a church door and put up with Jake's snoring until morning.

The journey continues and they finally arrive in Pesaro where the legendary Romagna Riviera opens up before them at last: the kingdom of Angels. Going north towards Rimini, they enter the first campsite on the right in Misano Adriatico, but luck is not on their side since it's already full. They decide to have breakfast in a bar near the entrance and wait. Their plan is to try again in the afternoon and hope that someone will have left. Their luck returns, the tent is pitched and the holiday continues on another shore. What's more, their camping neighbours have all the connotations of Angels, so they wait for the right moment to ask them if they know any place to go to have fun since the Bay of Angels is still closed. Talking generally about discotheques, they discover that the same situations are occurring here as in the places that the Loss usually go to.

'There were so many people, all Angels, camped everywhere... on the beach, on the street ... and we were all waiting for New York to open. But then, you could hear the residents and hoteliers complaining about us being there and even some of the tourists couldn't stand us and we were told that we couldn't stay there...'

'Aaaand, the worst came towards the end! Now and then, Police with dogs came and even raided people who were sitting quietly under a tree ...'

'And when they shut New York down, we tried to change places. We tried to go to the Altro Mondo, even though the music isn't ours, because they were talking about it as if it were a cool place with go-go girls dancing in some kind of tube aaaand spaceships around, but when we arrived at the entrance, they blocked us! One of us had white trousers with Indian sandals and they told us we couldn't get in because we weren't well dressed...'

'That's true! The thing is, these assholes won't let us in because we have long hair!'

'Poor excuse! Buuuut, now. Here at the moment. What are you goin' to do?'

'Calm down, brothers! There's the Cellophane. It's New York under a new name, ha, ha, ha!'

No sooner said than done. Saturday night is definitely Cellophane night and there is no lack of surprises.

'Stub! I've just met Carla, the one I had an accident with a while back. I asked her if she'd come for a ride and she told me to fuck off...'

'I just met Mila. She dumped me! I'm changing yoghurt brand...'

Although DJs Yano and Pery are no longer there, the music is still awesome, although songs of some time ago, such as "Jerky rhythm" by Erotic Drum Band, are occasionally revived.

Smoking breaks outside the disco are obligatory just to get a sense of what things are like.

'Most of the Angels moved to Mecca...'

'And the Bay of Angels?'

'They tried to open it under the name Nepentha, like the one in Turin, the Big Nepentha, but it wasn't possible...'

'Hey! Next up is Mecca!'

However, sunrise is near and the day to return home has come. A few hours' sleep are enough to recharge their batteries and soon they are dismantling the tent and loading the Vespas again. The first stop is a few kilometres from the campsite, in Gabicce, at the Bay of Angels.

There are endless stories regarding this club. Those which speak of people who stayed inside the Bay for two days and two nights without ever going out, and others about people who arrived in Sharks with "Long vehicle" on a yellow background stuck on the hatchback. Cars belonging to Angels usually stood out due to original bodywork painting, for example, palm trees, camels in the desert and the ohm symbol. One particular 2CV even had an actual smoke extractor coming out of the side window.

They set off again. The second time they stop, they are in a foreign country: San Marino. They stop for some chips and then continue on their expedition - Rimini, Ravenna, Ferrara. They leave the legendary Romagna Riviera behind, the mother of all holidays, immense expanses of deckchairs, umbrellas, clubs, restaurants, discos. After Ferrara, sleep takes them by the hand and accompanies them under a tree. They are woken by a buzz coming from the road. On raising their eyelids, their eyes are tickled by coloured lights. "How beautiful ", they think, "we are still on the Romagna Riviera." Instead, they find themselves surrounded by the fairy lights of a watermelon vendor. It's dark. They have to leave. The lights of their home town greet them late at night while Jake leaves a trail of Drakkar perfume in their wake.

☺

The only thing left to do is return to the parties organised by the clubs and continue to have fun.

DJ Meo and Daniele's party at the Small is fantastic, as is the Voodoo Party at the Boomerang. The Cosmic stages the

If yuh have a paper, yuh must have a pen. And if yuh have a start, yuh must have a end. (Yellowman - Zungguzungguguzungguzeng)

Stars Party, the Moon Party and the Spring Party where the Afro piece entitled "Oriental" by Peru is consecrated.

Where were you when I needed you. Well you could not be found. What can I do, oh I believed in you. (Greg Kihn Band - Jeopardy)

And then it's back to the Small for the Spring Party with Rubens and Mozart followed by a dive into the Sea Party at the Typhoon, not to mention the Summer Party back at the Cosmic.

'Even the sofas dance at these parties!'

Someone says.

☺

At last the time comes for being raised to heaven at what has become the Afro temple. The landmark where all Angels converge on magical summer evenings: the Melodj Mecca. The stories the boys hear continuously at the entrances to other discos are an invitation to go on a pilgrimage to this magical place and the Loss accepts wholeheartedly. Suri hardly has time to finish saying that they could go in his Dyane when someone has already loaded the tent in the car.

'Which way?'

'It's easy! It's so easy that cars going to the Riviera already know which way to go by themselves...'

They take the Emilia route along which there are more Angels than in heaven itself. Vespas criss-cross continuously, headlights constantly flash, arms are repeatedly raised in a sign of greeting. Some are going South; others are going North. They stop frequently along the way to join groups lounging on the grass equipped with a radio and tapes from some disco evening or other. A whole world unto itself. When they get close to Rimini, there have to look for a campsite that accepts Angels. They soon discover that they only have to ask any of the hundreds of Angels from all over Italy and abroad, who have invaded this part of the Riviera with tents and sleeping bags, and the name of a place will turn up. As soon as they find a campsite with vacancies, they pitch the tent as fast as possible because it's already evening and the tam-tam of Mecca is calling. It seems a little strange that most of the tents and caravans in the campsite are pitched and parked near the entrance. The area further back, towards the end of the site, which overlooks the countryside, is practically deserted. That is where they pitch their tent, far from the madding crowd. Once they finish sorting everything out, they jump back in the Dyane and head for the enchanted hill. Although a shuttle bus service to the Melodj Mecca is available, at sunset all the Angels who have descended onto the area, equipped with survival supplies, stream towards the disco on foot. The boys blend into the middle of this colourful cordon and, on reaching the car park below the disco, start to take note of overheard comments.

'Took me a fucking dayyyy! I left this morning, but I managed...'

'What did you expect, you freak? Coming from Verona by

Ciao!'
'Afro is bread for the sooooul, brings me happineeeess...'
'Stop talkiiiing, smokiiiig!'
Even though the terraced car park is very large, it struggles to contain the riot of French Citroen DS, CX Pallas, 2CV, Renault 4 and Dyane 6 cars with curtains on the back windows. All covered with stickers, some with interior lights, others with a spare wheel on the hatchback, big brand wheel covers. One chick arrives with a fluttering safi scarf tied to the aerial. The mixture is explosive: the summer, the Romagna Riviera, the music from stereos that, blaring out of speakers, blends with the other parked cars.

Aquarius and my name is Ralph. Now I like a woman who loves her freedom.   (The Floaters - Float On)

A white Shark with curtains stops near them. Some German guys get out, revealing leopard-skin seats, followed by a girl with straight, central-parted blonde hair that reaches halfway down her back. Her child-like body seems fragile. She's wearing a colourful Indian shirt and a pair of extremely tight, torn jeans tucked into a pair of light brown suede boots. She has a half-moon, leather handbag hanging on her shoulder from which a red sapphire safi dangles. The place is just magical. The night is magical, filling the air with infinite expectations.

They take the stairs that lead to the disco entrance. The area is a throng of boys and girls. Everywhere is a sea of hair, ragged blue jeans, Indian shirts, medallions, earrings, leather handbags, multi-coloured tights, miniskirts, thigh-length boots. Skimpy suede bodices that barely cover breasts, raw beards, mascara-painted eyes, red or deep purple lips. Due to the length of their hair, it is often hard to tell what gender the people are. The ticket office is a kind of kiosk and, after paying the entry fee, the path leads into a large park below the disco. There are a lot of vehicles parked here too: Vespas, motorcycles with plates from Florence, Siena and all over Italy. It's like being at a parade of originality and extravagance. There's another performance going on here: hippies and freaks in suede Clark's and bell-bottom trousers have set up stalls selling earrings, necklaces, bracelets, safi scarfs and other accessories alongside chillums and hookahs for smoking and a myriad of other objects, all strictly handmade. As they approach the entrance, they realise how wonderfully unique this club is. Apart from the outdoor gardens, which are covered in winter, the Melodj Mecca has three dance floors. The smallest is raised while the central and largest one dominates in front of the DJ's console. The third is located at the back near the bathrooms and is usually less crowded because there are no windows. The décor is predominantly white. The walls are white as are the concrete benches on which to sit. The canvas ceiling has yellowy-orange and white stripes and the windows overlook the beautiful outdoor garden. The style is undoubtedly oriental as the venue's name suggests. However, this vision is short-lived because the discotheque is becoming unimaginably full, both inside and out. The two bars are no longer visible. The two DJs, however, Meo from Les Cigales, and Pery from New York, are well in view. The evening promises to be amazing. History is about to consecrate Melodj Mecca as the most famous Afro disco in Europe.

    Until then, the boys had never had the pleasure of dancing with Pery but, knowing that he is the resident DJ's wingman and that he has been recognised and awarded as a revelation DJ in Italy, no introduction is required. His touch is immediately recognised by the opening theme song that he played at New York club: "Brown Rice" by Don Cherry. The oriental inclination at Melodj Mecca, as the name and décor suggest, is obvious, but it's the music that gives it that real touch of Arabian Nights. Dancing non-stop and tirelessly, if that's what you can call it, to tracks like "O Moena" by Tri Atma und Gyan Nishabda and until they play "Mysteries of the East" by Jhalib. The confusion is crazy. Everyone moves slowly. The bars are perpetually under assault, the psychedelic lights revolve madly, shooting myriads of colours from every angle. Afro music plays at stratospheric volume but time is also taken to see what's going on outside, which, in the opinion of many, is the best part. The disco stamp makes everyone free to come and go between the disco and the gardens as they please in order to smoke a joint in peace or pop to a nearby house where someone has set up an illegal chippie. However, the most exciting place is the terrace with its fabulous view. On the right, up into the hills is San Marino and, on the left, looking down, is the Adriatic Riviera with its twinkling lights, while just below, is the car park which is where the second musical gathering is taking place.

    'Our divine cars are parked!'
Someone says in a state of excitement.

Standing on the terrace, where a refreshing breeze blows in from the sea, the eyes also fall on the people wandering around the car park. Hairy junkies, freaks, Rastas, hippies; it's hard to know exactly which world you are in. Still, one thing's for sure, among these folk, it's easy to make new friends. With a pair of old jeans, a T-shirt and a sleeping bag, you all become brothers. Everyone is accommodating, nobody looks down on you. The atmosphere is unique.

'Peaaace bro, peaaace...'
An Angel passes by in some kind of mystic trance.
'I've got a message for you broooo; I've got a message for youuuuu...'
An Angel passes by cheerfully and almost falls over.

They go back inside to dance and spend ten minutes of fun with "War Dance" by Studio Project Kebekelektrik. And the dope dance goes on till late at night. Dawn is approaching and the Angels begin migrating towards the beach in front of the Columbus lido car park, where they had fled from police raids earlier in the day, to unroll their sleeping bags.

It's time to grab some sleep. Some doss down in a sleeping bag on the beach, others sit in a Dyane or more comfortably in a Shark, which many think of as their first home. Others choose to continue wandering barefoot, laughing and giggling under the full moon, perhaps even making out.

'On the Riviera, you go to bathe under the moon! The kiss of the moon! Not the sun!'
Someone says in the darkness.

Back at the campsite, even though Tex has stuck his feet outside the tent since it's a bit short, what makes the others relax is the coolness and the salty sea air. When melatonin secretion ends and gives way to sleep, the REM phase is interrupted by a vibration of cables that first seem to whip crazily in the air and then gradually fall into silence after a diminishing tinkle, similar to a child's toy. The rattling of the train rushes into the tent like a rumble of thunder. The gusts of wind from the passing wagons tickle the tarp until the convoy disappears into the depths of the night.

'Fuckin' hell! That's why they're all camped at the entrance! The railway line runs along here!'
The trains speed by every fifteen or thirty minutes. The only thing left to do is wait for daybreak and go back home.

☺

It's hard to break away from the Melodj Mecca world. The location is too far for them during the cold seasons but, to overcome this suffering, parties are organised on the legendary Afro DJs' invitation. The Happy New Year Party, Afro Party, Galactic Party and Light Party at the Cosmic are absolutely fantastic. They find out at these events that one of Melodj Mecca's three dance floors has been given over to a new type of music called Area House Music.

House music is a genre strongly influenced by disco, funky and electronic music. It originates from a Chicago club called Warehouse. The resident DJ Mancuso, is merited with shaping these genres and promoting one with exceptionally high rhythms. The first house record in history is "On & On" by Jesse Saunders, taken from "On and On" by Mach, which was the musical base of Space Invaders. Now at Melodj Mecca, people can go wild with Area House Music. The difference between house and funky can be heard in the song "Sunshine Hotel": Richard T Bear's version is a funky classic, while Jamie Lewis & Nick Morris' is house. We are in the music cradle. All the musical bases that were to come out from then on, come from these. "Muhammad goes to the mountain, I go to Mecca". Someone wrote.

Melodj Mecca club. The Mecca of Angels.

However, as time goes by, enthusiasm diminishes. Things are no longer what they were. While the Melamara has closed due to a terrorist attempt to burn it down, the Cosmic closes in general dismay. It appears that the problems are the same as those at the Bay of Angels, Les Cigales or New York. The news doesn't have much effect on the scenario. New Vinavil is born from the ashes of Vinavil but closes again. The Imperial Bay opens where the Bay of Angels was but everything is different. The theme is inspired by the Roman Empire and has nothing to do with the Angels. The New Vinavil re-opens under the name of Thriller. These openings and closures are confusing. Bad news also comes from Turin when the Big Nepentha closes. The Disco Arena also closes, but the most significant blow is the closing of the Typhoon. Just for the record, Thriller also closes but, what gives yet another twist of the knife in the wound is the bad news from Baricella. Even Chicago has closed.

It rains openings and closures. Someone attempts to try something new, but it seems that disco-bars are all the go these days. The end of the Angels has arrived. The Melodj Mecca closes.

'The Bay is dead. But the Angels are still alive.'

Someone says.

Soho, London.

STONED ANGELS

STONED ANGELS

The police closed Baia at the end of the 1978 season, saying, 'Its mere existence promotes drugs between young people'. We know it reopened for a final summer in 1979 with just Mozart at the decks and that it was closed for good that same year when someone died there, presumably from an overdose. Mozart started playing other clubs nearby, Baldelli went to a residency at a club called Cosmic near lake Garda. We know heroin was a big problem throughout Italy at that time and that the coolest car on the scene was the Citroen DS.

(Bill Brewster, Frank Broughton – Italian afro-cosmic)

The Cosmic Afro scene developed at the tail end of disco by a group of DJs in and around Rimini. Through unique mixing techniques, extreme EQing and plundering diverse genres of music they produced an eclectic tribal journey into sound and rhythm. In this provincial area of the country the DJ became the creator for the first time. The era was pre house. Paradise Garage and Studio 54 had just opened in New York, Northern Soul was taking off big style in the UK and Bambaata and Grand Master Flash were making their own experiments in the Bronx. Cosmic Afro was and still is the only music genre that was 100% homegrown without outside influence. It would be 10 years before Nicky Holloway and Paul Oakenfold would make that holiday to Ibiza and come back and create the myth that House was imported into Europe from Ibiza in '88. "When Ibiza blew up," commented Claudio Coccoluto, Italy's best known super-DJ, "we thought it was really commercial." In fact, it's a little documented fact that a lot of the DJs in Ibiza at the time were Italian, hailing from their own, by then established, dance music scene.

Back to 2002, weaving down a gravel track on the way to the middle of nowhere in central Italy on a what could be a wild goose chase to track down the founders of a unique electronic dance music movement that most the world doesn't know about, a mixtape from 1980 clicked onto play on the car stereo. Space age Funk, electronic bleeps, African percussion, Samba, twisted Disco, seamlessly mixed and continuously warped with EQ emerged. It didn't fit with any preconceived idea of Italian music.

There are a lot of foggy memories, but everyone agrees it all started at a club called the Baia degli Angeli (Bay of Angels) with two New Yorkers, Bob and Tom. The Baia first opened in 1974. Millionaire jet setter, Gian Carlo Tirotti, unusually for an Italian, travelled the world moving through exclusive circles of beautiful people. He returned to Italy to build his dream on the top of a hill overlooking a bay on the Adriatic Riviera. Constructed over different levels, terraces with panoramic views of the bay, swimming pools, internal and external dance floors, the club was more of an immense sprawling luxury villa complex than what would be thought of as a nightclub today. From a distance the shifting lights could be seen operated from the cabin of a mechanical crane, picking out the dance floors below. There was only one DJ console, housed in a four storey, fully functional glass lift, enabling the DJ to move between the dance floors at will. While other clubs were open until 2am, the Baia was the first club to close at 7am with the sunrise. The club was already a myth before it opened, strange graphics of the infamous angels appeared all over town with no explanation. The club opened and was a massive success. It was Italy's venue of the moment and anyone who was anyone had to be there.

Tirotti imported Bob and Tom (Bob Day and Tom Sison) as residents. Their impact on Italian club culture is the stuff of myth and legend. Some say they were from Studio 54, some say they were glass collectors even gay sailors. What is true, is that they were the first DJs to mix in Italy and that they had records that no one else had. They played an exclusive selection of Philadelphia Soul, Funk and Disco. The designer Elio Fiorucci, at the time was at the centre of New York's jet set was a regular complete with entourage of beautiful people. During their residency, Bob and Tom made a point of inviting a number of young, local aspiring DJs to the Baia to be schooled in the secret art of mixing.

When in 1977 Tirotti moved on, Bob and Tom disappeared from the club scene never to be heard of again. Before leaving, they suggested to the new owner that he should hand things over to two of their brightest pupils, Daniele Baldelli and Mozart. This unlikely duo began a journey into unchartered territory. The great adventure began.

Claudio Rispoli aka Mozart because of his classical music training, had been living at the Baia since the age of 16, leaving in the evenings to DJ locally and returning to sleep every night at the club. He spent his days hanging out with the owner and his entourage, living a life of excess. He became famed for his improvisation, musicality and sense of timing and his eclectic dark Funk mixes. In later years he reached international acclaim for his productions on Irma record's such as Double D's 'Found Love' and as one third of the group Jestofunk incorporating the talents of CeCe Rogers for 'Say it Again' (93) and 'Can We Live' (95) and. Back in 1977, however, Mozart, was busy being the wild child of the Adriatic DJ set and was about to be thrown together with an unlikely partner.

Daniele Baldelli, who had been DJing since 1968 was a geek, technical perfectionist and an avid record collector, searching for the funk in the electronic end of the music spectrum. Bob and Tom had picked him out too while he was DJing in a small club.

At the Baia, Mozart and Baldelli began using records to create a new sound, forging Disco, Funk and electronica into something new. They managed to beat mixed different genres of music with imprecise tempos, quickly moving on from the upbeat elitism of happy disco music and turned it into something darker and edgier.

When, in 1980, Baldelli saw an advert for the new Technics SP15 quartz turntables, he knew they were what he had been waiting for. Not only would they allow him to precisely orchestrate his set in advance, they would also solve the problem of skipping needles from going up and down in the lift between the dance floors.

They started to travel long distances in search of new beats and sounds. DJ shops with a convenient selection of playable tracks and listening facilities didn't exist. They hunted down specific sounds and tempo, plundering all genres of music, buying boxes of sealed records on a hunch that there would be something, no matter how small, that they could use. The regular turntables of the day were Thorrens and could only go to +/- 3. Baldelli's SP15s would go to +/- 10, giving them far greater scope producing a new hybrid sound which was taken even further by them playing tracks at the wrong speed, making them almost unrecognisable.

Within a short time, a phenomenon exploded. By 1978 there had been a cultural shift of seismic proportions and the Baia was the epicentre of the storm. It was now a completely different place to when Bob and Tom were in charge. There had been a change of drugs and public that had produced a new chemistry bringing in a new beat. Instead of Cocaine it was hash and poppers, instead of designer labels it was second hand vintage. Through mixtapes the word spread and the Baia became a mecca for a new generation of Italians, thousands began to make the pilgrimage. The crowd formed a new tribe. The second-hand clothes were as sought after as the DJs hunted down the music. Shops such as Gerard, which is still open today, in Florence, became famed for their selection of military and second hand. And like many changes in fashion, it too had it's curiosities: "At one point white clogs were in fashion. They took them to the cobbler and got the heels filed down so the toes would point up! The jeans were tight at the ankle and short so you could see the socks." remembers Luca Benini, now owner of the streetwear label Slam Jam, then regular clubber at the Baia. The customised Citroen DS' and 2CVs that filled the car park, packing super hi-fi systems and plastered with adhesives, had become official mascots for the scene.

The situation soon got out of control. The Baia packed in up to 4000 people, and thousands would be left outside unable to get in. Not that it mattered. Just being there was all that was important. Being an open-air club, they could still hear the music as they hung out on the surrounding hill and the consumption of illicit substances increased. The authorities decided to take the matter into hand. In August 1978, the military police violently stormed the waiting crowds camped outside the club and the Baia was shut down. It was too late, the virus had escaped and gone on to contaminate much of northern Italy.

The word had spread, fuelled by mixtapes. "I got hold of Mozart and Baldelli's mixtapes and they totally blew me away. They weren't playing records; they were creating music, which is totally different. I couldn't find the records, they didn't exist." Recalls Coccoluto just back off the plane from a weekend playing in Ibiza. "It's so disappointing, the international DJ community that find themselves in incredible venues on a beautiful island and all they do is play their safest most anonymous sets ever." He went on to lament. A far cry from the scene he cites as being the reason he started DJing in the first place. Coccoluto didn't go to the Baia from his native southern Italy. At the time, he says he wasn't into disco music at all; instead, electronic music was the sound that inspired him. "After hearing the tapes, I headed straight to the instrument shops and tried to work out how they'd produced the sounds". Research and the concept of encapsulating diverse musical genres into a format is something that has stayed with him ever since and formed the basis of his most well-known 1996 production, 'Belo Horizonti' which sampled Arito Moreira's "Celebration Suite" a classic Latin track from the Afro/Cosmic scene. "How they [the DJs] played it directly inspired my own production.

Following in Mozart and Baldelli's footsteps, new DJs began springing up, developing new strains of the genre. Ebreo and Spranga were ethnic and tribal, Mozart and Rubens journeyed further into Jazz Funk and Afro Beat, Fabrizio Fattori went into Brazilian but it was Baldelli and new partner TBC that took the electronic route even further at a new club called Cosmic at Lake Garda, northern Italy in 1979. The club was designed as a 'dance gymnasium' and comprised of a space age dance floor, no seating and was alcohol free. It was intended to be a cultural experience where people came to dance, lost in sound. Baldelli experimented with changing speeds of records, dropping artists as wide and varied as Klaus Shultze, Moebius, Kraftwerk, Yello, Airto Moriera, Fela Kuti, Manu Dibango, Weather Report, Kool and the Gang and Funkadelic into their sets. It was here that the word first spread outside of Italy. German and Austrian holidaymakers copied the sound and took it home with them. Cosmic Afro events are held to this day in Italy, southern Germany and Austria, a far cry however from the original spirit, style, innovation and magic of its origins.

Wherever this new pack of superstar DJs played, chaos was close behind. "I had a habit of closing clubs wherever I went," recalls Mozart from his home in the middle of the lush countryside. "Locals spray painted "Mozart go home!" on walls when I played somewhere," infuriated by the invasion. Thousands would turn up for to a 500-capacity club in the middle of nowhere, and those left outside would remain hanging around taking drugs. At the same time heroin entered the scene and caught up a lot of the DJs with it on a massive scale. The odd one out, Baldelli remembers "I ended up telling people I was sorted, so they'd leave me alone. At the time it wasn't cool not to be doing drugs." Things got negative and started to implode. The combination of massive crowds and smack, led to the inevitable crack down by the police and within 12 months, virtually every club in the scene was closed.

After the clubs were no longer an option, the scene moved to holding large Cosmic Afro gatherings where all the DJs from the scene would attract crowds of up to 12,000 in improvised venues in sport stadiums and fields. By then Italy was in full swing of a hippy revival and the scene had come to resemble more Woodstock than a club culture.

One of the most curious aspects to the phenomena is that the impact and importance of this scene has gone unrecognised and unreported. With the arrival of the international DJ circuit, DJs such as Ricky Montanari, Flavio Vecchi and Claudio Coccoluto passed on the tapes from the bygone era and surprised international DJs. No one bothered to contact the original DJs, in the production-fuelled era it didn't make commercial sense. There was nothing to sell; they didn't produce records, just mixtapes.

Has the scene been influential? Traces of the scene are there if you know how to recognise them. The 1989 classic house track 'Sueno Latino' is unmistakably a child of the Afro scene, a re-work of Manuel Gottsching's 'E2-E4', another Cosmic Afro classic.

New York's West End Record's Andy Reynold's says "Over here we were really into the Italian electronic stuff in the early 80s, stuff like Alexander Robotnik were filling up the Chicago and New York DJs sets." Italy's DJs today, renowned for their mixing skills and particular style credited this to their heritage of Cosmic Afro. Listening to DJ Harvey's Black Cock series and the Idjut Boys' cut up tape releases on their Noid imprint also instantly strike a chord. Maybe it's no coincidence that Italian DJ, Leo Young, seeded the tapes to a few London based DJs and producers in the mid nineties. "Leo brought me this Cosmic tape of Baldelli's to listen to and I thought it was technically amazing," recalls Faze Action's Simon Lee "that kind of music is really hard to mix, especially considering the date it was from: 1979." On whether it influenced him, "Yeah, I would say so. When we made 'Kariba' at the time I was listening more to Fela Kuti and Leo had given me the tape."

The tapes were nearly 20 years old by the time this new audience heard them for the first time. Since the early 90s on, Italy has been exporting house and techno, yet this earlier scene has remained it's best kept secret. Listening to their mixes today it's easy to be complacent. We've been exposed for over a decade to the idea of eclecticism on the dance floor by clubs such as Dingwalls in London, as a viable alternative from four to the floor. What happened in Italy twenty years ago was something completely different; the part they were missing was the music industry machine that has brought so many English-speaking artists to instant fame and notoriety. The Cosmic Afro DJs' approach to acoustics created a new concept of electronic music that coupled with the introduction of drum machines, analogical keyboards and sequencers, created a new sound. We've all seen live percussion introduced in DJ sets but it's a fairly recent innovation in the grand scale of dance music culture. To really understand what it was all about, you have to turn to the tapes. Listening to Fela Kuti's "Sorrow Tears and Blood" played end to end won't give you the answer, you have to listen to how they played it.

To really understand the impact it had on a generation of Italian kids, you would have to wipe your memory of musical experiences and return in a time capsule to Rimini in 1979. Failing that, go hunting for the tapes. They are around if you go looking. Just ask an Italian.

For proof on how amazing these guys were at mixing impossible disco tracks. Here's Mozart in 1979 at Baia Degli Angeli.

Many thanks to: Liam J. Nabb, Daniele Baldelli, Mozart, TBC, Claudio Coccoluto, Flavio Vecchi, Luca Benini, Fabio (Disco Inn), DJ Miki.

(Louise Oldfield - An Italian Music Scene: Afro/Cosmic)

Funny.

The word "afro" was invented by a girl or boy who occasionally heard tribal pieces at a Cosmic night. Since then, the name has gone viral enough to attribute this definition to the musical genre.

The pop star Madonna was one of the dancers behind Patrick Hernandez when he sang Born to Be Alive.

When the Les Pois club was demolished, Spain sued the municipality of Cavaion (Verona) for the destruction of the artistic-cultural heritage, as it considered it a work of art by the Spanish architect who had designed it.

Chicago nightclub was so named because Michele Torpedine liked the Chicago band. However, many clubs relied on the names of American cities.

To get the wet effect that gel gives to hair, a bay angel would have a bucket of water in his car and, once at his destination, dip in his hands and run them over his head.

The "woman with pot", one of the icons in the world of the Angels, is the singer Marsha Hunt, who became famous as Jimi Hendrix's lover.

STONED ANGELS

Write-up.

1978 - 1984 may have been the most and final prolific era for creative, talented music.
(Followtruth)

That's the music I've been starving for and thirsting for all my life! It touches the very deep of my heart and makes my soul dance! Thanks for sharing it with us, in spite of the fact that it's like almost 40 - years old tapes they sound fresh today, vivid, sweet and bright music that full of colours! Can't explain how delightful and beautiful this music sounds.
(Alex)

Acknowledgements.

- Bill Brewster and Frank Broughton. Last Night a DJ Saved My Life: The History of the Disc Jockey.
- Louise Oldfield. An Italian music scene, Afro Cosmic, 7 Magazine.
- Noise In My Head Radio. Melbourne.

Baia degli Angeli. Bay of Angels club.

Printed in Great Britain
by Amazon